THE TYRANNY OF TOLERANCE

THE **TYRANNY** OF **TOLERANCE**

A SITTING JUDGE BREAKS THE CODE OF SILENCE TO EXPOSE THE LIBERAL JUDICIAL ASSAULT

ROBERT H. DIERKER JR.

CROWN
FORUM
NEW YORK

Published in the United States by Crown Forum, an imprint of the Crown
Publishing Group, a division of Random House, Inc., New York.
www.crownpublishing.com

Crown Forum and the Crown Forum colophon are trademarks of Random
House, Inc.

Library of Congress Cataloging-in-Publication Data
Dierker, Robert H.
The tyranny of tolerance : a sitting judge breaks the code of silence to expose
the liberal judicial assault/ Robert H. Dierker, Jr. — 1st ed.
p.   cm.
Includes bibliographical references and index.
1. Judges—United States.   2. Justice, Administration of—United States.
3. Political questions and judicial power—United States.   4. Liberalism—
United States.   I. Title.

KF8775.D54 2006
347.73'14—dc22
2006028777

ISBN 978-0-307-33919-5

Printed in the United States of America

Design by Lenny Henderson

10 9 8 7 6 5 4 3 2 1

First Edition

To my beloved wife, Dotty

CONTENTS

THE TYRANNY OF TOLERANCE

INTRODUCTION

THE TYRANNY OF
TOLERANCE

THEY ARE THE PEOPLE who won't wish you a Merry Christmas; who think infants in the womb are just this side of fecal matter; who never met a criminal who couldn't be rehabilitated; who think that Hollywood is a better moral compass than the Vatican; who think that men and women are identical, except when it comes to a man making even mildly suggestive remarks to a woman; who deny the individual right to keep and bear arms (and who don't think much of the military, either); who think that perverted sexual conduct is a constitutional right; who think that racial quotas are salutary as long as they operate against whites and Asians; who think that public schools benefit from no discipline and no competition; and, above all, who think that God should be expunged from the public square.

What do you call these people? You can call them überliberal, radical liberal, liberal statist, liberal absolutists, licentious leftists. But today's liberals are, in fact, anything but liberal; they are illiberal, radical, and extreme. And these illiberal liberals are at the root of the constitutional crisis that we face today.

When I became a trial judge twenty years ago, I swore to uphold the Constitution of the United States, and I have tried to do so. I believed implicitly in fair and equal treatment for all litigants, and I steadfastly applied cases handed down by the United States Supreme Court—whether I agreed with them or not—to the best of my ability. But after those twenty years, and the years of practicing law that preceded them—much of it spent in public policy or constitutional litigation—I have come to realize that the Constitution I swore to uphold is not the same Constitution other lawyers and judges uphold. Slowly it has dawned on me that the notion of law as a tool to advance an agenda of the politically correct segment of society has supplanted the ideal of the rule of law that I learned from my father (a night law school graduate who worked seven days a week to nurture a small private practice) and from my other mentors—all members of the "greatest generation" and all believers in God and fundamental principles expounded in the Constitution and the Declaration of Independence.

As case after case has come down from the federal courts (and, increasingly, from state courts), it has become apparent that the law and the courts are no longer grounded in principle, in the text of the Constitution, in precedent, or in the traditions of our culture. Leading the way toward the overthrow of the real Constitution, and of moral and natural law as the foundation of all law, was at first a group that seemed to be confined to academe, babbling of "deconstruction" and "instrumentalism" and other shibboleths of a mutated Marxism. But as one established principle of law after another has been jettisoned in the name of "equality," or "privacy," or "loss spreading," I have realized that the mutants have seized the controls of the courts and the legal profession. They use the high-minded language of equal rights and social justice but actually stand for something quite different. These are the modern liberals, the illiberal liberals.

These are the people who regularly use the unelected federal judiciary to turn the Constitution—formerly a blueprint for limited government—into a weapon for advancing their agenda. These are the people who make war on traditional American values and ram their distinctly minority ideology down the throats of the American people without letting little things like democracy or free speech get in their way. These are the people who suppress dissent by those they sneeringly describe as "the religious right," "gun-toting fundamentalists," or even "fascists." These are the people who control the "mainstream" media, the universities, the law schools, the federal courts (and some state courts), and much of the legal profession.

The liberal agenda, they say, is "tolerance." Who can oppose tolerance? Who wants to be labeled intolerant? But tolerance in the liberal cosmos has a rather *intolerant* aura. Indeed, the illiberal liberals must be regarded as the practitioners of doublethink and doublespeak foretold by George Orwell—although he was a couple of decades too early.

"Tolerant" liberals are the ones who file lawsuits to kick the Boy Scouts out of public parks, to get sodomy made into a constitutional right, to throw peaceful abortion protesters in jail, to allow abortionists to pull babies three-quarters of the way out of the womb and kill them, to crush pro-lifers' rights of speech and assembly, to nullify the reproductive and parental rights of men, to bankrupt the firearms industry as a means of disarming a free people, to impose racial quotas on employers, to prevent the expulsion of punks from public schools, to prevent manifestly guilty multiple murderers from being executed, to tear monuments to the Ten Commandments out of public buildings, to eliminate God from the Pledge of Allegiance, to free foreign terrorists who then can return to the battlefield and kill more Americans, and to crown it all with taxation by decree. Not content with assaults on traditional morality and public safety, the radical liberals also bring class actions to make the rights of insects superior to the rights of property owners and to take away the rights of smokers, fast-food diners, and gun owners. While advocating for pornographers, perverts, and abortionists, they censor or suppress all speech that dares to contradict their dogma of tolerance.

Of course, liberals would not be the danger that they are if their lawsuits failed. But they win! Having taken control of the legal profession and the courts, they have subverted the checks and balances of the American Constitution to their ends. They have declared war on the laws of nature, the laws of reason, and especially on the law of God. The illiberal liberals have imposed a tyranny of tolerance on the American people.

The radical liberals' agenda is tyrannical because it brooks no dissent from the regime of tolerance. A Christian who voices opposition to his employer's policies favoring homosexuals loses his job, because he is "intolerant." A judge who insists on defending a monument to the Ten Commandments in a courthouse loses his job, because he is "intolerant." Airline pilots and air marshals who recommend that suspicious people who appear to be of Middle Eastern origin be kept off airliners are sued and must undergo "sensitivity training," for they are "intolerant."

The courts have become the liberals' most important weapon for enforcing their tyranny. Judges change the Constitution itself by judicial fiat. That way they can suppress views that run contrary to the regime of tolerance, and they can take critical decision-making powers away from our elected officials. Voting? It doesn't matter. Who needs free and honest debate and democratic elections when you can impose your views through litigation and by judicial fiat?

Liberal lawyers concoct spurious legal theories in the name of equality—the favorite alter ego of tolerance—and liberal judges accept the theories, destroying traditional values as they go, and encouraging liberal lawyers to dream up more theories to advance the tyranny. The rule of law becomes the rule of liberal lawyers and judges.

Don't kid yourselves, folks, the cases that I talk about in this book really happened, and they happened because radical liberals don't believe in law, only in power. To them, there is no truth, there is no natural law, there is no God; there are just arbitrary rules that they get to invent through their control of the judiciary.

This book is intended to awaken Americans to the dimensions of the struggle that lies before us. It is nothing less than a struggle to reclaim the republic. It is a struggle that must be waged in Congress, the state legislatures, and the courts. Unfortunately, it is likely to be a struggle that is won or lost in the courts—or in the selection of those who sit on the bench.

I know that in outlining why liberals have become so dangerous, and what to do about it, I am putting my job as a state judge at risk, even though this book is written on my own time and the views expressed are lawyer-brokered "class action settlements." We will see religious liberty eroded even further and God and morality completely excluded from our law. We will quite possibly see our war-making ability crippled and see captured terrorists set free to go kill Americans here and abroad. We will see licentiousness, not liberty, become the cornerstone of constitutional law, and we will see the parallel "deconstruction" of the family, the cornerstone of civil society.

We cannot fail. Now, to work.

CHAPTER 1

THE CLOUD CUCKOOLAND
OF RADICAL FEMINISM

*Differences [between men and women], including the products
of social inequality, make unequal treatment not unequal at all.*
—Catharine MacKinnon, "Reflections on Sex Equality Under Law,"
Yale Law Journal, **1991**

*This most illiberal Court . . . has embarked on a course of in-
scribing one after another of the current preferences of the society (and in some cases only the countermajoritarian preferences
of the society's law-trained elite) into our Basic Law.*
—Justice Antonin Scalia, dissenting,
***United States v. Virginia* (1996)**

D O   Y O U   T H I N K   J U D G E S should be able to write freely about
the law? Do you think that judges should sound the alarm if radicalism threatens to hijack the legal system itself?

Do you think judges should be truly independent of any dominant
legal elite?

I believe that judges can and must write freely about the law, and
that they have a positive duty to resist political forces that try to take
over the legal system. I believe that judicial independence actually

means more than never having your salary cut—that it means speaking and writing about threats to that independence from any source.

I have taken an oath to support the Constitution of the United States. I cannot in good conscience sit idly by and watch the destruction of that Constitution by a judiciary that is no longer independent. Despite a tradition of silence by judges on such topics, I can no longer keep quiet about what I, as an insider, have seen happening in, and to, our courts. I may be accused of unethical conduct and threatened with professional discipline, as I was in the past. If that is a risk I must take, so be it. Others before me have taken much greater risks in defense of republican government.

I have witnessed liberal totalitarianism on many fronts as both a lawyer and a judge, but it is fair to say that I probably would not have written this book if I had not had my own, very direct run-in with the tyrants of tolerance. That unpleasant personal experience forced me to do some serious thinking about what is happening to American law, how it is happening, and who is making it happen. And finally it convinced me to write this book, and to accept whatever consequences came from publishing it.

That run-in occurred when I dared confront one of the most active elements of liberalism: the radical feminists.

"MANIFESTING BIAS"

If Social Security is the "third rail" of American politics, then sex is the third rail of American law. Anyone who touches it, except in the manner approved by the tyrants of tolerance, is fried. In this realm, the tyranny of tolerance is best described as rule by the radical feminist cadre of liberalism. Like the rest of the illiberal liberals, femifascists display single-minded devotion to imposing their tyranny on the American people—and will viciously punish those who resist.

I learned this from painful experience.

In 1998, a case came before me in which a woman alleged that the male defendant, who apparently had been her employer, had inflicted emotional distress based on alleged sexual harassment. The defendant's alleged harassment involved making sexual advances and touching the plaintiff (in a manner that stopped well short of actual sexual assault). The plaintiff had previously litigated a claim of employment discrimination based on the same course of conduct of the defendant, and lost. So now she was recasting the claims, in part to avoid the statute of limitations that now barred the employment claims.

I carefully researched the law of Missouri to see whether the plaintiff's theories were defensible as a matter of law. As pleaded, they were not, I concluded. I had law clerks do independent research on the matter, and they confirmed my own view of Missouri law. At the time the case came before me, Missouri law on "sexual harassment" as infliction of emotional distress was sparse; it seemed the plaintiff wanted to import certain theories of federal employment law regarding "sexual harassment" into Missouri common law.

Having reached a conclusion based on impartial examination of the law, I wrote an opinion dismissing the woman's claim of infliction of emotional distress, but giving the plaintiff an opportunity to revise her claim to meet what I thought were proper legal standards.

In that opinion, I felt obliged to sound an alarm about the threat that radical feminist sexual harassment theories pose to common sense and common law, especially because such views could easily lead to fictitious claims and vexatious suits. I was blunt in my criticism of radical feminist views of sexual harassment law. "The question before this Court," I wrote, "is whether a wholesale extension of notions of 'sexual harassment' into tort law is warranted, without direction from the people through the [legislature]. The Court concludes that the common law does not enact Cardinal Newman's definition of a gentleman, nor [feminist scholar] Catharine MacKinnon's vapid maunderings, and that Plaintiff's petition at present fails to state a claim."

I concluded my opinion by observing the danger of imposing liability based solely on speech. "[T]he sexual harassment police," I wrote, "seem oblivious to the First Amendment as they eagerly enlist the courts as censors of words and literature in the workplace." More specifically, I noted that it seems clear to everyone "except for the denizens of the cloud cuckooland of radical feminism" that no court had ever held a sexual advance to be actionable in and of itself.

Although I did not expect liberals to applaud my opinion, and I probably expected a certain amount of controversy, I was comfortable with the complete freedom judges have had historically to say what they thought about the law. When writing opinions, especially on issues where precedent is unclear or conflicting, judges have a unique opportunity to criticize the parties' theories and to explain or instruct the public concerning the state of the law. I felt particularly comfortable because my dicta did not control my legal analysis of the main issue. I was doing nothing unusual—or so I thought. (My opinion is included as an appendix to this book, so you can see exactly what I wrote.)

Prepared for public criticism, I was unprepared for what actually happened. The opinion did not become the subject of open debate, but rather, I learned later, radical feminists began working behind the scenes within the St. Louis legal community to attack my integrity and accuse me of official misconduct for writing the opinion. (Never mind that, to this day, no competent lawyer has contended that I distorted the law in reaching the result that I reached.)

In Missouri, judges are subject to investigation and discipline through a body known as the Commission on Retirement, Removal, and Discipline. Unbeknownst to me, liberal Democratic governor Mel Carnahan had appointed virulent radical feminists (or "femifascists") to that body, women who openly expressed contempt for men and pressured judicial nominating commissions charged with selecting judges to discriminate against men. The femifascists thus had an ideal forum in which to mount their secret attack.

Some months after filing my opinion in the harassment case, the Discipline Commission notified me that someone had filed a complaint alleging that my opinion showed "preconceived bias against women, female lawyers, or sexual harassment suits." Under Missouri rules, I was not allowed to see the complaint itself or to know who filed it.

Although I can honestly say that I did not react to the complaint with the frenzied groveling of, say, Harvard president Larry Summers

after he foolishly speculated about differences in scientific ability between men and women,[1] I confess that I did beat a retreat of sorts. Perhaps it was weariness after two grueling years as chief judge of my
circuit (elected unanimously, I might add, by a highly "diverse" court),
perhaps it was fear or shock at the use of this weapon against me, but I
simply wanted the matter put to rest. So in my response to the Commission, I acknowledged the polemics and promised that I would use more
care in expressing myself in the future (self-censorship?). In the end, the
Commission did nothing but send me a "reminder" to avoid language
that "might" give rise to an "appearance" of bias in performing my official duties. (For the sake of full disclosure, I also include this correspondence in the appendix.)

In retrospect, I should have been prepared to sue the Discipline
Commission to vindicate the absolute right of judges to express their
views in their opinions. After all, don't judges have the right and duty
to "say what the law is"? If they can't say what they think, what happens to judicial independence?

As horrifying as I find the prospect that the tyranny of tolerance can
force judges to censor themselves (and conceivably even adjust their
rulings) to avoid the liberal hammer, I can't say I hadn't been warned
that this possibility existed. But such warnings made no sense to me
given the freedom judges have long enjoyed to express their views on
the law.

The warnings came from several lawyers shortly after I was elected
chief judge of my circuit. These attorneys were aware that in 1992 I
had written a scathing review of a report issued by the Missouri "gender and justice" commission, which was set up in the early 1990s to
study Missouri courts and laws for sex bias and to recommend cures.
Femifascists had successfully pressured state and federal courts around
the country to create such commissions. The Missouri commission, like
those of other federal and state jurisdictions, was under the thumb of
radical feminists, and its report was replete with dubious conclusions
based on thin or misleading data, all used to demand changes to discriminate in favor of women and against men. In addition to writing a

critical review of the commission's report, I presented to the Missouri Judicial Conference a resolution condemning it. My resolution was supported by half of the members of the conference executive council and a substantial number of Missouri judges, but it failed to win a majority vote of the conference.

When the resolution did not pass, I saw no point in continuing the battle, and I thought that was the end of the matter. Little did I know that, like dissenters in the Soviet Union, I was now marked for retaliation by the PC police.

THE FEMIFASCIST LEGAL ASSAULT

Although I evaded the sensitivity gulag, my run-in with the tyranny of tolerance made me realize how thoroughly liberals have remade American law over the past several decades. If the femifascists and radical liberals can hijack the courts and intimidate judges into remaining silent in the face of subversion of the law, then what's left of constitutional government? Worse, if these people actually control the judiciary, what happens to democracy?

It was entirely fitting that my direct encounter with the tyranny of tolerance involved that cadre of liberals known as femifascists. Liberals certainly do not confine their efforts to fighting for special treatment for women; as we will see throughout this book, their favored groups range from racial minorities to homosexuals to the disabled to criminals to terrorists. But the femifascists offer a revealing look at how liberals have seized power through the judiciary, allowing the law to be rewritten without regard to the democratic process. Both bench and bar have cravenly acquiesced to the femifascists and signed on to their radical agenda.

The femifascist confluence with liberalism has spawned a truly horrible jurisprudence. Concluding that the law should not treat men and women equally, but should treat women *better* than men to "compensate" women for centuries of oppression, radical feminists exclude men from any reproductive rights and attack traditional marriage, with its implied contractual rights of both men and women. (Indeed, femifascists do not disguise their hostility to the institution of marriage and to the role of women as mothers.)[2]

Perhaps the clearest example of how femifascists have used the law to replace the supposed oppressors with the oppressed is found in the legal treatment of "sexual harassment." If sexual harassment was a means by which men kept women in a subordinate societal role (something that need not be conceded), it is clear at this point that sexual harassment law threatens to become a weapon by which the femifascists can ensure the oppression of men. The judiciary enacted this radical change.[3]

What we know today as sexual harassment law resulted largely from Title VII of the Civil Rights Act of 1964, which forbade discrimination on account of sex in terms and conditions of employment. Liberals pushed the courts to apply Title VII in a way Congress never contemplated. Building on principles developed to prevent employers from intimidating black employees into leaving their jobs, the courts expanded the notion of a "hostile and oppressive work environment" to so-called sexual harassment.[4]

The femifascists' first step was to establish the basic principle that a female employee could suffer sex discrimination as a result of harassment on the job, even if she could not show any tangible job detriment, such as demotion or loss of pay. Another principle established was that the "harassment" could be "unwelcome" even if it involved voluntary, consensual sexual relations. Of course, once liability can be established without reference to any objective criteria such as loss of promotion or pay, the limits of liability are hard to come by. So the courts solemnly decreed that the harassment had to be "severe" and "pervasive."[5] And just to give employers an additional incentive to censor employee speech and to police contact between the sexes in the workplace, the courts held out the largely illusory prospect that the employer could evade liability if it had a specific policy proscribing sexual harassment backed up by a grievance remedy that encouraged victims to come forward.[6] Finally, despite centuries of employment law to the contrary, the courts decided that an employer would be liable for words and acts of nonsupervisory employees acting outside the course and scope of employment. The Equal Employment Opportunity Commission (EEOC) has gone so far as to claim that employers can be held liable for the words of nonemployees![7]

The femifascists gleefully embraced sexual harassment law,[8] as it gave them the whip hand in enforcing standards for male behavior in the workplace. The courts' creation of sexual harassment law prompted many employers to establish speech and conduct codes, ostensibly neutral, but primarily aimed at men. The new standards were also rapidly written into professional conduct codes for lawyers and judges. Every man was immediately placed at risk if he made any remark that was even claimed to be off-color, to a woman.[9]

In fact, the changes sparked tremendous pressure to take disciplinary actions aimed at men who "offended" women or merely made sexual remarks. In another case that came before me, the record showed that an employee had been disciplined for remarking "nice legs" to his boss's wife; Judge Robert Bork relates the story of the male student accused of a "mini-rape"—whatever that is—for commenting about a female student's appearance; arbitration rulings show that male employees have been disciplined merely for banter that included sexual remarks; writers on employment discrimination law emphasize discipline of any alleged harasser as the most effective step an employer can take when confronted with a sexual harassment complaint.[10]

The Supreme Court's "pervasiveness" standard did not satisfy the femifascists. They demanded that the standard be revised so that challenged conduct be assessed by what was hostile or abusive in the eyes of a reasonable *woman*.[11] That effort failed, but the radical feminists achieved other successes. Notably, many courts soon began to ignore the "pervasiveness" standard, or, as is often their way, to quote it and apply it in a manner that essentially ignored it. Thus, in one case, an employer was subjected to a trial because a female fire department lieutenant claimed that she was subjected to a male subordinate's obscene tirade, even though the male subordinate was off duty at the time and not on the employer's premises. The federal court of appeals found that the male firefighter's comments were somehow attributable to the employer, who presumably should have fired the male for comments made in a public forum. The court said that the single incident was somehow "severe and pervasive."[12]

One of the most significant aspects of sexual harassment law is that it never demands any actual objective harm to the claimant, whether financial or psychological. Before liberals engulfed the law, words alone had seldom been actionable, unless they were defamatory; at the very least, to prove infliction of emotional distress, one had to show substantial mental or emotional injury.[13] Now, thanks to the femifascists' tyranny of tolerance, words alone can bring serious consequences to the speaker, even if they result in no tangible harm to the listener. Heretofore, freedom of speech meant just that: freedom to speak, without fear of consequences. Now, employers and their employees have lost freedom of speech, and the federal courts joyfully enforce this new censorship.[14]

One recent case illustrates the idiocy of sexual harassment law. In 2001, the U.S. Supreme Court had to be bothered to weigh in on the case of *Clark County School Dist. v. Breeden*.[15] In that case, a male employee had the effrontery to utter, in the presence of a female coworker, the sentence, "I hear making love to you is like making love to the Grand Canyon." The man didn't direct the remark at the female coworker; he simply read it aloud from a psychological evaluation report in a job applicant's file. But then the male employee who read the remark had the unmitigated gall to look at the woman and say, "I don't know what that means." Whereupon another man present said he would explain it later, and they both dared to chuckle. This conduct led the woman to complain to her superiors. When they did not exact the obligatory pound of male flesh from the utterer, she filed suit, contending that she had been punished for complaining about this illegal behavior, and therefore her employer had violated Title VII by "retaliating" against her for complaining about her coworker's supposedly illegal behavior.

The female employee's claim of sexual harassment was so ridiculous that not even Justice Ruth Bader Ginsburg swallowed it. But somehow at least two judges of the federal court of appeals had bought into the claim. And that is my point: It is ludicrous that such a claim could even get in the courthouse door, let alone up to the United States Supreme Court. But that is exactly what the femifascists want. The claim in *Breeden* failed, but few employers are willing to fight the issue all the way to the Supreme Court.

CAVING IN TO THE FEMIFASCISTS

Sexual harassment law is by no means the only weapon the femifascists use in the battle to impose their views on our government and society. As we have seen, I tried, and failed, to limit the damage done by another of the femifascists' weapons: the gender and justice commission. These commissions, which state and federal courts created and populated with femifascist-friendly liberals in the late 1980s and 1990s, studied supposed "disparate treatment" of men and women in the law. Just as the Missouri commission did, gender and justice commissions around the country used the flimsiest of evidence to "prove" horrible discrimination against women in the justice system—from podiums in courtrooms that were too high for women lawyers (but is the difference in average height between men and women a "real" difference between the sexes, or just a construct?) to wrong-headed ideas about the presumption of innocence in "domestic violence" cases.[16]

Virtually every gender and justice commission demanded major changes in the way the courts and lawyers treated women, but not with a view to achieving equal treatment of the sexes. These commissions demanded quotas in judicial appointments, not with reference to the relative proportions of men and women lawyers (the qualified applicant pool), but with reference to the relative numbers of men and women in the general population. In Missouri and Iowa, for example, radical feminists insisted that at least 50 percent of appointments to the state judiciary be female.[17] This arbitrary standard was plainly at variance with established law concerning employment discrimination,[18] but in accord with the femifascist political agenda to supplant men with women decision makers at every opportunity.

For every ill perceived by the gender and justice commissions, they demanded special "training" of judges and lawyers. Such training was a thinly veiled effort to reeducate judges and lawyers to toe the femifascist line in every case, but especially in domestic violence, sexual assault, and similar cases. Judges were to "encourage" prosecutors to pursue rape cases to trial, regardless of the merits of the case—and regardless of the proper role of the judge as neutral arbiter in an adversary system. The issue of consent was to be eliminated from sexual assault cases, because, as radical feminist "scholars" such as Susan Estrich (Michael Dukakis's campaign chief in 1988) could show, even when women say yes, their consent is merely the product of centuries of oppression.[19] Neglecting no aspect of the process, the Missouri gender and justice commission even suggested that juries be *ordered* to elect women as foremen—er, forepersons.

The gender and justice commissions also demanded enactment of speech codes that required judges to become censors of lawyers and other judges.[20] The powerful duumvirate of illiberal liberals and femifascists has compelled censorship of the language itself: Every rule, statute, regulation, opinion, brief, or whatever must be "gender neutral." The all-inclusive male pronoun must be banished from the language of the law—although everybody knows that the English language provides no ready substitute. In effect, they resurrected the old English rules of licensing speech.

More important, as my own case illustrates, a judge must never, ever criticize femifascist jurisprudence. My opinion in the sexual harassment case was attacked not for faulty legal analysis, but because my rhetoric was too polemical. Why? Were the femifascists afraid that my criticism might strike a responsive chord in the public, in the legal profession, in the courts? The complaint against me focused on my diction. Indeed, the notice of the complaint said so: "The complaint alleges that the language used in the order indicates a preconceived bias."

Ultimately, what are we talking about? *Ideas.* And the femifascists, like the rest of illiberal liberals, will allow no ideas at odds with their doctrines.

SPECIAL TREATMENT

At its core, the femifascist agenda is based on hatred for men. Hatred is not too strong a word to apply to the most radical feminism. For example, Catharine MacKinnon, one of the foremost exponents of radical feminist legal doctrine, attacks the basic premise of the equal protection clause, comparing it to Nazi legal doctrine. She also believes that white men are the root of all evil and injustice in America, and that the law must strip power from them to compensate women for their past oppression.[21]

In a rational legal order, the femifascists' venomous hatred for men (particularly white men) would be condemned as vigorously as any other hatred based on race or sex. That it is *not* condemned, but rather exalted, exposes the hypocrisy of the liberal legal order. As in the realm of race discrimination, it does not follow that the sons are to be punished for the sins of the fathers; but to liberals, such replacement of oppressors follows as a matter of course. And this state of affairs will continue so long as liberals, including the femifascists, remain in control of the judiciary.

The liberal philosophy of judicial absolutism is made to order for the femifascists. They readily distort the law to achieve their ends of special treatment for (some) women at the expense of men and other women who do not subscribe to their agenda. To understand the truly discriminatory purpose of the femifascists' agenda, consider that the ACLU and other liberal organizations have actually called for the drug laws to be enforced differently for women.[22]

The femifascists' philosophy of enforcing special treatment for women creates some striking inconsistencies. They maintain that the differences between men and women are mere "constructs" and denounce laws that treat women differently, but their entire legal campaign is predicated on the idea of affording women special protections or compensations—different kinds of protections and compensations from what the law formerly provided, to be sure, but protections and compensations just the same.[23]

As a result of the femifascists' legal efforts, the courts, too, have been inconsistent. The schizoid femifascist philosophy—which oscillates between demanding equality with men and demanding better treatment than men—leads the courts to do much backing and filling.

In 1882, the Supreme Court held that a state could legitimately restrict membership in the bar to men.[24] The femifascists love to dwell on the concurring opinion of Justice Joseph P. Bradley, who declaimed about the proper roles of men and women as devised by the Creator. But the gravamen of the decision was simply that the judgment about who was suited to be lawyers should be made by the legislature. The decision did not write into the Constitution any requirement that lawyers be men.[25] In this regard it is a far cry from what we see today from liberal judicial activists.

In 1908, in the case of *Muller v. Oregon*,[26] the Supreme Court held that protective legislation designed to limit the working hours of women was constitutional. At the time, the decision was thought to be progressive. Indeed, the attorney who argued successfully for protecting women from long work hours, Louis Brandeis—later to become a Supreme Court justice—would probably be quite surprised to learn that his case is now just one more count in the indictment against the oppressive white male patriarchy. Here, again, the Court was not writing anything into the Constitution that *required* women to be limited in working hours or anything else. It quite simply—and quite properly— found that the Constitution did not forbid such protective legislation.

At this time, it is constitutional for Congress to exclude women from military draft registration (and presumably from combat),[27] for legislatures to grant special tax exemptions to women but not men,[28] for Congress to provide different standards for men and women in determining whether they are dependents of their spouses for purposes of computing Social Security benefits,[29] and for federally assisted colleges to abolish men's sports in order to provide additional athletic scholarships for women.[30] It also is apparently constitutional to treat pregnancy differently from other physical conditions requiring medical treatment,[31] although such differentiation in the employment context has been forbidden by the Pregnancy Discrimination Act, amending Title VII of the Civil Rights Act of 1964.

It is unconstitutional, however, to exclude women from historically all-male military schools,[32] to exclude men from women's colleges,[33] to forbid the sale of 3.2 percent beer to men between the ages of eighteen and twenty-one but not to women,[34] and to exclude women from juries by the use of what are called peremptory challenges (in which the litigants get to eliminate a prospective juror from sitting on a trial jury).[35]

In achieving its varying results, the Supreme Court simply created a special standard of assessing claims of denial of equal protection to women, calling it "intermediate scrutiny" or "exceedingly persuasive justification." These phrases are nowhere to be found in the Constitution, but the courts adopted them so they could strike down legislative distinctions between the sexes with which they did not agree.[36] In other words, when five justices want to show how "up-to-date and right-thinking" they are "in matters pertaining to the sexes" (as Justice Antonin Scalia once put it[37]), they simply strike down the law they disagree with. This is not constitutional law; it is social policy making in robes.

Justice Felix Frankfurter, by no means a hidebound conservative, expressed the traditional notion of how the courts should view laws distinguishing between the sexes:

> The fact that women may now have achieved the virtues that men have long claimed as their prerogatives and now indulge in vices that men have long practiced, does not preclude the States from drawing a sharp line between the sexes. . . . The Constitution does not require legislatures to reflect sociological insight, or shifting social standards, any more than it requires them to keep abreast of the latest scientific standards.[38]

Try telling that to Catharine MacKinnon or Ruth Bader Ginsburg! For them, shifting social standards, or creating new social standards, is what modern constitutional law is all about.

Again, the point is not that the legislation in question is right, or the best policy, but that the courts should not substitute their notions of social policy for those of the legislature, either as a result of liberal dominance or femifascist intimidation. In 1908, Louis Brandeis mustered the best "scientific" support he could find, to support protective legislation for women. In 2005, such "science" would be derided by Justice Ginsburg. Who decides what "science" should be followed? The courts, or the people's representatives?

As Justice Scalia has written, "The virtue of a democratic system with a First Amendment is that it readily enables the people, over time, to be persuaded that what they took for granted is not so, and to change their laws accordingly. That system is destroyed if the smug assurances of each age are removed from the democratic process and written into the Constitution." Referring specifically to claims of discrimination on the basis of sex, Scalia added, "Even while bemoaning the sorry, bygone days of 'fixed notions' concerning women's education, the Court favors current notions so fixedly that it is willing to write them into the Constitution by application of custom-built 'tests.' This is not the interpretation of a Constitution, but the creation of one."[39]

FORCED COMPLIANCE

The liberal notions of sexual harassment and sex discrimination generally have little to do with law and everything to do with power. The courts exist to do liberal bidding, and if a state judge dares utter a contrary word, then remove him! My own case illustrates how much radical liberals, and especially the femifascist cadre, oppose a truly independent judiciary. That opposition leads them to make the meanest and most vicious attacks on highly qualified judicial nominees who do not subscribe to their view of the law and the judiciary. The equal rights amendment failed in the political process, but the femifascists know that a liberal judiciary can and will render the amendment unnecessary.

The orthodoxy of radical feminism should have no greater claim to monopoly in the marketplace of ideas, or in the language of the law, than any other political orthodoxy. The equal rights amendment failed precisely because there are, and always will be, significant differences between men and women. These warrant recognition in the law, *if* desired by a majority of the people (women *are* a majority) speaking through their elected representatives. The "tolerance" and "sensitivity" and "compensation" demanded by femifascist liberals is really tolerance with a brown shirt and the sensitivity of the reeducation gulag.

Of course, it is the duty of an independent judiciary to ensure that the law and the judiciary are not subverted in favor of special interests. So why aren't the courts doing their job? Because the illiberal liberals have hijacked the judiciary to distort and pervert the Constitution in service of their agenda—and not just in matters of sex.

CHAPTER 2

MAKING SOME AMERICANS MORE EQUAL THAN OTHERS

All persons born or naturalized in the United States, and subject to the jurisdiction thereof, are citizens of the United States and of the state wherein they reside. No state shall make or enforce any law which shall abridge the privileges or immunities of citizens of the United States; nor shall any state deprive any person of life, liberty or property without due process of law; nor deny to any person within its jurisdiction the equal protection of the laws.

—Fourteenth Amendment, U.S. Constitution

All animals are equal, but some animals are more equal than others.
—George Orwell, *Animal Farm*

W HY?" CRIED MY TEENAGE DAUGHTER, vexed and near tears after enduring pitying looks and silence from her teammates. "Why were the rules different?" She had just lost a tennis match to a girl in a wheelchair who was playing by "special" rules. At the time, I had no answer, except to mutter about affirmative action.

Well, my dear, the answer to your question is what this book is all about. How did we arrive at this point when the rules are changed to benefit one person over another? And not just on the tennis court, but in courts of law, where everybody is supposed to be treated equally. Just as we saw with the femifascists, illiberal liberals don't want equality; they want to make some people *more equal* than others.

And they've made it happen through their dominance of the courts over the past seventy-five years. Liberals have converted the courts from the "least dangerous" branch of government envisioned by the Founding Fathers to the most dangerous.[1]

EQUAL PROTECTION GOES OUT THE WINDOW

The liberal jurisprudence this country has witnessed amounts to an egregious abuse of power. This is not to say the courts have no power at all. Indeed, I firmly believe that the power of judicial review—the power of a court to declare an act of the legislature void as contrary to the Constitution—represents an essential part of American constitutional government.[2] Though the Constitution does not expressly grant this power to the courts, the Constitution would be meaningless if the legislature could enact laws in direct conflict with it, as Alexander Hamilton observed in *The Federalist No. 78*.[3] In Chief Justice John Marshall's words, judges must have the power to "say what the law is."[4]

But by abusing that power, by turning it from a power to enforce the Constitution as written into a power to rewrite the Constitution itself, the liberal courts have perverted the Constitution, basic legal principles, and our system of limited government, so as to impose their own brand of tyranny on the American people.

The radical liberals' favorite weapon in imposing the tyranny of tolerance has been the Constitution's Fourteenth Amendment, which was passed by Congress and ratified by the states in the wake of the Civil War. Just as the Civil War centered on the issue of slavery, the three constitutional amendments adopted after the war dealt with slavery as well—namely, by abolishing slavery itself and assuring the basic political rights of freed slaves. The Thirteenth Amendment abolished slavery in so many words. The Fifteenth Amendment forbade denial of the suffrage on the basis of race, color, or "previous condition of servitude."

Sandwiched between these was the Fourteenth Amendment. And thereby hangs the tale.

The Fourteenth Amendment had one main purpose: to ensure equality under the law for former slaves by limiting the power of the state governments over their citizens. It had other purposes, of course, such as assuring the primacy of the federal government's debt, disqualifying from office certain rebels, and compelling the states to grant the vote to the freed slaves, on pain of reduced representation in the U.S. House of Representatives—sort of a reverse "three-fifths compromise" (when the Founding Fathers agreed to count three-fifths of the number of slaves in Southern states for purposes of allotting seats in the new House of Representatives). But the overriding purpose was to ensure that the state governments treated all their citizens, including freed slaves, as equal in their citizenship.[5]

So how in the world did the Fourteenth Amendment become about guaranteeing special preferences to certain Americans on the basis of race, color, sex, "sexual orientation," "disability," economic status, marital status, fluency (or lack thereof) in English, or atheism?

From the beginning, the courts' approach to the Fourteenth Amendment has been a study in dishonest judicial review. Initially, the Supreme Court confined the amendment within relatively narrow boundaries. So narrow, in fact, that the Court effectively read out of the amendment its central purpose of assuring freed slaves the full rights of citizenship. In a prescient comment in a dissent in *The Civil Rights Cases*,[6] decided in 1883, the first Justice John M. Harlan observed:

> The [1875 Civil Rights Act], now adjudged to be unconstitutional, is for the benefit of citizens of every race and color. . . .
> Today, it is the colored race which is denied, by corporations and individuals wielding public authority, rights fundamental in their freedom and citizenship. At some future time, it may be that some other race will fall under the ban of race discrimination. If the constitutional amendments be enforced, according to the intent with which . . . they were adopted, there cannot be, in this republic, any class of human beings in practical subjec-

tion to another class, with power in the latter to dole out to the former just such privileges as they may choose to grant.

The Supreme Court limited Congress's power to ensure civil rights of all citizens, out of concern (not altogether misplaced) that such power, if recognized, could extend to every facet of private life. That concern evaporated when the New Deal liberals gained control of the Court. At that point, the Fourteenth Amendment's equal protection clause (and the Constitution itself) underwent radical revision, from a basic assurance of equal treatment under the law, to an elaborate mosaic of "suspect classes," "fundamental rights," and "compelling interests," none of which has any root in the language or intention of the amendment, but all of which advance the agenda of favored treatment for select classes of Americans.[7]

What classes get more than equal status? The most important are the "suspect classes." The original suspect class was composed of black persons, the ones the Fourteenth Amendment was designed to protect. But any group identified by liberal judges as deserving of special protection could be designated a suspect class at any time. If a suspect class is involved, the courts will strike down almost any differential treatment.

In recent years we've seen a variety of cases that evince this liberal "deconstruction" of the equal protection clause. The affirmative action cases are a prime example. In one such case, Justice Ruth Bader Ginsburg, second to none in illiberal liberalism, frankly admitted that, in her cosmos, equal protection does not forbid racial discrimination altogether; rather, she said, such discrimination is permissible when its purpose is to favor "minorities."[8] Justice Sandra Day O'Connor adopted the "more than equal protection" credo in her ludicrous concurring opinion in the Texas sodomy case.[9]

NO LIMITS

Paralleling the radical revision of the equal protection clause was an equally radical revision of the Fourteenth Amendment's due process clause. The due process clause is straight out of the Fifth Amendment, part of the original Bill of Rights. The meaning of due process of law admittedly is vague, but given its roots in language in Magna Carta, it really means that the government cannot take away life, liberty, or property without following established legal procedures, or without having authority in the law to do so. It is a limitation on the power of the government to act arbitrarily and capriciously, as medieval monarchs were wont to do.

During the nineteenth century, the Fourteenth Amendment's due process clause became the darling of judicial activists who saw it as a means to curb state regulation of economic liberty. Since the clause expressly protects liberty *and* property, there is some textual basis for treating the language as limiting state regulation of economic pursuits. But the nineteenth-century activists decided that the clause had a "substantive" meaning—that is, even when the government acted on the basis of a statute or established common law precedent, the law itself had to be reasonable . . . and of course the judges got to decide what was reasonable. Populists and later New Deal liberals screamed bloody murder at this judicial activism—because it protected economic conduct that they wanted to stifle or control.[10] Note, however, that this form of "substantive" due process was strictly a defensive weapon: It placed certain regulatory activity off-limits, but it definitely did not impose a different social policy. Thus the nineteenth-century courts used the due process clause entirely within the established norms of judicial review: Statutes or regulations were declared unconstitutional and unenforceable in court.

When the liberals got control of the judiciary, they quickly renounced the nineteenth-century substantive due process doctrine—*as to economic regulation.* Just as quickly, they decided the doctrine had great utility in expanding liberal control of other aspects of social policy. Here, they jettisoned not only nineteenth-century jurisprudence but also a carefully crafted construction of the Fourteenth Amendment explicated by one of their own.

Justice Benjamin Cardozo, a liberal icon, was perhaps the first jurist in the twentieth century to attempt to define the "substantive" content of the Fourteenth Amendment's due process clause. Despite Cardozo's liberalism, however, he was essentially an apostle of judicial restraint and was profoundly skeptical of all sorts of government regulation, including economic regulation.[11] Therefore he attempted to define the substantive content of the due process clause by very careful reference to established law, deciding that the due process clause should be construed to apply only to matters involving rights that were "fundamental" or "of the very essence of a scheme of ordered liberty."[12] In finding such rights, he did not peer into his own private sense of the meaning of life, but rather looked to the express provisions of the Constitution and to the history and traditions of our people. Cardozo concluded that freedom of speech, press, and religion were about the most fundamental rights imaginable. He did not think the specific criminal procedure elements of the Bill of Rights ranked up there as fundamental, although a fair hearing was fundamental. So he read the First Amendment into the Fourteenth. He called this "absorption."

It was only a matter of time before liberals took Fourteenth Amendment jurisprudence to extremes Cardozo never hinted at. Soon they "incorporated" other provisions of the Bill of Rights into the Fourteenth Amendment and made them binding on the states.[13] But not all rights were incorporated (forget that pesky Second Amendment), nor were the rights always incorporated in exactly the same form as they appeared in the original Bill of Rights. The due process clause, far from becoming well defined by simply reading the Bill of Rights into it, became even more protean than feared by critics of the Cardozo approach. The notion of "substantive" due process and the doctrine of "incorporation" meant that the due process clause could be given the shape as desired by any five justices of the Supreme Court at any given time.[14]

Liberals quickly put substantive due process to use in their quest to remake American culture (without ever letting the people vote on their "reforms"). Thus, abortion on demand and sodomy are now part of a "liberty" that cannot be denied with or without a hearing. Assisted suicide could be such a liberty if liberals got one more vote on the Supreme Court.[15] And it will not be long before homosexual "marriage" is included.[16]

EGALITARIANISM RUN AMOK

The liberal courts have been at their most radical in transforming a fairly straightforward command—treat people equally under the law—into something convoluted.

Initially, of course, liberals undid the incorrect racial discrimination jurisprudence of the nineteenth century—a jurisprudence clearly at odds with the text and purpose of the Thirteenth, Fourteenth, and Fifteenth Amendments. But the liberals did so as a first step toward a broad assault on what they considered to be mistreatment of "discrete and insular minorities," not just racial minorities.

Cardozo's jurisprudence of fundamental rights at least had the virtue of seeking an anchor in history and tradition, and, in its first applications, of seeking to protect religious expression.[17] But as liberals ground away at the evils of racial discrimination, they invented radically new doctrines that melded substantive due process with "more than equal" protection. Thus, they discovered all kinds of "fundamental" rights that might be "burdened" by legislative classifications. An early favorite was the "right to travel."[18] This supposedly fundamental right, the Supreme Court found, was infringed by state requirements that persons could not be eligible for welfare benefits unless they had resided in the state for a certain period. Treating new residents differently from long-term residents was invidious discrimination, the Court said, because the classification "burdened" the "fundamental" right to travel.

Once this "new" equal protection took hold, the illiberal liberals expanded it to invalidate all sorts of regulations with which they disagreed. And the beauty of it was that the people getting the benefit of this new law did not need to be "similarly situated" to others at all—indeed, they could and would be differently situated, but the differences would be placed off-limits to legislative classification.

This "new" equal protection is egalitarianism run amok. There are no differences between men and women, so single-sex educational institutions go out the window.[19] There are no differences between heterosexuals and homosexuals, so regulations designed to suppress homosexual behavior or which preclude homosexual "marriage" are ipso facto a denial of equal protection.[20] There are no differences between citizens and aliens, so illegal immigrants are entitled to free public education, welfare, and other benefits provided by the taxpayers.[21] There are no differences between the mentally retarded and normal people, so group homes for the mentally retarded are really the same as single-family residences (but the "retarded" cannot be executed for murder, because they are different).[22]

The "new" equal protection authorizes racial discrimination in voting, public university admissions, public contracts, and other areas.[23] It also condemns "irrational disability discrimination," and so it authorizes Congress to mandate "accommodation" of the handicapped at all costs in education, employment, and public buildings.[24] And it allows liberals to nullify abortion regulations, promote the homosexual agenda, make the death penalty an almost impossible exercise, and generally wage war on traditional values of the American people—especially against religion.[25]

THE ENFORCERS

How do the radical liberals enforce their tyranny of tolerance? Ironically, they resort to the same weapon used by nineteenth-century judges to suppress labor unions and forestall economic regulation: the injunction. But liberals have used injunctions in ways never contemplated by the Founding Fathers when they made provision for the "judicial power" in the Constitution.

The injunction is, quite simply, a decree, a dictate. In Anglo-American legal history, it was an order issued by a court of equity. Equity was a body of rules imported into English law to give the King's Chancellor the ability to circumvent problems created by English common law technicalities. Equity rules come from the Roman law, an authoritarian jurisprudence ideally suited for rule by decree, emphasizing discretion in the judge and not recognizing the role of the jury. During the seventeenth century, as the Founding Fathers well knew, there was a power struggle between the common law courts, championed by Sir Edward Coke, and the equity courts, favored by the king; Sir Edward lost.[26] The Founding Fathers were careful not to create separate equity courts, and they effectively abolished any distinction between equity and common law courts when they provided that the judicial power would extend to all cases in law or equity. The Founding Fathers certainly never intended the judiciary to enjoy the unfettered power of the equity courts resisted by Coke. The idea that a court could enjoin action by a coequal branch of government never occurred to the Founders.

Until the late nineteenth century, the courts seldom, if ever, purported to issue injunctions against other branches of government.[27] But during the labor strife of the late nineteenth century, corporate lawyers saw great promise in injunctions as a way to break strikes. Undoubtedly the most famous use of this weapon was in the great Pullman Strike of 1894, when federal courts enjoined the strike on the dubious premise that it interfered with the transport of the U.S. mail. Eugene Debs, the renowned socialist and labor agitator, felt the full force of the injunction, as he wound up jailed for contempt for violating it—a judgment that was upheld by the Supreme Court.[28]

At about the same time, the federal courts also began to issue injunctions against state officials to prevent enforcement of economic regulations and other laws deemed unconstitutional. Although the Supreme Court had, after the Civil War, expressed doubt that it had the power to enjoin actions of the president,[29] the Court decided in 1908 that it need have no such reservations about enjoining conduct by state officials, despite the Eleventh Amendment, among other things.[30]

When liberals took over, they saw no limits to their use of injunctions. Not only could they prevent state actions with which they disagreed, but they quickly decided that they could also mandate actions to achieve their preferred policy objectives. The injunction thus became an offensive weapon. To make it so, the illiberal liberals jettisoned hundreds of years of common law teaching that the judiciary, via the common law writ of mandamus, could compel government action by a government official only when the official's duty was clear, simple, and easily stated.[31]

When liberals combined the authoritarianism of injunctions with the power of judicial review, the result was an imperial judiciary, ready, willing, and able to impose its will on society. When the segregationists went to extreme lengths to resist equal treatment of blacks, liberals were ready with a weapon that they knew they could wield with powerful public support.[32] Naturally, they didn't stop there. Once having tasted absolute power, they rapidly swept into other areas of social policy that they disliked. Basic rules like the separation of powers wouldn't stop them from interfering.

"EVOLVING" TO SUIT THE ILLIBERAL LIBERALS

The capstone of the tyranny of tolerance is found in the liberal notion that the Constitution is not fixed and definite, but malleable—that it "evolves."

It is one thing to decree that a law cannot be enforced because it runs contrary to the Constitution. It is quite another to decree that the Constitution has no fixed meaning, but can be revised or emended at the will of the courts, who will then decree that affirmative or positive steps must be taken to enforce these revisions, often at great public expense.

The liberal notion of an "evolving" Constitution and an "evolving" concept of equality is clearly expressed in *City of Cleburne v. Cleburne Living Center*,[33] a Supreme Court case decided in 1985. The issue was whether a group home for the mentally retarded could be subject to a special use permit requirement. Of course, the city ordinance under attack used the term "feeble-minded" and required special use permits for homes for the insane, the feeble-minded, alcoholics, and drug addicts. Even in 1985, it was plain that no law appearing to discriminate against the "feeble-minded" was going to stand up in the federal courts, although the district judge courageously concluded that the ordinance was rationally related to the city's legitimate interests in the legal liabilities of the group home's operator, as well as the safety and fears of the residents in the adjoining neighborhood. The proposed group home was expected to house thirteen retarded men and women, who would be under the "constant supervision" of the operator's staff.

Not a single Supreme Court justice could find a rational basis for the city ordinance—although the district judge could and did. And the arch-liberals—William Brennan, Thurgood Marshall, and Harry Blackmun—weren't happy with the majority's decision to hold that the ordinance was invalid as applied to the group home in question. They wanted more. They wanted the "retarded" to be recognized as yet another special group of Americans entitled to "more than equal" protection.

The opinion of Justice Marshall is most revealing. Without regard to the language or intent of the Constitution, he is simply not content with allowing the legislature to make the call on how to treat admittedly differently situated classes—if the classes in question are classes favored by judges:

> Courts, however, do not sit or act in a social vacuum. Moral philosophers may debate whether certain inequalities are absolute wrongs, but history makes clear that constitutional principles of equality, like constitutional principles of liberty, property, and due process, *evolve over time*; what once was a "natural" and "self-evident" ordering later comes to be seen as an artificial and invidious constraint on human potential and freedom. . . . Shifting cultural, political, and social patterns at times come to make past practices appear inconsistent with fundamental principles upon which American society rests, an inconsistency legally cognizable under the Equal Protection Clause. . . .
>
> For the retarded, just as for Negroes and women, much has changed in recent years, but much remains the same; out-dated statutes are still on the books, and irrational fears or ignorance, traceable to the prolonged social and cultural isolation of the

retarded, continue to stymie recognition of the dignity and individuality of retarded people. *Heightened judicial scrutiny of action appearing to impose unnecessary barriers to the retarded is required in light of increasing recognition that such barriers are inconsistent with evolving principles of equality embedded in the Fourteenth Amendment.* [Emphasis added.]

So who decides what groups get favored treatment under the law, giving them a judicial veto of legislation democratically adopted and subject to democratic repeal? *The judges, of course!* And how do the judges get this special insight into what groups should be more equal than others? Well, let's let Justice Marshall regurgitate a little more:

No single talisman can define those groups likely to be the target of classifications offensive to the Fourteenth Amendment and therefore warranting heightened or strict scrutiny; experience, not abstract logic, must be the primary guide. . . .

The discreteness and insularity warranting a "more searching judicial inquiry," . . . must therefore be viewed *from a social and cultural perspective* as well as a political one. *To this task judges are well suited,* for the lessons of history and experience are surely the best guide as to when, and with respect to what interests, society is likely to stigmatize individuals as members of an inferior caste or view them as not belonging to the community. Because prejudice spawns prejudice, and stereotypes produce limitations that confirm the stereotype on which they are based, a history of unequal treatment requires *sensitivity* to the prospect that its vestiges endure. In separating those groups that are discrete and insular from those that are not, as in many important legal distinctions, "a page of history is worth a volume of logic."[34] [Emphasis added.]

Here we have in a nutshell the liberal judicial philosophy: The equal protection clause, like the rest of the Constitution, "evolves." Where once the idea of equal protection required only that the law treat similarly situated people alike and that any classifications be based on real (not racial) differences between groups, this was not enough for radical liberals. Certain judicially favored groups needed special protection. We started out with race, then we added "alienage" and national origin; then we added sex. The illiberal liberals decide who is "different" and what classifications are "rational," and they do this on the basis of "evolving standards" and "increasing recognition" (by whom?) that certain class-based distinctions are just *bad*. To implement their own notions of equality and due process, they use their handy injunctions. Often these are very elaborate "remedial" decrees, prescribing everything from tax rates for desegregation of schools to the temperature of the coleslaw in county jail kitchens.[35]

EQUAL OUTCOMES, OR EQUAL OPPORTUNITY?

The ultimate irony of liberal "equal protection" is that, at bottom, it is no different from the legal philosophy underlying the infamous *Dred Scott* and *Plessy v. Ferguson* decisions: The judiciary decides what good social policy is and revises the Constitution to impose it. As the first Justice Harlan predicted, when the courts abandon the true meaning of the Constitution, everyone is at risk. The liberal "evolution" permits, indeed mandates, unequal treatment of men, white persons, Christians, the military, gun owners, middle-class property owners, and persons of Asian descent—all to benefit favored groups.

Radical liberals fail to see, or refuse to acknowledge, that you can't discriminate in favor of somebody without discriminating *against* somebody else. The liberal approach necessarily conflicts with the rights of all individuals.[36] By all means give every citizen equal *opportunity*. But the illiberal liberals won't settle for that. Their radical egalitarianism seeks to impose equality of *outcome* rather than equality of opportunity. That's what the tyranny of tolerance is all about.

CHAPTER 3

"BENIGN" DISCRIMINATION

[I] deny that any legislative body or judicial tribunal may have regard to the race of citizens when the civil rights of those citizens are involved. . . . [I]n view of the Constitution, in the eye of the law, there is in this country no superior, dominant, ruling class of citizens. There is no caste here. Our Constitution is color-blind, and neither knows nor tolerates classes among citizens.
—Justice John M. Harlan, dissenting in *Plessy v. Ferguson* (1896)

The Court today resoundingly reaffirms the principle that State-imposed racial segregation is highly suspect and cannot be justified on the ground that " 'all persons suffer . . . in equal degree.' " . . . While I join that declaration without reservation, I write separately to express again my conviction that the same standard of review ought not to control judicial inspection of **every** *official race classification. [Emphasis added.]*
—Justice Ruth Bader Ginsburg, concurring in
Johnson v. California (2004)

I FACED OFF AGAINST the tyranny of tolerance well before I became a judge. Many times, in fact. The liberal assault is so broad-ranging that it would have been impossible to avoid.

When I was practicing employment and local government law in the 1970s and 1980s, I frequently locked horns with liberals on matters involving alleged racial discrimination. The crusade against racial discrimination lies at the heart of the tyranny of tolerance. After all, how can one be tolerant and not be racially "inclusive"? Have not blacks suffered centuries of disadvantage at the hands of whites? Is there not conscious and "unconscious" racial bias by whites affecting every facet of our society? Sure, contemporary whites are not guilty of illegal discrimination just because they're white, but does that really matter? Don't the social, educational, and economic disadvantages of blacks require something more than nondiscrimination?[1]

This was the kind of liberal thinking I was up against when I practiced employment law. The problem was that the Supreme Court had endorsed such fuzzy logic. Most notably, the Court had, in the 1970s, embraced the doctrine of "adverse impact" or "disparate impact."[2] By this vague standard, a plaintiff presenting himself as the victim of illegal discrimination no longer needed to provide any evidence that the employer actually intended to discriminate; if statistics (no matter how questionable) showed that hiring or promotion did not match up with statistically "expected" patterns, then the employer was guilty of discrimination.[3]

The real-world implications, as I saw firsthand, were deeply troubling. Statistics could easily show that merit-based hiring had an "adverse impact" on blacks—especially because, as Thomas Sowell has demonstrated, the statistical methods routinely relied on by employment discrimination plaintiffs never control for the variables that can affect test outcomes.[4] Private employers simply turned to unwritten and unacknowledged quotas. The Equal Employment Opportunity Commission (EEOC) assured them in so many words that employment practices would not be scrutinized if they generated the minimum number of black hires. The EEOC rule of thumb was the "80 percent rule"—that is, if blacks were hired at a rate equal to 80 percent the selection rate of whites, everything was A-OK.[5]

State and local governments did not cave so quickly. They tried to adapt the concept of merit-based hiring to the EEOC's and the liberal judiciary's standards for "professionally validated" tests, which the Civil Rights Act of 1964 had expressly permitted for hiring or promotion.[6] It was a futile effort. If statistics prove anything, they must be said to have proved one thing about civil service testing (the objective standard used for government hiring): Virtually 100 percent of such tests were not valid. Amazing.

I represented the City of St. Louis in a long-running lawsuit over promotions in the fire department. The city spent quite a bit of money in developing a test for promotion to fire captain. Whites and blacks participated in the development process. Did it work? No. The city fell short of the EEOC's 80 percent rule by two promotions. That is to say, if just two more black firefighters had been promoted, the U.S. Justice Department (which was suing the city) would not have attacked the test. As it was, the Justice Department offered to settle the case if the city would simply adjust the test results to promote two more black firefighters. But St. Louis officials refused.[7] We would fight it out.

We won in the district court, but then the action shifted to the federal court of appeals in St. Louis, a court composed almost entirely of the most radical liberals on the bench anywhere, anytime. Even though the case went to the appellate court at a preliminary stage (that is, before a full trial on the merits), the court of appeals ordered the city immediately to fill one-third of all fire captain vacancies by promoting black firefighters—an unprecedented quota. The court also ordered the city to develop a new test, and ordered the Justice Department and the plaintiffs to hire experts to "help" St. Louis. The city paid for the plaintiffs' expert, of course.[8]

So a new test was developed with the aid of the same expert from the Justice Department who had never found a valid test in use in his life. A new test was produced, using every method suggested by the Justice Department guru, and guess what? It had adverse impact! So what did the Justice Department expert say? He said it was valid. Though the black plaintiffs disagreed, even the court of appeals had little choice but to back the Justice Department.

Such convoluted reasoning and unnecessary litigation recur again and again because liberals have decided to ensure not that all citizens are equal regardless of race, but that citizens of certain races are considered *more equal* than others.

Even more disturbing, the liberal courts have used racial discrimination as the spearhead in their fight to take control of American culture. No one would argue for the preservation of government-sponsored or -mandated racial discrimination against blacks. But in the name of fighting for civil rights, the courts have consolidated their power. In combating unconstitutional racial discrimination, liberals found an issue that most Americans would accept to justify draconian judicial decrees. Thus, the spectacle of a crazed mob threatening black kids trying to go to school led the country to accept the Supreme Court's arrogation to itself of a role superior to the Constitution and led the president of the United States to use federal troops to vindicate the will of the Court.[9] A few years later, a similar spectacle at a state university, engendered by a black man's effort to enroll, led to more court orders and further intervention by federal troops to vindicate the court's orders.

Ironically, the legal regime of racial segregation that provided the occasion for the liberal judiciary's coup de main resulted largely because the Supreme Court refused to enforce the Constitution according to its plain meaning and intent. The Fourteenth Amendment was intended to secure political and legal equality for freed blacks—indeed, for blacks everywhere. But in the case of *Plessy v. Ferguson* (1896), the Court simply ignored the plain meaning and intent of the Fourteenth Amendment, authorizing racial segregation under the rubric of "separate but equal."[10] Unfortunately, when the Court finally recognized the patent unconstitutionality of government-imposed segregation, it proved to be but a first step in the liberal coup.

QUOTAS? NEVER!

No, overturning the doctrine of "separate but equal" would not suffice for the illiberal liberals. They needed to do more. They need to show black citizens that they were truly serious about tolerance and equality.

But how? Through "affirmative action." Does that mean quotas? Perish the thought! No, we have only "goals." Reverse discrimination? There is no such thing. We don't discriminate. We merely want "diversity."

The idea of "affirmative action" was given expression by President Lyndon Johnson (author of so many of our modern societal disasters) in Executive Order 11246, which decreed "goals and timetables" for increasing "minority participation" in federal contracts. In no time, this rendition of affirmative action spread from federal government contracting to local government contracting, employment, education, and voting. It also mutated from "goals and timetables" to "set-asides."

The Supreme Court, confronted with repeated challenges to this blatant discrimination in favor of blacks, women, and other "disadvantaged groups," did a creditable imitation of a drunk trying to walk a straight line, zigzagging crazily from approval of set-asides to disapproval of set-asides, from approval of hiring quotas to disapproval of hiring quotas, from disapproval of college admissions quotas to approval of admissions quotas. The inconsistency reflects liberal judges' categorical unwillingness to enforce the Constitution when favored "minority" groups don't want it enforced. Under the regime of illiberal liberalism, the *Plessy* doctrine has come full circle: Separate but equal is unequal and illegal, but separate and "more equal" is quite all right, as long as the ones who are more equal belong to a favored minority.

The Supreme Court first confronted affirmative action in 1974 in a case known as *DeFunis v. Odegaard*.[11] In that case, the lower courts had forced the University of Washington Law School to admit the white plaintiff, who had been rejected by the school despite the fact that his test scores were higher than those of some of the minority students admitted. But here the justices simply ducked the issue, because the plaintiff would graduate before the case could be decided. The odd thing about the case, though, was that a leading liberal, William O. Douglas, broke ranks with the other liberals, denying that racial criteria were lawful for any purpose whatever. He departed from the court soon after; his replacement, John Paul Stevens, would soon come to see the virtue of "benign" racial classifications.[12]

After dodging the issue in *DeFunis*, the Supreme Court was forced to face affirmative action in *Regents of the University of California v. Bakke*.[13] In that case, the University of California at Davis decided to reserve sixteen of one hundred medical school slots for selected minorities. Four Supreme Court justices said that this obvious quota was unconstitutional as well as in direct conflict with the plain language of Title VI of the Civil Rights Act of 1964 (barring discrimination in federally funded programs). But four other justices—the most reliably "tolerant" of the bunch, William Brennan, Thurgood Marshall, and Harry Blackmun, along with the so-called moderate Whizzer White— said that the school could admit students on the basis of race. Stevens, surprisingly, condemned the UC-Davis quota this time, but that would change. The decisive vote came from Justice Lewis Powell, who split the difference, saying on the one hand that the UC-Davis quota was illegal and Bakke should be admitted to medical school, but on the other that "diversity" was a compelling governmental interest that could be served "by a properly devised admissions program involving the competitive consideration of race and ethnic origin." Thus, the hallowed notion of "diversity" was enshrined in the law.

During the 1980s and 1990s, the Supreme Court continued to bob and weave about the equal protection ring, with the so-called moderate justices obviously uncomfortable with "benign" racial discrimination but equally uncomfortable with the idea of actually enforcing the Fourteenth Amendment. Sounds like the *Plessy* majority, doesn't it?

THE DEATH OF OBJECTIVE STANDARDS

Before and after the *Bakke* case, actual racial quotas had been approved in one major arena: employment discrimination cases. As my experience in the St. Louis firefighters' case indicates, courts imposed hiring and promotion quotas on the premise that identifiable black employees had been denied jobs or promotions and so were entitled to be hired or promoted into the jobs they had been illegally denied. This makes sense when we're talking about a specific individual or group of individuals (like Allan Bakke) who lost specific job opportunities.[14] Of course, sometimes the quota mentality got out of hand, as liberal lower federal courts decided to impose quotas that had no relationship whatever to the actual harm found. This is exactly what the court of appeals did in the St. Louis case. These excessive quotas undoubtedly were motivated by a desire to punish employers and "white" labor unions, who stubbornly refused to throw in the towel when accused of discrimination.

Perhaps the most pernicious consequence of the courts' approval of quotas is that it leads to the idea that certain people don't have to adhere to the same standards as everyone else, because those standards—no matter how objective—are tainted by history. As seen with the St. Louis firefighters' case, even the most rigorously developed civil service testing could be found to have an "adverse impact" and thus to be invalid. Obviously, the best way to ensure proportional hiring of blacks by government and private employers was to destroy all objective hiring or promotion standards.

It wasn't just the courts that attacked objective standards. During the Carter era, Congress mandated "minority business enterprise" set-asides—that is, quotas in government contracts. If contractors did not demonstrate the participation of a sufficient number of "minority business enterprises" (MBEs) or "women business enterprises" (WBEs), then they would lose the contract, even if they had the low bid.

The set-aside gimmick was attacked at the federal level, but the Supreme Court upheld it as a proper exercise of congressional power to "remedy" discrimination. Surprisingly, Justice Stevens still stood resolutely with the first Justice Harlan.[15] So did Justice Potter Stewart, seldom a "moderate" in civil rights litigation; Stewart noted that in enacting racial entitlements, the Court displayed sentiments similar to those of the majority in *Plessy*.[16]

The liberal judiciary, aided by liberal legislators, thus fosters a form of corruption of blood: Because the government practiced racial discrimination in the past, we are all tainted by those former practices. Such a doctrine not only unfairly stigmatizes (a liberal expression, I know), but it legitimizes and even encourages black racism, insisting that blacks, no matter what their personal achievements or so-cial status, are and always will be victims of conscious or "uncon-scious" racism.

Here, as in most other arenas, the radical liberals are wrong—morally, ethically, and legally. They continue to wrap themselves in the mantle of the civil rights battle because it gives them political ad-vantages, especially the political loyalty of blacks, that they can't live without. But in reality, the civil rights battle has been won. Look at the facts.

Liberals often claim, for example, that voter registration proce-dures disadvantage black citizens. I represented the City of St. Louis in one case when liberal activists attempted to take over voter registration procedures because those procedures supposedly were unfair to blacks and "the poor." But as we demonstrated to the federal court, the facts showed that blacks were actually registered in disproportionately *larger* numbers than whites.[17] Since blacks aren't actually excluded from the voting booth anymore, liberals must manufacture voting rights challenges based on election outcomes. Professor Lani Guinier, the notorious civil rights activist, has demanded that elections be rigged, by giving black and women voters weighted votes or otherwise discounting white and male votes, to produce the "right" proportion of blacks and women in elective office.[18]

Once again, we see that the illiberal liberals' real concern is not with equal opportunity but with equal outcomes.

Liberals cannot stomach the notion that perhaps American society is *not* the racist hellhole that they portray. I have observed hundreds of trial juries in the city of St. Louis, juries truly drawn from a fair cross section of the city. These people are drawn together at random, thrust into an uncomfortable role as decision maker in disputes involving everything from minor auto collisions to the death sentence; they listen, discuss, and render verdicts, or agree to disagree, without allowing any racial bias to prevent them from doing their duty. If racial bias affects deliberations, nearly always it is because the black community has been and is being taught to hate the police and distrust the law.[19]

Of course there are instances of discriminatory behavior by some

whites against some blacks, motivated, at least in part, by racial bigotry. But there are now effective remedies in place to address injuries
inflicted by such conduct. On the other hand, there are equally discriminatory acts taken by some blacks against some whites, also because of
racial hatred. The same remedies should be available to address injuries
caused by this conduct as well, but the judicial system does not respond
as readily to these injuries.

Indeed, the liberal doctrine of more equal than others has become
firmly entrenched in American law. When the Supreme Court attempted
to modify the adverse impact rule ever so slightly in 1989,[20] liberals
screamed "Segregation!" and "Racism!" and passed the Civil Rights
Act of 1991. President George H. W. Bush, in perhaps the most courageous action of his administration—next to the appointment of Justice
Thomas—vetoed it. The veto was sustained, but then a curious thing
happened: The Republicans cut and ran, and a "compromise" bill was
enacted that not only restored the old rule of adverse impact but added
punitive damages and jury trials to the mix.

QUOTAS ENDURE

The quota mentality has taken root most deeply in academe, dominated as it is by liberals. Relying on Justice Powell's endorsement of
the "competitive consideration" of race and ethnicity in college admissions in *Bakke,* the universities quietly have imposed their own
admissions quotas, usually well disguised, but always producing the desired numerical results. Inevitably, liberal academics ventured closer
and closer to outright quotas, while the Supreme Court started to zag
away from racial preferences. In a series of cases in the 1980s, the
Court allowed white employees to challenge and sometimes stop the
continuation of hiring quotas if there was no longer any connection
between the quota and the previous discrimination; it rejected racial
preferences in teacher layoffs; and it held that minority set-asides in
awarding public contracts had to be justified as remedying past racial
discrimination.[21] Lower courts began to question the racial preference

rules for college admissions approved by Justice Powell in *Bakke* and actually struck down some of them.[22] So a lot was on the line when, in 2003, the Supreme Court took up two cases involving admissions quotas used by the University of Michigan: *Gratz v. Bollinger*[23] and *Grutter v. Bollinger.*[24] With these decisions, the Court showed the continuing strength of the liberal notion that some are more equal than others.

Gratz v. Bollinger involved a number of clever ploys to give black and other selected minority groups a leg up in getting into the University of Michigan undergraduate school. The most direct measure simply gave minority students an extra twenty points in a scoring system that determined who was admitted to the university and who wasn't. Every single judge on the Supreme Court admitted that this was a racial classification. So did every judge agree to strike it down? Of course not. Every liberal (Stevens, Ginsburg, Souter, and Breyer) said that "benign" racial preferences are perfectly constitutional. Breyer was especially canny. He *concurred* in the judgment striking down the twenty-point preference, so that he didn't have to try and defend the indefensible, but stated that "in implementing the Constitution's equality instruction, government decisionmakers may properly distinguish between policies of inclusion and exclusion, . . . for the former are more likely to prove consistent with the basic constitutional obligation that the law respect each individual equally."[25] What does that mean? That ditching the white and Asian kids is a way to "respect each individual equally"?

The fact that the Supreme Court struck down the undergraduate quota does not mean that the idea of more equal than others has been laid to rest. Not by a long shot. The undergraduate "bonus" system failed because, in Justice Sandra Day O'Connor's decisive view, it was "nonindividualized" and "mechanical."

To find an "individualized" and "nonmechanical" way to discriminate against white and Asian kids, you have only to look through Justice O'Connor's peculiar constitutional prism at the warm and fuzzy race discrimination used by the University of Michigan Law School.

That system was upheld in *Grutter v. Bollinger*, decided the same day as *Gratz*, but reaching the "tolerant" result.

The law school, as befits a squad of brilliant lawyers, played the race card in a way that cribbed directly from Justice Powell's opinion in *Bakke* and from the Harvard admissions policy commended by Powell. That process set as its "goal" a "critical mass" of minority student enrollees, who would achieve "diversity" and all of the hypothetical benefits of this "diversity." The trial court found that the process discriminated in fact against white applicants. Ordinarily, appellate courts defer to a factual finding of discrimination, but when "tolerance" and "diversity" are at stake, the ordinary rules go by the boards. Justice O'Connor, "moderate" legal goddess that she is, had nary a word to say about the trial court's findings, which she treated as virtually nonexistent. Drawing her facts not from the findings of the trial court but from unsupported generalities set out in the law school's brief and briefs of the amici curiae ("friends of the court") supporting the law school, she resolved all uncertainty in the law of equal protection: "diversity" is a "compelling state interest" that justifies racial classifications.[26] The only question is whether these classifications are "narrowly tailored" so as to not "unduly" harm the innocent and are structured to last only so long as necessary to eradicate the evil in question.

Never mind that the law school saw to it that, for six straight years, the percentages of blacks and Hispanics admitted corresponded almost exactly with the percentages of those groups who applied to the law school.[27] Such correlation is remarkable indeed, but less so when one recalls the testimony before the trial court indicating that the admissions director demanded and got daily "tracking reports" of the percentage of favored minorities being admitted to the school. Although the director denied that he intentionally boosted admission rates for minorities, the trial court obviously did not believe him—for good reason, given the data. But again, the trial court's findings and inferences carried no weight with Justice O'Connor.

The most inspiring aspect of Justice O'Connor's opinion in *Grutter* is her conclusion that these racial classifications cannot go on forever.

They are subject to reasonable "durational limits" (sorry, but that's how judges write these days; in ordinary language, they must come to an end some time). So what's reasonable? Well, *Brown v. Board of Education* was decided in 1954. Every black kid in school in 1954 has moved on, but so what? *Bakke* was decided in 1978. Again, every black kid in school at that time has moved on. Well, let's give it another twenty-five years. Yep, in 2028, 160 years after the adoption of the equal protection clause, we won't need this kind of "benign" racial discrimination.[28]

Oh, but wait a minute. Let's look at the true blue liberals. Justice Ginsburg: We're neck-deep in conscious and *unconscious* racism, so let's not be too hasty in setting limits here. Only when we get absolute equality of outcomes in all areas of American society can we be sure that we don't need "benign" racial classifications.[29] (Note also that Ginsburg and Souter would uphold the blatantly discriminatory "bonus" system used in the Michigan undergraduate school.)

There you have it, folks, the liberal concept of equal protection of the law. Quotas for everything—even when these "benign" classifications end up hurting whites and Asians.[30]

THE GOSPEL OF DIVERSITY

There was a time when the courts sat to try to vindicate individual rights on a case-by-case basis. They also tried, under American constitutional principles as they used to exist, to restrain government from depriving its citizens of life, liberty, and property, or treating citizens differently based solely on skin color. The illiberal liberals don't believe that the courts should sit for these purposes. Rather, they sit to remake society in the image of the liberals.

Is this due process of law? Is this equal protection? A qualified white or Asian student is denied admission to an elite educational institution solely because of skin color. Other benefits, like employment, or government contracts, are awarded according to preordained percentages. Is this going to eliminate racism, or exacerbate it? Does it liberate us, or impress a badge of servitude on all of us? If we continue to maintain quotas, how will we know when we don't need them anymore?

Perhaps Justice O'Connor's twenty-five-year limit for racial discrimination in education will prove prophetic. The striking down of the barrier against racial intermarriage, a barrier rightly struck down,[31] may prove to be the undoing of the radical liberals' quota society. People are continuing America's melting-pot tradition, whether liberals and black politicians like it or not. Indeed, it is very likely that concepts of distinctive "races" may evaporate as the mapping of the human genome and the proliferation of DNA profiles shows us that we really are brothers under the skin, and that there is no meaningful way to distinguish among us. Perhaps then the judiciary will realize that it is better to enforce the equal protection clause as it was intended and leave to the good sense of the American people the completion of progress toward one nation, under God—oops! The illiberal liberals can't stand God, either.

The problem is that nothing has really changed since 1896. The judiciary still rewrites the Constitution to suit itself. Now, instead of "separate but equal," we must contend with the tyranny of tolerance and its gospel of diversity. Not "separate but equal," but "more equal than others."

CHAPTER 4

"OZZIE AND HARRIET ARE DEAD"

Opinion leaders . . . continue to tout irresponsible sexual behavior as a mere lifestyle choice and disparage firm standards of conduct. They embrace a misplaced "tolerance" that sees family forms as equivalent and refuses to condemn variants as dysfunctional. . . . At this juncture in our civilization, their outlook is the ultimate act of bad faith. Sexual freedom and political correctness for the advantaged have come at the price of broken families for the vulnerable.

—Amy Wax, "What Women Want,"
Wall Street Journal, August 29, 2005

Today's opinion dismantles the structure of constitutional law that has permitted a distinction to be made between heterosexual and homosexual unions, insofar as formal recognition in marriage is concerned.

—Justice Antonin Scalia, dissenting in *Lawrence v. Texas* (2003)

"OZZIE AND HARRIET ARE DEAD," declared Congressman Richard Gephardt of Missouri, during his 1992 campaign for president.[1] This trenchant phrase confirmed his conversion from a relatively moderate, pro-life, antibusing midwestern Democrat to a lapdog of the radical liberal wing of his party (though it failed to win that wing's support for his presidential campaign). The phrase epitomizes the liberal attitude toward the family and sexual morality—symbolized by the 1950s television show *The Adventures of Ozzie and Harriet.*

Ozzie and Harriet, for those of you unfamiliar with television comedies from the 1950s and early 1960s, were the prototypical monogamous, hardworking, law-abiding, clean-living suburban American parents, piloting a family of clean-cut, obedient children. They also epitomize virtually everything despised by the liberals who control our courts: They were white, they were heterosexual, they were temperate, they were churchgoers, and they were *married.*

So it is not surprising that by 1992 a leading Democratic candidate for president could pronounce that they were "dead." By that, of course, he meant that the American standard for the family was dead. In his world, the radical liberal world, he was right. In the world created by the illiberal liberals, through Lyndon Johnson's Great Society welfare state, he was right. In mainstream America, he was only partly right: Ozzie and Harriet are not dead, but they are plainly fighting a rearguard action, under assault from an array of liberal constituencies, including femifascists and homosexual activists. And here, too, the courts are in the forefront of the assault on traditional norms and values.

THE FAMILY UNDER ATTACK

It is not so easy to pinpoint the beginning of the legal assault on the family. Although liberals tout several early twentieth-century Supreme Court decisions that limited legislative authority to control how people raised and educated their kids, they do not cite these cases because they are really interested in preserving the traditional family. Rather, they use these decisions as building blocks for their doctrine of "privacy," a powerful legal weapon to destroy majoritarian laws aimed at preserving traditional moral standards in society.

There can be little doubt that, at the time of the foundation of the Republic, the law regarded the nuclear family as the cornerstone of civil society. Indeed, the Christian family, composed of husband-father, wife-mother, and children of the marriage, had been the template for civil society in England from earliest times, forming at once the basic unit of society and the locus of succession of property ownership. As one of the greatest of English legal historians puts it, "The sanctity of inheritance as the great safeguard of family security is a theme which runs continually through the history of property."[2] Whatever inheritance rules were applied, marriage and children of the marriage were of crucial importance.[3]

As the American welfare state evolved under the superintendence of the illiberal liberals, the continuing primacy of the family became a threat to the omnipotence of the government. The best way to attack that threat was to destroy its favored position in the law. To do that, it was necessary first to attack the "sanctity of inheritance," and then to attack the essential terms of the marriage contract itself, by destroying the rights of men and unborn children in the relationship.

The modern attack on the family as the fundamental prop of society surely began with the employment of the liberals' favorite tool, the equal protection clause. This weapon was used to attack the very essence of the family, the idea that children of a marriage occupied a status at once different from and superior to illegitimate children. (Oh, by the way, the modern, politically correct law school profs don't use the term "illegitimate," since that term is obviously "insensitive" and, even worse, "normative." The old law frankly used the term "bastards," but now we use the phrase "nonmarital children,"[4] so that we don't imply that bastardy carries any sort of taint.)

In the 1968 case *Levy v. Louisiana,*[5] the Supreme Court found unconstitutional a Louisiana statute that barred unacknowledged illegitimate children from filing legal actions for the wrongful death of the parent. Delivering the opinion of the Court, Justice William O. Douglas wrote: "[W]e have been extremely sensitive when it comes to basic civil rights and have not hesitated to strike down an invidious classification even though it had history and tradition on its side."[6]

This is liberal law in a nutshell. History and tradition count for nothing; the language of the Constitution itself counts for little; the only criterion is whether a ruling will advance the liberal agenda.

Although the Supreme Court did not chart a consistent course in invalidating legal distinctions based on legitimacy, the liberals on the Court never wavered. They voted to strike down every distinction that came before them, displaying their contempt for traditional notions of family and morality.[7] But these cases merely served as the precursor to a real liberal assault on the family—the fight for abortion.

FROM CRIME TO CONSTITUTIONAL RIGHT

Abortion, though not itself a homicide (unless the child was born and then died as result of the abortion), was a crime at common law.[8] It was a crime when the Constitution was ratified. It was a crime when the Bill of Rights was ratified. It was a crime when the Fourteenth Amendment was ratified.[9]

Then came *Roe v. Wade*.[10] Suddenly abortion was no longer a crime; it was a constitutional right. This deeply flawed ruling remains as a monument to the absolute power of the liberal judiciary. The consequences have been frightening.

Have you ever seen a "partial birth" abortion? I have. I am probably one of a relatively small number of nonabortionists who have had that . . . what? Privilege? Opportunity? In my case, it was duty.

As an attorney, I had a brief set-to with the abortion industry when I represented the City of St. Louis. Abortionists sued to invalidate a city ordinance that required abortions after the first three months of pregnancy (trimester) to be performed only in hospitals. The lawsuit came to an abrupt end when the Supreme Court invalidated such requirements in 1983.[11] Although the suit was soon over, we took enough pretrial depositions to learn that the abortion business was a very good business, with very few performed for free. This experience with abortion as a lawyer was followed by one case on the bench when I dismissed a suit by a husband seeking an injunction to bar his wife from aborting their child. Even though the defense lawyer in that case had been my opponent in the city ordinance case, he knew I would follow the law. He was right. The law was clear that the husband had no rights.

So it was with this limited experience with abortion that I confronted one of the most challenging cases of my career.

In 1999, Missouri, along with many other states and the federal government, adopted a law forbidding "partial birth abortions," with the sole exception if necessary to preserve the mother's life. Missouri's liberal Democratic governor, Mel Carnahan, vetoed the law, but the legislature promptly overrode the veto, with many Democrats voting in favor. Scarcely had they done so when the usual happened: The abortionists hastened to federal court and got an injunction against enforcement of the law. Missouri's Democratic attorney general had no stomach for defending the law, so he retained a special counsel. Then a funny thing happened: The federal court of appeals (now populated by Reagan-Bush judges) held that the federal judge was supposed to "abstain," or wait, and let a state court decide what the law meant, before the federal courts could decide if it was constitutional. The special attorney general filed suit in St. Louis circuit court to get a declaration of the meaning of the law, and the suit eventually came to me.

By the time I got the case, known as *State of Missouri v. Reproductive Health Services,* the 2000 presidential election campaign was in full swing, and the United States Supreme Court was hearing a challenge to a Nebraska law also aimed at partial birth abortion. Although the Supreme Court nullified the Nebraska law,[12] the differences between that law and Missouri's compelled me to hold a trial on the issues in the Missouri case.

For several days I was treated to evidence from prominent abortionists and obstetrician/gynecologists on the basics of abortion, as well as many finer points, as practiced in modern medicine. The pièce de résistance was the videotape.

What do "D&E" and "D&X" mean to you? Probably nothing. I'll tell you what they mean. "D&E" refers to an abortion procedure that occurs from about twelve to twenty-four weeks' gestation, when the infant is fully formed in the womb and is usually "quickened"—that is, moving about in the womb. The "D&E" abortionist literally pulls the child apart inside the womb and pulls the pieces out one at a time. It is analogous to twisting a boiled chicken to pieces. This is a recognized, constitutionally protected form of abortion.[13]

"D&X" is partial birth abortion. This procedure is employed after twenty-four weeks, when the infant's bones are too far developed to permit the butchery known as "D&E." In the "D&X" procedure, the child is extracted feet first from the uterus, up to the head. The abortionist (the temptation to call him a baby butcher is strong) then sucks the brain out of the skull, collapsing it, and permitting the infant to be removed completely from the uterus. Justice Antonin Scalia noted that the description of the procedure evokes a shudder of revulsion;[14] in a sane legal system, it would do more than evoke a shudder, it would evoke swift condemnation. Yet the courts have thwarted efforts to limit or prevent the use of the "D&X" procedure on the flimsiest pretext that somehow, somewhere, the health of a mother might require abortion of her unborn child by "D&X."

The "inventor" of partial birth abortion, a fellow named Haskell, was so enamored of the procedure that he videotaped himself performing it, to show it at a conference of abortionists. When Ohio outlawed partial birth abortion, Haskell sued and his videotape was put into evidence, but never released to the public. After much procedural jockeying, the Missouri special attorney general succeeded in getting the federal judge who struck down Ohio's law to share the videotape with me. It was agreed that the video would not be made public. Surprisingly, nobody, not even the media, objected. During the testimony of the state's expert witness, the videotape was played for the witness, counsel, and me.

I was present at the birth of each of my three daughters, so the delivery of a baby is not a mystery to me. What was and is a mystery is how anyone could participate in a partial birth abortion, which is simply delivering the baby up to the head and then killing him or her by crushing the skull.

I suppose watching a partial birth abortion could be compared to watching an execution, except that the abortion is messier and involves an innocent infant. Perhaps the more apt analogy is to watching a murder. Is this part of the "evolving standard of decency" that motivates liberals to oppose the death penalty? If it's part of decency to extract an unborn infant and crush his skull, then the liberal notion of decency needs some work. We seem to be evolving away from decency and back into barbarism if killing infants in this way is a constitutional right.

After my brush with the femifascist PC police in the sexual harassment case in 1999, I carefully adhered to the blandest and most dispassionate language in dealing with partial birth abortion. After all, I was not called upon to rule on the constitutionality of the law; the feds had kept that for themselves. My job was to say what the Missouri statute meant, what abortion procedures it outlawed, and what defenses or exceptions would apply. Because the statutory language was murky in key places, this was a difficult task.

In retrospect, I believe I spent a great deal of effort to no purpose in *State v. Planned Parenthood*. I was seduced by the sophistries employed by both sides and produced an opinion that fell into the trap of adjudicating hypothetical questions. I should have said that the statute applied only to the "D&X" procedure—the true partial birth procedure—which it did, and to nothing else. Then I should have said that it implied an exception for preserving maternal health, and let it go at that. Instead, I produced a turgid, David Souter–like opinion, attempting to define with great precision many things that really needed no defining. The reality was that no one was likely to be prosecuted under the law—especially when Missouri's premier abortionist testified that he had performed just two partial birth procedures in thirty years, and both were clearly in circumstances where the mother's life was at stake.[15]

The struggle over partial birth abortion will be renewed during the 2006–07 term of the Supreme Court. Before the Court will be cases attacking the new federal statute forbidding the procedure, backed up by congressional findings that the procedure is never necessary to preserve the mother's health.[16] As with racial preferences, Justice Anthony

Kennedy will in all probability be the decisive vote. He voted against partial birth abortion in the 2000 Nebraska case. Will he do so again, when his "moderate" credentials are at stake? Will his thirst for praise from the *Washington Post* overwhelm him?

We are forced to ponder such questions because in 1973, in a masterpiece of revisionist legal history, the Supreme Court decided that abortion is a constitutional right. Criticism of *Roe v. Wade* has been unremitting and unanswerable since the decision was handed down. Unfortunately, unlike the infamous rulings in *Dred Scott v. Sandford*,[17] which also ignored established law in striking down a statute disliked by a majority of the Supreme Court, and in *Plessy v. Ferguson*,[18] which ignored the plain language and history of the Fourteenth Amendment, *Roe* remains on the books.

Roe purported to identify a corollary to a right of privacy, subsumed under the liberty guaranteed by the due process clause of the Fourteenth Amendment. As the rationale of *Roe* evolved, however, it became clear that what was at issue was not the right of privacy. What *privacy* is there in the destruction of unborn life? A pregnancy, absent intervention of a syringe, requires the participation of two people, and results in the creation of a third—who had, even in the womb, formerly enjoyed legal protections and indeed legal rights, foremost of which had been the right to inherit.[19] And remember, too, that termination of a pregnancy involves doctors, nurses, hospitals, or clinics. This is privacy?

No, at stake with *Roe* were the "reproductive rights" of women, to the exclusion of husbands and fathers, and perforce to the exclusion of traditional ideas of the family. Part and parcel of the marriage contract is the procreation of children. This is not some artifact of Roman Catholic doctrine; it was a real and vital part of the marriage contract under the law. To be sure, no one could be compelled by the government to procreate, but certainly a great object of the marriage contract was children, born and reared within the marriage.[20] *Roe* nullifies the central purpose of the marriage contract, and the correlative rights and obligations of husband and wife in that regard.

This is the way of modern constitutional adjudication by liberals:

Women were subordinate to men for too long in our history; this subordination manifested itself (they claim) in abortion laws, which compelled women to bear unwanted children (unwanted by whom?). Nothing must stand in the way of making women now more equal than men in this most essential aspect of human life. Who (except the ineffable Catharine MacKinnon) can deny that the abortion "right" establishes, not equality, but superiority—superiority both to men and to unborn children?[21]

In the liberal legal cosmos, the institutions of marriage and family are inconsequential when held up against the almighty *right to choose*. Of course, the right is not found in the Constitution or in Anglo-American legal history or tradition. Liberal judges have invented it to justify decisions that advance their political agenda on everything from abortion to sodomy.

Ah, the right to choose. Where has that right taken us? Abortion on demand. Abortion for minors whose every other medical treatment would require parental consent.[22] And not just abortion when the child is in the earliest stages of embryonic development. No, we get abortion by some of the most revolting procedures ever witnessed outside concentration camp medical experiments.

CHILDREN AND MEN OVERBOARD

The liberal fight for abortion is not just about the defense of baby butchery; it is part of the multipronged assault on the traditional family. Perhaps no court decision validated these left-wing legal efforts more than the U.S. Supreme Court's 1992 ruling in *Planned Parenthood v. Casey*.

That case featured the infamous opinion written jointly by Justices Sandra Day O'Connor, Anthony Kennedy, and David Souter, which held that a state could not require a wife to notify her husband of a planned abortion. Relying on "scientific" data—really extrapolations of statistical extrapolations grossly exaggerating the incidence of spousal abuse (indeed, the data clearly show that spousal abuse is trivial in comparison to abuse by unmarried cohabitants)—the *Casey* majority determined that husbands had no marital rights, because some husbands mistreat their wives. And apparently women are too weak to adhere to an abortion decision if their husbands vigorously oppose it. So, presto! Husband-fathers have no reproductive rights. The abortion decision is that of the woman alone, even if she is part of an apparently intact, functioning family. Only she has the "right to choose" to carry to term the child jointly conceived in a relationship that once was the most sacred contract known to the law.[23]

So let's see, unborn children have no rights until they are "viable" (and try to get a liberal to admit when viability occurs during pregnancy—they won't). Fathers have no reproductive rights whatsoever, even if they are also husbands. Women are the sole arbiters of reproduction. All of this in the name of due process and equal protection.

FROM FAMILY TO FORNICATION AND BEYOND

If we've destroyed the evil patriarchal model of the family, what's next? The cornerstone of the family itself: marriage.

For years, the Supreme Court protected rights of marriage and family in a manner in keeping with the common law, history, tradition, and the meaning and central purpose of the Fourteenth Amendment. The earliest cases on state interference with the family involved not marriage itself but the rights of parents to decide where their children went to school and what languages they could learn.[24] These cases obviously rested on what everybody knew was true: The family, as an institution, predated the state, and the power of the state to control the family was limited. So far, so good.

In 1967, the Supreme Court ruled that antimiscegenation laws—that is, laws forbidding interracial marriage—interfered with the fundamental right to marry.[25] Once again, the Court was right: It hardly needs much discussion to know that laws creating racial classifications were exactly what the Fourteenth Amendment was all about. If black and white citizens are equal in law, how can they be forbidden to marry one another?

But next we see the full power of the liberal dominance of the courts. Suddenly, the Supreme Court moved from protecting marriage and family as sacred rights to inventing the right of "reproductive freedom." By the Court's ruling, contraception became a constitutional right for married people. Then the crusade began for unmarried people. *Unmarried people have babies, too, don't they? So it's a constitutional right for them as well; there's no compelling state interest to restrict this fundamental right.*

Wait a minute! What fundamental right? We started with fundamental rights of marriage and family. We then arrived at a fundamental right of contraception, implying an equally fundamental right of fornication.[26]

From marriage and the family to fornication. Simple logic, right? Well, of course, it's all about liberty: "At the heart of liberty is the right to define one's own concept of existence, of meaning, of the universe, and of the mystery of human life." Thus sayeth the three wise persons of *Planned Parenthood v. Casey*.[27] So marriage and family are fundamental rights, but it's not really about marriage and family, it's about liberty—the liberty to define "one's own concept" of the mystery of life. That means the state can't define certain things for us. And among those things it can't define are—marriage and family!

In Anglo-American legal history, no court has ever had to define marriage or order the executive or legislature to make provision in the law for the institution. The institution existed prior to, and independently of, the common law and American constitutional law.[28] It existed (and exists) because men and women exist and have basic natural instincts and functions in the matter of procreation. It existed (and exists) because reason (to say nothing of religion and natural law) compels recognition of a union of a man and a woman as the cornerstone of the family. For centuries, the law recognized the special place occupied by marriage and family, and many legal rights and liabilities are founded on the normal, universal concept of marriage and family.

For centuries, likewise, the law condemned deviate sexual intercourse, primarily that between homosexual men. When Blackstone wrote of the "detestable and abominable crime against nature, not to be named among Christians," only revisionist history written by homosexual partisans supports the idea that he meant anything other than homosexual sodomy, particularly anal intercourse.[29]

But enter the illiberal liberals. "Minorities" are to be protected from majority "oppression" at all costs. Homosexuals are obviously a minority. What could be more "oppressive" than criminalizing the conduct that is central to homosexuals?

The first frontal assault on sodomy laws was defeated in the Supreme Court by one vote in 1986 in a case called *Bowers v. Hardwick*.[30] As usually happens when liberals lose by only one vote in the U.S. Supreme Court, they did not give up, but redoubled their efforts. They got the American Bar Association to sign on to their agenda on behalf of sodomy. They got the law schools to do the same. But then democracy reared its ugly head. The American people reacted against the liberal campaign to grant favored status to sexual activity that had been condemned by the law (and the broader society) for centuries; the people themselves, by initiative and referendum, adopted laws forbidding special treatment for homosexuals, or repealed laws that had been passed to put homosexuality on the same footing as race in the matter of discrimination. So what did the radical liberals do? They turned to the courts and got the people's laws invalidated.

The death knell of the *Bowers* decision was sounded in 1995 with the Supreme Court's ruling in *Romer v. Evans*. That case declared unconstitutional a Colorado state constitutional amendment that annulled statutes forbidding discrimination against homosexuals and forbade the enactment of new ones. In his dissent, Justice Scalia trenchantly explained the effect of *Romer*:

> In holding that homosexuality cannot be singled out for disfavorable treatment, the Court . . . places the prestige of this institution behind the proposition that opposition to homosexuality

is as reprehensible as racial or religious bias. Whether it is or not is precisely that cultural debate that gave rise to the Colorado constitutional amendment (and to the preferential laws against which the amendment was directed). Since the Constitution of the United States says nothing about this subject, it is left to be resolved by normal democratic means, including the democratic adoption of provisions in state constitutions. This Court has no business imposing upon all Americans the resolution favored by the elite class from which the Members of this institution are selected, pronouncing that "animosity" toward homosexuality is evil.[31]

From *Romer* it was just a short step for the Supreme Court to enshrine homosexual sodomy as a "right." The Court did exactly that in 2003, handing liberals their most significant victory to that point in *Lawrence v. Texas*.[32] Once again, Justice Scalia identified exactly how the judiciary had perverted the Constitution and the democratic system. In his dissent he wrote, "State laws against bigamy, same-sex marriage, adult incest, prostitution, masturbation, adultery, fornication, bestiality, and obscenity are likewise sustainable only in light of *Bowers'* validation of laws based on moral choices. Every single one of these laws is called into question by today's decision; the Court makes no effort to cabin the scope of its decision to exclude them from its holding." He added that since the Supreme Court had cast aside "all pretense of neutrality" and thrown its weight against "moral disapprobation of homosexual conduct," there could no longer be any possible justification "for denying the benefits of marriage to homosexual couples exercising '[t]he liberty protected by the Constitution.'"

SCALIA WAS RIGHT

Having decreed that sodomy is a constitutional right, and having condemned "discrimination" against homosexuals as evil, the courts did exactly what Justice Scalia said they would do. What happened next illustrates the deep roots that the tyranny of tolerance has put down in the judiciary, and the lengths to which liberal judges at all levels are prepared to go to ram that tyranny down the throats of the American people.

Homosexual activists began to attack the institution of marriage and other legal distinctions based on homosexuality or homosexual conduct in the early 1970s, at the same time other liberals were attacking abortion regulations. The early attacks on marriage generally failed, with the courts giving short shrift to contrived arguments based on due process and equal protection. And when the United States Supreme Court rejected the claim of a right to engage in homosexual sodomy in *Bowers,* homosexual activists and their liberal allies adjusted their tactics. Realizing that the tyranny of tolerance had begun to permeate the state courts as well as the federal courts—and had even come to dominate in some jurisdictions—they shifted the battle to states like Hawaii, Vermont, and Massachusetts.

Hawaii led the way. In 1993, the state supreme court held that even though homosexual sodomy was not a fundamental right, the Hawaiian constitution's equal protection clause required the state to show a *compelling* governmental interest in "excluding" homosexuals from marriage.[33] Here the court deployed the classic liberal weapon: taking something not the same, and mandating that the government treat it the same, or prove that different treatment is necessitated by a "compelling" interest, like national security or prevention of vote fraud.

The Hawaii court insisted that defining marriage in terms only of the union of a man and a woman was discrimination on the basis of sex. It equated the "exclusion" of homosexuals with the limitation on interracial marriage in the miscegenation case *Loving v. Virginia* and heaped scorn on religious objections to homosexual conduct by quoting a Virginia court's justification of the antimiscegenation law on the basis of that court's perception of divine law.

Hawaii's twisted notion of equal protection—which other courts have subsequently adopted in mandating recognition of homosexual "marriage"—ignores the plain, incontrovertible fact that homosexuals are not the "same" as heterosexuals, certainly insofar as marriage and procreation are concerned. It further ignores the plain truth that the definition of marriage, as presupposed by the Constitution and the common law alike, as a union of a man and a woman, treats all persons exactly the same. All men and all women have exactly the same right to enter into marriage. The antimiscegenation laws placed a racial classification on this right: Blacks could not marry whites. Blacks and whites were therefore treated differently because of their race—a facial violation of the Fourteenth Amendment.

To say that homosexuals are not treated the same by the received definition of marriage is simply wrong. There is no distinction based on sex insofar as the exercise of the right to marry is concerned. To say that prohibiting men from "marrying" other men is sex discrimination is a bit like saying that throwing a baseball out of the playing field is the same as hitting the ball out of the playing field; you are talking about two different sorts of conduct.

This "apples are oranges" reasoning permeates the liberal assault on the institution of marriage. The illiberal liberals have decided that homosexuals are an oppressed minority and that "discrimination" against them is wrong. The remedy is to convert the oppressed into the oppressors and destroy the rights of the majority to make judgments about the kind of civil society in which we live and the very definition of basic institutions in that society.

The objection to elevating homosexuals to the same level of constitutional protection as racial minorities is rooted not in bigotry or ignorance, as liberal nonpareil Justice John Paul Stevens would have it (writing in the Boy Scouts case), but rather in the simple, undeniable fact that homosexual *conduct* is the problem. There are no laws discriminating against homosexuals as a class. They are not and never have been precluded from voting, holding public office, sitting at the same lunch counter, or sitting in the front of the bus. Even the statute authorizing discharge of homosexuals from the military is based on *behavior*, not status. The hypocrisy of the jurisprudence of tolerance in this regard is manifested by the insistence that regulations aimed at condemning homosexual conduct are "class-based" regulations. This is no more logically sound than equating laws against prostitution with laws against women as a class. But logic is irrelevant in liberal law; all that matters is tolerance. Every hint of intolerance of sodomy must be erased from our law and public life—by judicial decree.

The decisions of the Vermont Supreme Court and the Massachusetts Supreme Judicial Court in favor of homosexual "marriage" do not differ materially in their reasoning from the Hawaii Supreme Court's decision.[34] What is the sum and substance of the homosexual "marriage" cases? It is that the institution of marriage itself is unconstitutional! Tell that to the Founding Fathers. Tell that to the men who stood at Gettysburg. Tell that to the Congress that proposed and the legislatures that ratified the Fourteenth Amendment. Tell that to the overwhelming numbers of people who have voted in favor of state constitutional provisions to preserve the institution of marriage.

The methods of operation of the tyranny of tolerance are nowhere more stark than in the assault on any and all forms of "intolerance" of homosexuality: First comes the broad denunciation of traditional standards, then comes the suppression of dissenting opinion, and finally comes the full implementation of new standards and "affirmative action" to advance the interests of the favored class. And it all operates in the guise of constitutional law: unvoted, unelected, and unchangeable except by constitutional amendment.

ATTACKING THE BASIS FOR DEMOCRATIC GOVERNMENT

The utter and complete liberal judicial arrogance that permeates the homosexual "marriage" cases bodes horribly for the future of democratic government. Even trial judges have presumed to dictate to the legislature what laws must be passed. The Vermont Supreme Court effectively decreed that the legislature must adopt "civil union" legislation or risk judicial mandate that homosexuals would be entitled to regular marriage licenses. A trial court in Oregon did the same. Fortunately, the Oregon voters mooted that decision by adopting a constitutional amendment destroying the constitutional basis for the judicial ukase.[35]

But don't think that the passage of state constitutional amendments excluding homosexual "marriage" means anything to liberal judges. Under the reasoning of *Romer,* it is doubtful that either voters or the legislature can do anything that purports to limit or exclude homosexuals in any way. The federal Defense of Marriage Act has so far withstood homosexual attack, but it is difficult to tell how long that will last.[36] State supreme courts have upheld state marriage amendments, but lower federal courts are already questioning them.[37]

And, by the way, you who disagree with the tyranny's rescripts had better not try to stand up for your beliefs. Do you think you have a constitutional right to keep homosexuals out of your child's Boy Scout troop leadership? Think again. Do you think you have a right to vote on the definition of marriage? Ha! Are you worried that your barracksmate may harbor sexual desires for you when you shower together? What right do you have to be worried about that? He has every right to define his own destiny; he has every right to his perverted sexual fancies, and you have no right even to publicly disapprove! Ask the employees across the nation who have lost their jobs for daring to criticize employers' pro-homosexual policies.[38] Ask the military recruiters, who are relegated to the modern university's version of "the closet," because a democratically elected Congress has made a judgment that the military and buggery do not mix (as we will see in Chapter 10).

Just think about the actions and behaviors liberal courts have elevated to the level of a constitutional right over the past fifty years:

- *Drug addiction.* No, we can't make that a crime. That's punishing someone's *status,* which is "cruel and unusual punishment." But the right to be a drug addict does not embrace the right to buy and sell drugs—yet.[39]
- *Obscenity.* Possession of obscene literature can't be a crime. That's punishing private conduct.[40] Everybody has a right to be let alone

with his depravities. Well, sure, a pathetic loser poring over his porno in the privacy of his apartment may not produce harm to the public—unless, of course, it motivates him to go out and commit rape. And a right of possession doesn't mean a right to buy and sell, does it? Not yet.[41] Oh, by the way, we'll make an exception for possession of child pornography—children must be protected at all costs.[42]

- *Abortion.* That can't be a crime; that can't even be regulated in such a way as to create an "undue burden" (in whose judgment?) on the "right" to an abortion. That interferes with a woman's right to define her destiny—and besides, most married women consult with their husbands before butchering their children, so why bother to permit democratically elected legislators to choose innocent life over selfishness, convenience, or radical feminist philosophy?

- *Sodomy.* The unenlightened judges in *Bowers* simply made up all that stuff about sodomy being condemned by the law for centuries. But let's not talk about a constitutional right to engage in homosexual sodomy. That might conjure up images of Caligula's court and suggest a decadence in our civilization that we don't want to admit, and don't care about anyway. No, it's that business about personal autonomy and destiny and liberty "in its more transcendent dimensions" and "the right to be let alone."

GOVERNMENT OF PHILOSOPHER KINGS

The ongoing judicial assault on traditional marriage and family reveals the liberals' contempt for everything but their own power. That contempt was perfectly expressed in Justice Anthony Kennedy's penultimate remarks in *Lawrence v. Texas*:

> Had those who drew and ratified the Due Process Clauses of the Fifth Amendment or the Fourteenth Amendment known the components of liberty, in its manifold possibilities, they might have been more specific. They did not presume to have

this insight. They knew times can blind us to certain truths and later generations can see that laws once thought necessary and proper in fact serve only to oppress. As the Constitution endures, persons in every generation can invoke its principles in their own search for greater freedom.[43]

Well, if the Founding Fathers did not know what liberty was, they certainly knew what liberty was not. It was not licentiousness. Nor was it "tolerance." And it certainly was not judicial autocracy, masquerading as enforcement of the Constitution, which was designed to preserve and protect liberty. In other words, it was not slavery to the whims of five judges who fancy themselves philosopher kings—or queens.

Justice Kennedy's remarks expose the attitude of the illiberal liberals for all to see: The language of the Constitution, the intent of the framers and ratifiers, the traditions and usages of our people over unbroken generations—all are irrelevant. Every generation of judges is entitled to rewrite the Constitution to suit themselves, as long as those judges include five Supreme Court justices. In effect, then, we have no Constitution. Nor do we have a democracy, for the people cannot work their will through the ballot box on any issue that liberal judges decide to write into "their" Constitution. The tyranny of tolerance is complete. The tyranny of tolerance, not the Constitution, is the supreme law of the land.

Ozzie and Harriet may not be dead, but the radical liberals are certainly very close to killing them.

CHAPTER 5

TAXATION FOR TOLERANCE

Scutage or aid shall be levied in our kingdom only by the common counsel of our kingdom. . . .
—Magna Carta, 1215

Taxation without representation is tyranny.
—James Otis, 1763

He has combined with others to subject us to a jurisdiction foreign to our constitution, and unacknowledged by our laws; giving his Assent to their acts of pretended legislation: . . . For imposing taxes on us without our Consent. . . .
—Declaration of Independence, 1776

ON APRIL 18, 1990, the Constitution as we had known it for two centuries died.

On that day, five members of the United States Supreme Court made us all serfs on the liberal plantation. In an opinion of consummate hypocrisy, the five life-tenured justices, even while admitting that federal courts had no power to impose taxes, insisted that judges could order local governments to impose unlimited taxes on the people in the name of school desegregation.

After that decision, judges quickly jumped at the chance to wield ultimate political power to advance liberal ends. The beauty of it was that they seldom had to order tax increases; the mere threat was enough to compel local governments to act—whether it was to build new jails, increase welfare benefits, provide expensive medical care to criminals in prison, or compel unbelievably expensive gold-plating of school districts that were trapped in school desegregation litigation.[1]

The rallying cry of the American Revolution was "No taxation without representation," and later, the framers of the Constitution made sure that the power to tax was limited to the elected branch of government. But on April 18, 1990, five philosopher kings in Washington overrode all that and installed taxation by decree.

Welcome to taxation for tolerance.

EYEWITNESS TO JUDICIAL TYRANNY

The Supreme Court's decision in 1990 amounted to a massive seizure of power. But that power grab did not occur out of nowhere. The first step toward this landmark change occurred several years earlier in St. Louis, Missouri, during a school desegregation case known as *Liddell v. Board of Education*.[2]

As it happened, I represented the City of St. Louis in that case. Thus I became an eyewitness to the liberals' manipulation of the federal judiciary to undo the Constitution.[3]

The *Liddell* case took a radical turn in 1980, after the school desegregation plaintiffs, spearheaded by the NAACP, won a claim that the St. Louis public school district was illegally segregated.[4] Immediately after the plaintiffs won that decision, the St. Louis school board switched sides, joining with the plaintiffs to milk the maximum amount of money possible out of the taxpayers. Initially, this took the form of ordering the state of Missouri to fund all of the forced busing and special educational programs devised jointly by the plaintiffs and the school board. The "remedy" called for the state to spend about $50 million each year, or approximately $1,000 per pupil (in 1980 dollars!)—all in addition to the $3,000 per pupil that the city district already spent. The programs devised by the plaintiffs and the school board padded the school board payroll, created lucrative "renovation" contracts to hand out to favored contractors, and relieved the school district of its dependence on the voters to approve tax increases. The federal court's decree proved to be such a good deal that the school district welcomed continued federal judicial oversight.[5]

The school board also joined with the NAACP in urging the federal court to venture into issues of *housing* segregation, on the premise that school segregation resulted from illegal housing segregation. This was the brainchild of Gary Orfield, a notorious liberal professor who advised in countless school desegregation cases, doing major harm. I came in when the city—a plaintiff in the case, too—was directed to help devise some sort of housing desegregation plan to supplement the school desegregation. As counsel for the city, I first focused on preventing the school board and NAACP from turning the case into a massive housing case and giving Professor Orfield free rein to try out his housing desegregation theories. I soon discovered an even bigger threat when, at one of the first hearings on the "remedy" within the city district, I learned that the St. Louis school board wanted unlimited property tax increases by judicial fiat.

The St. Louis school board and the NAACP both recognized the total failure of expensive "magnet" schools to attract anything but contractors and bureaucrats. The school board (perhaps I should say the school board lawyers and bureaucracy, as the members of the board themselves seemed to be so many puppets during this stage of the case) saw even greater opportunities for money and personnel by seeking to expand the federal court's field of supervision. So the NAACP plaintiffs and the school board tried to suck the suburban school districts into the case, to create a metropolitan school district that in effect would be controlled by the city school board, the NAACP, and its political allies. But there was a problem: In 1974 the U.S. Supreme Court had ruled in the *Milliken v. Bradley* case that suburban districts must be found guilty of actual illegal segregation before a federal judge could take over the districts.[6] That was a difficult standard to prove, given that most suburban schools districts were created after 1954 (the year of

Brown v. Board of Education) and thus had never had formal policies of segregation in place.

Given the *Milliken* ruling, the NAACP and the St. Louis school board knew that winning a trial and obtaining a federal decree abolishing the suburban school districts would be difficult. The district judge in charge of the case (a former Democratic congressman) evidently thought so, too. So instead of proceeding to a trial against the suburban school districts in the usual way, the NAACP and the St. Louis school board persuaded the federal judge to proceed in the best *Alice in Wonderland* tradition: sentence first, verdict afterward. The judge agreed to hold a hearing first on the remedy to be imposed *if the school districts lost.* Only *after deciding how to abolish them* would the judge hear the issue of whether the districts had done anything illegal. At the first hearing, the St. Louis school board and the NAACP presented an elaborate plan to divide the St. Louis metropolitan area into three "super" school districts, sweeping away some twenty suburban districts and subjecting thousands of students (white and black) to forced busing to schools many miles from their homes. The federal judge endorsed this plan, "suggesting" that the parties try to settle the case before he scheduled a trial to see if the suburban school districts were guilty of illegal discrimination.[7]

The *Liddell* "interdistrict" case was settled through negotiations that excluded the United States Department of Justice (by this time under the management of the Reagan administration), the State of Missouri (led by John Ashcroft, the state's attorney general), and my client, the City of St. Louis (led by a Democratic mayor who had no desire to sign on to massive forced busing or court-ordered taxation). The negotiators were the attorneys for the suburban school districts, St. Louis County (St. Louis County and the City of St. Louis are separate entities), the St. Louis school board, and a "special master" appointed by the district court. This special master was a liberal Washington University law professor. I don't know how it was decided to exclude the federal, state, and city governments, but I know that my client, the city, was not invited to participate. Only after a settlement plan was agreed to did the special master make any effort to talk to me.

The settlement gave black parents the option of having their kids transfer to suburban school districts. Each suburban district was assigned a quota for black transfer students. If the district met and maintained its quota for long enough, it would be exempt from further litigation. To counterbalance the one-way busing of black kids, the settlement established an even more elaborate system of "magnet" schools and further gold-plating of the city public schools. *All* of the costs were to be paid for by the State of Missouri and the taxpayers of the City of St. Louis. As soon as the settlement was approved by the district judge, he stripped city taxpayers of a property tax rollback intended to offset part of a sales tax increase that had been approved by the voters and earmarked for public schools.[8]

The State of Missouri and the City of St. Louis appealed. The appeal required some courage on the part of the mayor, but he agreed to go forward with it because the settlement's taxation by decree would fall on city taxpayers. I argued the case before the full federal court of appeals in St. Louis, which also heard arguments from attorneys for the state, the St. Louis school board, the NAACP, and the suburban school districts. Despite the outrageous judicial taxation in the *Liddell* case and the unprecedented burdens the settlement placed on the city and state taxpayers to pay for a settlement of claims that had never been proved, we lost the case. For the first time in our history, the court of appeals held that federal judges had the power to raise taxes to fund "remedies" of constitutional violations.[9]

That ruling did not come as much of a surprise, as the court of appeals at that time (1983–84) was still dominated by some of the most notorious liberals who ever rode roughshod over separation of powers. One in particular, Gerald Heaney, a radical liberal from Minnesota, was known for never ruling in favor of state or local governments in race discrimination cases, and for conducting his own investigations of the facts of cases, going outside the trial record to do so—something totally improper for any judge, much less an appellate judge.[10]

The *Liddell* settlement ended up costing Missouri taxpayers nearly a billion dollars during the time (nearly fifteen years) it was fully in force. Black transfer students got a good deal, since they were able to flee the city public schools without actually having to move to the suburbs. The suburban public schools got a good deal, as the state-financed busing offset declining enrollments. The city public school district got a *very* good deal, as it collected hundreds of millions of dollars from the State of Missouri to pay for magnet schools, extensive capital improvements in many other schools, and huge increases in personnel. But these "good deals" came at a very high cost to the taxpayers, and at an even higher cost to constitutional liberty. And it all arose by judicial decree. No need for those troublesome elections.

To be fair, in the later stages of the *Liddell* case the district judge apparently awoke to the dangers of judicial taxation, and he never gave the St. Louis school board the blank check on the taxpayers that it demanded. Instead, he forced the board to go to the voters. In all modesty, I may say that I lost the battle, but I won the war.

Still, the people of Missouri had become acquainted with judicial tyranny. Soon enough, an even greater judicial tyrant would emerge on the other side of the state.

KING CLARK

One night in 1987, the good people of Kansas City, Missouri, went to bed under a Constitution and laws that protected them from taxation without their consent. They woke up to a regime of judicial taxation, imposed by a single federal judge.

The change arose, once again, from a school desegregation case. In many ways the Kansas City case paralleled the St. Louis case: First there was a suit involving only the center city school district, in which a judicial decree required forced busing and educational improvements; then came the claim that the suburban school districts were also guilty. The NAACP lawyers in Kansas City were even more radical than those in St. Louis, since they tried to bring Kansas school districts into the case as well as the Missouri school districts. Not even the federal court of appeals could swallow that. But the NAACP lawyers found their George III in the federal judge assigned to their case, the ineffable Russell Clark.

After the *Liddell* appeal was decided and the power of federal judges to tax was recognized, at least in the Eighth Circuit (which covers seven states), the Kansas City case took a dramatic new twist. The plaintiffs abandoned efforts to create a metropolitan school district, joined with the Kansas City school board (represented by the same Washington, D.C., lawyers hired by the St. Louis school board), and tried to create such opulent programs and facilities in the Kansas City central school district as would inevitably draw white suburban students into the district. To this end, the abominable Judge Clark approved "petting farms," Olympic-sized swimming pools, and some $260 million in other improvements to the school facilities and programs.[11]

How was the gold-plating of the Kansas City district to be paid for? Not only did Judge Clark raise the school property tax, but, perhaps recognizing that it was unfair to expect the residents of the city district to bear the burden entirely, he also imposed an income tax surcharge on all persons living or working in the district. No piker, King Clark fixed the income tax surcharge at 1.5 percent of gross income.[12]

County officials fought King Clark. Surprisingly, the court of appeals panel, which included Judge Gerald Heaney, overturned Clark's income tax surcharge. But it also approved his property tax on the strength of the *Liddell* holding. Here, then, was a situation wholly without precedent in American history: A federal judge had ordered property taxes to be increased beyond the authority of the local government to do so, without the consent of the people.

This time, the U.S. Supreme Court could not evade the issue, as it had done in *Liddell*. The Court handed down the result in *Missouri v. Jenkins* on that infamous mid-April day in 1990.[13] Five members of the Court, led by the execrable Byron "Whizzer" White,[14] decided that the American Revolution didn't count, and neither did the U.S. Constitution. They imposed the radical liberal notion of unlimited judicial power.

As is usual with illiberal liberals, the Supreme Court's opinion in *Missouri v. Jenkins* rests on a breathtaking combination of revisionist history and hypocrisy. Relying on nineteenth-century cases that permitted courts to compel local governments to levy and collect *statutorily authorized* taxes, the five justices insisted that the federal courts could compel local governments to ignore all limits on taxation "where there is reason based in the Constitution for not observing the statutory limitation." Of course, the reason is never actually based in the Constitution, but only in liberal views of how the Constitution should be enforced on behalf of favored groups.[15]

Since even the liberals could not say that federal courts enjoyed independent powers of taxation, the justices devised an end run that preserves the shell of separation of powers without the substance: No limits on taxation can get in the way of federal court decrees. Federal judges may not say that they are imposing the taxes; they simply order the local officials to impose the taxes! This was too much even for Justices Anthony Kennedy and Sandra Day O'Connor—not the most stalwart champions of limited government when racial injustice is the battle cry. Justice Kennedy's dissent (would he adhere to it today?) exposed the hypocrisy of *Missouri v. Jenkins* for what it was:

> I do not acknowledge the troubling departures in today's majority opinion as either necessary or appropriate to ensure full compliance with the Equal Protection Clause or its mandate to eliminate the cause and effects of racial discrimination in the schools. Indeed, while this case happens to arise in the compelling context of school desegregation, the principles involved are not limited to that context. There is no obvious limit to today's discussion that would prevent judicial taxation in cases involving prisons, hospitals, or other public institutions, or indeed to pay a large damages award levied against a municipality under 42 U.S.C. §1983 [a general federal civil rights statute]. This assertion of judicial power in one of the most sensitive of policy areas, that involving taxation, begins a process that over time could threaten fundamental alteration of the form of government our Constitution embodies. James Madison observed: "Justice is the end of government. It is the end of civil society. It ever has been, and ever will be pursued, until it be obtained, or until liberty be lost in the pursuit." . . . In pursuing the demand of justice for racial equality, I fear that the Court today loses

sight of other basic political liberties guaranteed by our constitutional system, liberties that can coexist with a proper exercise of judicial remedial powers adequate to correct constitutional violations.

THE POWER TO DESTROY

Missouri v. Jenkins constitutes perhaps the most extreme illustration of how liberals use the judiciary to destroy the liberty of all to advance the interests of some. As Justice Kennedy indicated with his reference to "the demand of justice for racial equality," liberals have gladly ignored the right of every citizen not to be taxed without his consent, because taxation by judicial decree advances "racial justice," the ne plus ultra of the regime of tolerance.

Two hundred years ago Chief Justice John Marshall recognized that the power to tax is the power to destroy. With *Missouri v. Jenkins*, the Supreme Court handed that incredible power to federal judges. As Justice Kennedy observed, the power is not limited to school desegregation cases. Federal judges can use *Jenkins* as a weapon to saddle the people with all sorts of taxes for special groups, all to meet the judges' notions of sound policy. With the connivance of government bureaucrats, who thrive on money from any source, the courts can funnel practically unlimited funds to prison reformers, mental health advocates, school boards, welfare recipients, and others.[16] And as we'll see in a later chapter, the shocking ruling in *Jenkins* may ultimately embolden activists to file lawsuits against federal, state, and local governments demanding huge sums of money as "reparations" for slavery, payable to . . . wait a minute, payable to whom? Oh, the illiberal liberals don't need to concern themselves with minor details like that; the tyranny of tolerance is all about "righting wrongs."[17]

Missouri v. Jenkins fostered the idea of judicial omnipotence, which has so deeply permeated the American judiciary that state after state now confronts the specter of judicial taxation and spending in the name of equality. Liberals are applying in state courts the lessons learned in federal civil rights litigation, and the state judges are falling into line with the theory of judicial omnipotence. Public school bureaucracies and liberals in Ohio, Nevada, North Carolina, Arkansas, and other states have formed the same alliance that the NAACP and the Kansas City school board formed in *Jenkins* to attack supposedly discriminatory public school funding regimes. (Never mind that source after source after source reveals that per-pupil expenditures are typically very high in the urban school districts.)[18]

What has happened in recent years?

- The Nevada Supreme Court used the cloak of public education simply to order the legislature to ignore a voter-approval requirement for new taxes.[19]

- The Kansas Supreme Court ordered the Kansas legislature to appropriate $285 million more for education in a single fiscal year.[20] The Kansas constitution provides only that the legislature "make suitable provision for finance" of the public schools. Until the era of judicial imperium, how much is "suitable" was a matter for the legislature to decide, not the courts.

- The supreme court of Ohio ruled that it had the power to order the legislature to write laws to suit the court, and spend money as directed by the court: "the power to declare a particular law or enactment unconstitutional must include the power to require a revision of that enactment, to ensure that it is then constitutional."[21] It is one thing to declare a law unconstitutional. It is quite another to command the legislature to rewrite laws in particular ways, and appropriate certain amounts of money, or levy certain tax rates.

When the courts act as though the American Revolution never happened, something is seriously wrong. The usurpation of the powers of taxation and spending began with the federal courts and, like a venereal disease, has spread to the state courts. This disease is pandemic because the Constitution died on April 18, 1990, as a direct result of the liberal pursuit of racial "equality."

CHAPTER 6

NO RIGHT TO KEEP AND BEAR ARMS

I cannot help but suspect that the best explanation for the absence of the Second Amendment from the legal consciousness of the elite bar, including that component found in the legal academy, is derived from a mixture of sheer opposition to the idea of private ownership of guns and the perhaps subconscious fear that altogether plausible, perhaps even "winning" interpretations of the Second Amendment would present real hurdles to those of us supporting prohibitory regulations.

—Professor Sanford Levinson,
"The Embarrassing Second Amendment," *Yale Law Journal,* 1989

The right to keep and bear arms is the Palladium of liberties of a republic.

—Supreme Court Justice Joseph Story,
Commentaries on the Constitution of the United States, 1833

THE LIBERAL NOTION of constitutional law is especially egregious when it comes to rights specifically mentioned in the Constitution, but with which liberals don't agree. The most obvious example is the right to keep and bear arms.

The Second Amendment to the U.S. Constitution is as simple and straightforward as the First Amendment: "A well regulated Militia, being necessary to the security of a free State, the right of the people to keep and bear Arms, shall not be infringed." Until the advent of the liberal judicial imperium, the meaning of the Second Amendment admitted of no doubt. The right to keep and bear arms was seen as a natural right,[1] and the reference to the "militia" was no more than a recognition that every able-bodied male citizen over the age of sixteen constituted the reserve armed force of every state.[2] The amendment therefore operated at two levels: It recognized the militia as a potential military force, which could be regulated (indeed, the Constitution states that the militia was subject to congressional regulation), and it recognized the individual right to keep and bear arms, which could not be infringed.

But along came the illiberal liberals, to whom armed citizens are anathema. They tried to force the Second Amendment out of the picture.

In waging war on the Second Amendment in the judiciary, liberals have attempted to revise history and rewrite the Constitution. In many ways their tactics mirror those of Professor Michael A. Bellesiles of Emory University, who wrote the book *Arming America: The Origins of a National Gun Culture*. The good professor undertook to demonstrate that colonial Americans didn't really own or want guns, and that the "right" guaranteed by the Second Amendment was of no significance until the National Rifle Association made it so for political reasons in the late twentieth century. Liberal media and academe fawned all over Professor Bellesiles, awarding him the prestigious Bancroft Prize for outstanding historiography. Oops! Some critics, including some intellectually honest liberals (yes, there are some), noticed a few problems with the good professor's research. Much like Dan Rather's reporting on President Bush's National Guard service, Professor Bellesiles's work unraveled under scrutiny. It seems that he fabricated data, among other things. So the liberal academic elite had to swallow its fawning and rescind the Bancroft Prize.[3]

Like Professor Bellesiles, liberals have a way of ignoring the truth about the right to keep and bear arms. They ignore the plain and simple words of the Constitution, as well as the statements of the Founding Fathers indicating that the Founders knew very well that they were securing a personal right to keep and bear arms.

Liberals also have a way of applying their legal doctrines very selectively so that they don't have to deal with the inconvenient right protected by the Second Amendment.

PORNOGRAPHY, SODOMY, ABORTION . . . BUT NO GUNS!

Consider the "rights" that the Supreme Court has suddenly discovered in recent decades.

In a case called *Stanley v. Georgia*,[4] Supreme Court Justice Thurgood Marshall, one of the icons of liberalism, grandly proclaimed, "We hold that the First and Fourteenth Amendments prohibit making mere private possession of obscene material a crime."

In *Lawrence v. Texas*, Justice Anthony Kennedy—a Republican appointee who has come to embrace the radical liberal agenda, or been "Blackmunized"[5]—read homosexual sodomy into the Constitution.

And, above all, in *Roe v. Wade*, the Court created the "right" to abortion on demand.

So according to the Court, pornography, sodomy, and abortion are all fundamental rights. Sure, they are mentioned nowhere in the Constitution, but they are premised on a concept of "privacy"—which is also not mentioned in the Constitution but has been manufactured as part of the "liberty" protected by the Fourteenth Amendment's due process clause. And in the *Stanley* case, the Supreme Court fell back on the so-called incorporation doctrine, whereby specific parts of the Bill of Rights—selected by liberal judges—are "incorporated" in the due process clause and made applicable to the states.[6]

Let's see. The due process clause protects porno, sodomy, and abortion. The Fourteenth Amendment "incorporates" those portions of the Bill of Rights deemed "fundamental" to "ordered liberty" or to a "fair trial."[7] So the right to keep and bear arms, a right that, like freedom of the press, is expressly protected by the plain language of the Bill of Rights, must be "fundamental" and must apply to the states. Right?

Ha! Let's not underestimate the capacity of the illiberal liberals to dance around their own doctrines when it suits them.

ATTACKS ON PERSONAL FREEDOM

In 1981, the federal Seventh Circuit Court of Appeals was confronted with an ordinance from the town of Morton Grove, Illinois, that banned all possession of handguns. Citizens sued, alleging that the ordinance violated both the state and federal constitutions.

Of course, the citizens lost. The court's majority said that the Second Amendment does not apply to the states, and even declared that the right guaranteed by the Second Amendment is not a personal right at all, but a right of the states to organize and arm a militia if they choose to do so.[8]

One judge, John Coffey, dissented. In the process he exposed the hypocrisy of liberal constitutional law:

> I believe that Morton Grove Ordinance No. 81-11, as a matter of constitutional law, impermissibly interferes with individual privacy rights. I join others who throughout history have recognized that an individual in this Country has a protected right, within the confines of the criminal law, to guard his or her home or place of business from unlawful intrusions. In my view, today's majority decision marks a new nadir for the fundamental principle that "a man's home is his castle." It has been said that the greatest threat to our liberty is from well-meaning, and almost imperceptible government encroachments upon our personal freedom. Today's decision sanctions an intrusion on our basic rights as citizens which would no doubt be alarming and odious to our founding fathers.[9]

The U.S. Supreme Court never heard the case. Why not? Why does the Constitution protect pornography, sodomy, and abortion but not the right to keep and bear arms, the right expressly set out in the text of the Bill of Rights?

The liberals' stated objections to the Second Amendment don't hold up to scrutiny. First, as noted, the Second Amendment operated at two levels—recognizing the existence of the militia and also recognizing the individual citizen's right to keep and bear arms. So the Seventh Circuit was simply wrong that the Second Amendment does not protect a personal right.

The liberals don't like the Second Amendment because, to them, it's discriminatory. Take the definition of "militia" at the time of ratification of the Bill of Rights: males between the ages of sixteen and sixty. Obviously anything that smacks of "patriarchy" must be worthless and should be discarded in the age of ovarianism. And of course we must assume that blacks were excluded from the protection of the Second Amendment. So, to illiberal liberals, the Second Amendment really shouldn't be in the Constitution at all, and we can ignore it.

This is where radical liberals ignore the language not only of the Second Amendment itself but also of their own favorite constitutional amendment, the Fourteenth. The plain language of the Fourteenth Amendment promises equal protection. The debates in Congress after the Civil War clearly indicate that the right to keep and bear arms was one of the cherished rights the Fourteenth Amendment was intended to guarantee to blacks.[10] As for women, the liberals had no difficulty in ruling in the case involving the Virginia Military Institute (VMI), *United States v. Virginia*,[11] that women are equally entitled to be part of the military, so why can't we deem the militia to include all citizens capable of bearing arms? The Second Amendment can protect every citizen, male or female, of whatever race, because the Fourteenth Amendment commands that all citizens be treated equally by the states.

So if the common objections to the Second Amendment don't hold up, why don't we enforce the amendment? It seems there's a simple answer: Liberals, who have controlled the judiciary since the 1930s, just don't want to. After all, no "enlightened" society sees any need for an armed citizenry. The United Nations is trying to outlaw private possession of weapons,[12] and we know how important international law is in interpreting our Constitution—Justice Anthony Kennedy tells us so.

The Founding Fathers understood that a militia did not mean people like Oklahoma City bomber Timothy McVeigh, but rather was almost inseparable from the citizenry as a whole. The rights of speech, assembly, and bearing arms were part and parcel of liberty as understood by the Founding Fathers. But totalitarian regimes cannot tolerate (if you'll pardon the pun) guns in the hands of the citizen—and the illiberal liberals are nothing if not totalitarian in their tolerance. They prefer to tolerate pornography and sodomy rather than the right of owning and bearing arms.

And as Judge Coffey observed in his *Morton Grove* dissent, what about the vaunted right of privacy? If you can have porno in your own home, if you can have deviant sexual intercourse in your home, if you can have an abortion on demand, then why can't you have a gun? Obviously, the scope of the right of privacy is limited after all. Pornography represents spiritual degeneracy—in the liberal cosmos, nothing at all to worry about. Indeed, radical liberals are devoted to licentiousness. On the other hand, they really have no use for true freedom—precisely what the right to keep and bear arms represents. Consequently, for all their stirring talk of "liberty" and "privacy," liberal jurists like Ruth Bader Ginsburg and David Souter care not for the issues Judge Coffey raised in his dissent.

FIGHTING BACK

The courts' refusal to enforce the Second Amendment, or even to recognize that it guarantees individual rights, may soon be put to the test.

Inspired by lawsuits against the tobacco industry in the 1990s, trial lawyers and liberals joined forces with liberal-dominated state and local governments to try to destroy the domestic firearms manufacturing and distribution industry, and thereby effectively destroy the personal right to keep and bear arms. They argued that gun manufacturers were negligent in failing to keep their products out of the hands of criminals. It didn't matter that the guns got to criminals through third parties, including unscrupulous gun retailers. Nor did it matter that gun crimes are committed by individuals, not gun manufacturers—after all, individual responsibility for individual acts is not a principle of law that has meaning to radical liberals. Gun violence is a social problem. Gun makers, not punks and thugs, are a cause, perhaps *the* cause, of this social problem. And every social problem gets a liberal judicial solution.

The judicial campaign against gun makers and sellers provoked a revolutionary attempt by Congress to give force to the Second Amendment. In 2005 the House and Senate passed, and President George W. Bush signed, the Protection of Lawful Commerce in Arms Act. The Act declared:

> The Second Amendment to the United States Constitution protects the rights of individuals, including those who are not members of a militia or engaged in military service or training, to keep and bear arms. . . .
>
> The possibility of imposing liability on an entire industry for harm that is solely caused by others is an abuse of the legal system. . . .
>
> The liability actions commenced or contemplated by the Federal Government, States, municipalities, and private interest groups and others are based on theories without foundation in hundreds of years of the common law and jurisprudence of the United States and do not represent a bona fide expansion of the common law. The possible sustaining of these actions by a maverick judicial officer or petit jury would expand civil liability in a manner never contemplated by the framers of the Constitution, by Congress, or by the legislatures of the several States. . . .
>
> The liability actions . . . attempt to use the judicial branch to circumvent the Legislative branch of government. . . .[13]

Outside the realm of civil rights legislation, one seldom finds such forceful phrases resonating through an act of Congress. In a sense, however, we are dealing with civil rights legislation, albeit a civil right that liberals wish to repeal.

During the civil rights struggle in the latter half of the twentieth century, Congress acted to enforce the Fourteenth and Fifteenth Amendments by "appropriate legislation," such as the Voting Rights Act. In doing so, Congress practically put elections in many states and cities into receivership, with the Justice Department authorized to supervise the minutest changes in electoral laws. The Supreme Court upheld this congressional legislation, and even proclaimed, in the case of *Katzenbach v. Morgan*,[14] that Congress could create rights enforceable under the Fourteenth Amendment beyond those that the amendment itself actually guaranteed. Although the *Morgan* doctrine was modified later, when the Supreme Court struck down the Religious Freedom Restoration Act,[15] the illiberal liberals continued to maintain this sweeping view of congressional enforcement powers under the Fourteenth Amendment.

So what will the courts do with the Protection of Lawful Commerce in Arms Act? After all, one of the act's stated purposes is "to guarantee a citizen's rights, privileges and immunities, as applied to the States, under the Fourteenth Amendment. . . ."[16]

I am not sure what the current U.S. Supreme Court will do, but we already know what some liberal federal judges will do: They will ignore the act.

Judge Jack Weinstein, a Lyndon Johnson appointee to the federal district court of New York, is the very model of the modern liberal judicial activist. From litigation over the use of the defoliant Agent Orange in Vietnam to tobacco to asbestos and now firearms, Judge Weinstein has gone out of his way to assume ultimate authority to cure any perceived wrong presented by his favored groups. I directly encountered his brand of judicial imperialism in asbestos litigation when he tried to assume control of all asbestos suits involving certain companies nationwide in the 1990s. At the time, I was handling the asbestos cases in my circuit, and I was disposing of them expeditiously when Judge Weinstein purported to enjoin proceedings everywhere in the country that involved Keene Corporation. I considered his order entirely beyond his jurisdiction and rejected its enforceability. Sure enough, the federal court of appeals in New York reversed him, strongly objecting to his methods.[17]

Undeterred by appellate rebukes, Judge Weinstein has continued to act as supreme arbiter of social justice. When Congress passed the Protection of Lawful Commerce in Arms Act, he was hearing a case known as *City of New York v. Beretta U.S.A. Corp.* and was all set to force the gun industry into a trial on various novel theories concocted by the City of New York in an effort to put the entire firearms industry under federal judicial supervision. Then, based on the plain language of the new law, the gun industry defendants moved to dismiss the lawsuit. But in a masterpiece of judicial sleight of hand, Judge Weinstein took the language in the congressional statute providing exceptions for lawsuits based on violations of laws "applicable to" the sale or marketing of firearms and turned it into a gigantic loophole allowing the New York suit. He based his ruling on a New York general criminal nuisance statute that said nothing whatever about the sale or marketing of firearms. The judge had already said, *in the very same case,* that improper marketing of firearms could be a public nuisance within the meaning of New York law. So, presto! The general nuisance law was applicable to the sale or marketing of firearms, and so exempt from the Protection of Lawful Commerce in Arms Act.[18]

Judge Weinstein's tour de force illustrates what liberal judges do all the time: Like Humpty Dumpty in *Through the Looking Glass,* they insist that everything means exactly what they choose it to mean. The actual language of a statute or the Constitution means nothing.

Judge Weinstein's game plan ran into another obstacle, however. Perhaps sensing that the judiciary could not be trusted to apply the Protection of Lawful Commerce in Arms Act, Congress prohibited the federal government from sharing data on gun transfers with anybody who wanted to use it for litigation against the gun industry, and forbade any such information from being used in evidence. The database law threatened to throw a spoke into the wheels of the New York lawsuit, because the only way the plaintiffs could prove that guns marketed by the defendants were used in crimes in New York would be to use the federal database to trace the ownership history of the guns. No history meant no proof that the defendants sold the guns used by the criminals. Never one to give up, Judge Weinstein figured out a way around that.[19] He simply ruled that the law did not apply to information that New York had *already* obtained before the statute was passed, even though the statute said in plain words that data from the federal database "shall be inadmissible in evidence, and shall not be used, relied on, or disclosed in any manner, nor shall testimony or other evidence be permitted based upon such data."[20]

What will happen if Congress passes another law to squelch Judge Weinstein? I would hazard a guess that he or some other liberal judge will take the next step and simply declare any limitation on gun lawsuits to be unconstitutional. To this end, liberal judges will embrace doctrines of strict construction and federalism that they categorically reject everywhere else.[21] They will deny that Congress can act as though the Second Amendment applies to the states, for, they will say, only the federal judiciary can do that. They will say that guns have nothing to do with privacy, that there is no fundamental right of self-defense or defense of property. They will say that the Second Amendment means only that the states can have a militia if they want, and only members of the militia can carry guns, and only when on duty. They will say that the states have the authority to decide whether gun makers and sellers can be sued in state court, and that Congress cannot immunize an industry from state tort suits based on nuisance or other distorted common law theories.

Contrast the treatment of gun owners and makers with the treatment of abortionists and their patients. Here we have a right not even mentioned in the Constitution, but the liberal judiciary strains every nerve to thwart efforts to regulate it and even citizens' efforts to protest against it, picket against it, and hand out leaflets arguing against it.

Why? Because liberal abortion doctrine is part and parcel of the tyranny of tolerance, and gun ownership is not.

THE CONSTITUTION MEANS WHAT WE SAY IT MEANS

As one who thinks that the idea of "selective incorporation" of the Bill of Rights into the Fourteenth Amendment was simple liberal arbitrariness, do I think that the Second Amendment applies to the states? Absolutely. Does that make me a hypocrite? Not at all.

In applying the due process clause, one looks to see if the right at stake is such that neither liberty nor justice would exist if it was sacrificed. Is it a fundamental principle of liberty and justice that lies at the base of all our civil and political institutions? Is it so rooted in the traditions and conscience of our people as to be ranked as fundamental? Is it of the very essence of a scheme of ordered liberty? Yes, the right to keep and bear arms is all of these. Supreme Court Justice Joseph Story was correct when he described the right to keep and bear arms as the "Palladium," or safeguard, of all our liberties.

In fact, the need for an armed citizenry seems particularly acute during the age of the war on terror. Our borders are porous, and parties of armed citizens living on the Mexican border have performed an important public safety task by patrolling the border and intercepting thousands of illegal aliens—some of whom may be Islamic terrorists.[22] The clear and present danger of terrorist attack in our metropolitan areas also highlights the need for an armed citizenry. If terrorists mount an attack sufficient to disrupt communications and paralyze standard law enforcement agencies, to whom do we turn? The militia, in the classic sense. Indeed, it is high time that some thought be given to the importance of the ancient institutions of the militia and the posse comitatus in an era when regular institutions may fail us.

But don't tell that to the illiberal liberals. They would rather that you and your property be at the mercy of terrorists or looters—as well as ordinary criminals in ordinary times. Let's tolerate all manner of terror, rapine, and degeneracy before we tolerate guns in the hands of decent citizens.

The prime mover in the trampling of the Second Amendment is, of course, the liberal judiciary. In this arena, their paeans to "penumbras" and "emanations" and "fundamental rights" are exposed as the hypocritical legal ordure that they really are. Nowhere is the fundamental premise of the liberal judiciary better illustrated: The Constitution means nothing except what we say it means. If this be a constitution, then Nathan Hale and thousands of others died for nothing, and the assembly of demigods in Philadelphia labored in vain.

CHAPTER 7

CRIME BUT NO PUNISHMENT

The [Eighth] Amendment must draw its meaning from the evolving standards of decency that mark the progress of a maturing society.
—Chief Justice Earl Warren, *Trop v. Dulles* (1958)

Today, obscured within the fog of confusion that is our annually improvised Eighth Amendment, "death is different" jurisprudence, the Court strikes a further blow against the People in its campaign against the death penalty. Not only must mercy be allowed, but now only the merciful may be permitted to sit in judgment. Those who agree with the author of Exodus, or with Immanuel Kant, must be banished from American juries—not because the People have so decreed, but because such jurors do not share the strong penological preferences of this Court. In my view, that not only is not required by the Constitution of the United States; it grossly offends it.
—Justice Antonin Scalia, dissenting in
Morgan v. Illinois (1992)

THIS CHAPTER COULD FILL a book on its own.

Liberals' insistence on tolerance has made a mess of criminal justice in this country. Insisting that the rights of the lawless trump the rights of the law-abiding—and even that the rights of the killer trump the rights of the victims—federal courts have done everything possible to protect criminals. Most notably, they wage ceaseless war against the death penalty (which they see as racist, even if they can't prove it) and persistently interfere in the management of jails and prisons.

According to the illiberal liberals' twisted worldview, tolerance demands that we coddle the guilty—even when that means putting the innocent at greater risk.

DEFENDING KILLERS OVER THE INNOCENT

On March 29, 1989, fifteen-year-old Ann Harrison left her home in Kansas City, Missouri, to catch the school bus. A few minutes later, her mother heard the school bus horn. She looked out and saw the bus, and saw Ann's jacket, books, and other items lying near the mailbox by the road, scarcely fifty feet from her front door—but no Ann. Her mother waved the school bus on and started to search. She looked in the house, the yard, and the area around the house. No Ann. She called the police. The search intensified, covering the area where Ann's house was located. Still no Ann. Hours passed; night fell; and still, no Ann.

The next evening, police responded to a report of a suspicious auto in a nearby suburb, not very far from Ann's home. The car had been stolen. The owner and her boyfriend came to collect it. While inspecting the car, the boyfriend opened the trunk. He found Ann.

Ann Harrison had been abducted by Michael Taylor and Roderick Nunley, two convicted felons, who saw her as they cruised about in the stolen car after a nightlong cocaine binge. They seized her, took her to the home of Nunley's mother, raped her, bound her, and put her in the trunk of the car. At that point, they decided to kill her, and stabbed her numerous times in the neck and chest.

Nunley and Taylor pleaded guilty to murder early in 1991. A few months later, they were sentenced to death.

But after that, the guilty parties were able to grind the criminal justice system to a halt. As of 2006—a full *fifteen years* after being sentenced to death—Nunley and Taylor still have not been executed. And it is doubtful that either guilty party will be executed for several more years, if at all.

It wasn't always this way. Once upon a time, a criminal got a trial and, usually, a direct appeal. Unless something very unusual happened, that was that. Cases might drag on for years, but they seldom dragged on for decades. For example, in Missouri in the 1950s, there was a famous case known as the Greenlease kidnapping. Little Bobby Greenlease was kidnapped in Kansas City and held for ransom. The perpetrators collected the ransom, but they killed the little boy. Apprehended, they pleaded guilty. They were executed *three months* later.

What happened in the fifty years between the Greenlease case and Nunley and Taylor? Simply put: radical liberals. They took control of the courts and began a decades-long assault on the death penalty, and on criminal justice more broadly. What has happened—or rather, *hasn't* happened—with Nunley and Taylor perfectly illustrates what liberals have wrought with their war on capital punishment.

First the convicted murderers filed an appeal in state court. In 1992, as the judge who heard the case, I upheld the pleas and death sentences. The next year the Missouri Supreme Court reversed that decision. New sentencing hearings were held in 1994, and new death sentences imposed. More postconviction proceedings and appeals ensued. In 1996, the Missouri Supreme Court finally affirmed Nunley and Taylor's convictions and death sentences. The defendants then shifted the action to federal court. Nunley's case was still in limbo as of the summer of 2006, with a district judge who apparently refused to act on it. In Taylor's case, the federal court of appeals in 2004 denied his claim for federal habeas corpus (quoting portions of my 1992 opinion), and the Supreme Court denied review. So Taylor has been executed by now, right? Wrong. On February 1, 2006, on the eve of Taylor's execution, the federal court of appeals granted a stay of execution; the Supreme Court would not vacate the stay.

What have been the grounds for these endless appeals? The same we see recur in capital punishment cases. The tyranny of tolerance attacks the death penalty for the same reason that it opposes most other standards of law and justice in our society: The death penalty, liberals maintain, is discriminatory and "morally unacceptable." Odd how liberals prate about morality when it comes to saving vicious killers from a richly deserved fate, but have no breath to spare for the lives of the innocent, born or unborn.

Taylor and Nunley, like hundreds of other condemned killers over the past thirty years, trade on three principal claims. The first is routine: Their lawyers were incompetent. The second is made to order for the tyranny of tolerance: They are victims of race discrimination. The third is the newest gimmick, and perhaps the most hypocritical: Death hurts! If execution inflicts pain, then it must be *cruel,* and if it's cruel, well, it's unconstitutional.

The competency of the defense attorney is raised in every capital case (and nearly every other felony case, for that matter) after direct appeals are exhausted. Since every defendant is entitled to the assistance of counsel, it follows that such assistance must be *effective.* What makes lawyers constitutionally ineffective defies simple explanation, and I won't attempt it. Suffice it to say that the cases go around in circles. In one case that I tried, the defense counsel were two of the best criminal trial lawyers in the state, but the federal court of appeals found them to be ineffective—even though I and the state supreme court and the federal district court had all found the attorneys to be competent. The problem, it seemed, was that the lawyers chose not to put on psychiatric evidence showing that their client, who had killed two women, was dangerous to women. Result: death sentences set aside.

In Taylor's case (we still don't know about Nunley), the federal court rejected the claim that his lawyers were incompetent.

The claims of race discrimination in the Nunley and Taylor case came up in the initial postconviction proceedings in state court. I know, because I was the judge who sat on those proceedings.[1]

In those initial proceedings, the lawyers for the guilty parties suggested that Nunley and Taylor had been subjected to death sentences because they were black and their victim was white. To support their claims that the death penalty was applied on a discriminatory basis, the defendants presented data on homicides in Kansas City for a three-year period. But the data showed that only 20 percent of the several hundred homicides were interracial, and of that group, only two cases—far less than 1 percent—involved whites killing blacks. So any comparison between rates of death sentence for whites killing blacks and blacks killing whites was simply meaningless, as the sample of white killers of blacks was just too small to demonstrate any trends. As for the other cases in which death sentences were imposed on blacks, the U.S. Supreme Court had already, in the 1987 case *McCleskey v. Kemp*,[2] rejected statistical proof of racial discrimination as a basis for overturning death sentences. The Court noted that there is really no way to show statistically that a specific killer was sentenced to death on account of race, since every capital case is unique. Statistics prove nothing, because there are too many variables to consider, and statistical studies can control for only so many of them.[3]

That is why I rejected the claims of discrimination and upheld the death sentences back in 1992. In 2006, when it looked like the law would finally catch up with him, Taylor joined the latest, and perhaps most dangerous, liberal offensive against the death penalty. Missouri, like many other states, uses lethal injection as its method of execution, replacing the old gas chamber. Lethal injection was adopted in the 1990s as liberals began polishing a new theory: Capital punishment in the abstract may be constitutional, but the way it is carried out (electric chair, hanging, gas chamber, firing squad) inflicts needless pain and suffering. Therefore, while it is not cruel and unusual to sentence someone to death, it *is* cruel and unusual to carry out the sentence.

As usual, the judiciary paved the way for the latest onslaught against the death penalty. The courts discarded centuries of precedent and allowed criminal defendants to sue for injunctions against their execution, even though all criminal appeals had been denied. Once upon a time, there was a principle that courts would not issue injunctions against criminal proceedings.[4] The Supreme Court jettisoned this principle in an Alabama case in which the defendant's veins were so bad that the execution would require an incision to reach a vein capable of receiving the needle; the defendant (naturally) claimed that this would be cruel and unusual.[5]

Most recently came *Hill v. McDonough*,[6] in which the defendant was actually on the gurney (decades after his crime) when the Supreme Court stopped the execution. The Court ruled once again that the federal courts could grant injunctions against particular methods of execution when it is alleged that there is a "foreseeable risk of gratuitous and unnecessary pain" in the manner of death.

Sure enough, the Court's rulings opened the floodgates for "all manner of method of execution challenges," just as the states and the Bush administration had warned they would. Taylor's case is typical. He claimed that the method of using three drugs to execute him *could* cause needless pain. He provided no proof that any prior execution in Missouri had in fact needlessly inflicted pain. Instead, he showed that the doctor retained by the state to supervise executions (a "board-certified" surgeon) may not have been the most meticulous medical professional, and in fact was dyslexic. (Isn't that a good thing? Shouldn't we accommodate his disability?) The federal judge hearing the case concluded that there was an "unacceptable risk" of inflicting needless pain. And that was all the judge needed to take control of executions in Missouri.[7]

Federal judges are not simply enjoining one method of execution and leaving it to the states to develop another; no, they are doing everything, including prescribing the drug dosage! In Taylor's case, the federal district judge imposed specific standards to be followed by the state, even though the Supreme Court said nothing about approving such mandatory relief. One of the standards was that a board-certified anesthesiologist must supervise the preparation and administration of the lethal drugs.

Guess what? A board-certified anesthesiologist could lose certification if he participates in an execution. That's right, performing abortions is okay in the modern American medical profession, but executing killers is not. So the federal judge has imposed an impossible condition on the state. It just goes to show the lengths liberal judges will go to undermine the death penalty.

AN EVOLVING STANDARD OF IDIOCY

In the Nunley and Taylor cases we see the essential tactics and strategies liberal legal warriors employ to eliminate the death penalty, or at least to make it next to impossible to carry out.

The claims of racial discrimination in the Nunley and Taylor cases represent a tactic liberals have used for years to derail capital punishment. It is no coincidence that liberals' war on the death penalty began shortly after they commenced their judicial war on racial discrimination. After all, to liberals, the death penalty discriminates against the poor and the powerless. How do we reach that conclusion? Well, look at the numbers. How many millionaires go to the gallows? (Or, as we say in Missouri now, the gurney?) And of course the predominant subset of the poor and powerless are blacks. So the death penalty is discriminatory. End of discussion.

The first flaw in the liberal approach is obvious: Who commits the most murders? Millionaires? In my two decades on the bench in St. Louis, there have been two millionaires prosecuted for murder. The other thousand or so killers had considerably less net worth. The fact is that most criminals, and definitely most murderers, are "the poor" and the "powerless." In any case, the claim of powerlessness is a mere shibboleth of the liberals. Criminal defendants, especially capital murder defendants, are far from powerless. From the moment capital charges are preferred, the defendants have ranged on their side the whole panoply of liberal judges and lawyers, whose paramount mission is to ensure that they cheat the gallows. (Besides, just how "powerless" are you when you have exercised the power of life and death over another human being?)

As the tyranny of tolerance strengthened its grip on the federal judiciary, the first effort was to eliminate the death penalty outright. This attack began shortly after Chief Justice Earl Warren equated the Eighth

Amendment's "cruel and unusual punishment" language with an "evolving standard of decency."[8] The peculiar thing about the standard is that it evolved only one way: in favor of criminals. Gradually, the liberal federal judges shut down executions in the nation, as frontal attacks on the death penalty percolated up through the state and federal courts. If the "evolving standard" meant anything, it had to mean that if society never executed anybody in fact, then society must have effectively rejected the death penalty, even if the legislatures never changed the law and even if juries kept demanding death for brutal killers.

In the Supreme Court case *Furman v. Georgia,*[9] in 1972, liberals failed in their effort to wipe away the death penalty completely. Two justices, Potter Stewart and Byron White, weren't convinced that "decency" had gone all the way over to abolition. Instead, they focused on the "arbitrary" way in which people were sentenced to death. The gist of their position was that the states weren't executing enough murderers or rapists (both were eligible for death sentences then) to show that the system really picked the murderers and rapists most deserving of execution. The extreme liberal justices (William O. Douglas, Thurgood Marshall, and William Brennan) decided that the death penalty was excessive and morally unacceptable, and therefore unconstitutional.

As to the issue of discrimination, even Justice Marshall admitted that the higher rate of black executions was "partially due" to the higher rate of black crime,[10] but neither he nor anybody else spent any substantial effort to correlate the rate of conviction and sentence for murder with the rate at which specific groups committed murder.

Furman forced the states and the federal government to adopt elaborate capital sentencing procedures, to try to show Justices Stewart and White that the system was picking the worst of the murderers for the supreme penalty. Much to the liberals' chagrin, forty states and Congress promptly reenacted the death penalty. Some states tried to remove all discretion from the process by mandating the death sentence for selected murders (much as early American law specified death for all "premeditated" murder).[11] Well, decency couldn't tolerate that. That system allowed *too little* sentencing discretion. No, the problem with discretion in capital sentencing is a one-way street: Discretion to impose the death penalty has to be severely limited, but discretion to reject it must be unlimited.

Soon the Supreme Court limited death sentences even further, to apply only to murder. In 1977 the Court ruled that rape isn't serious enough to warrant a death sentence.[12] It was certainly true that 90 percent of executions for rape were of black defendants, mostly in southern states. But this does not mean the death penalty was unconstitutional; it means only that, in regard to rape, there was good reason to be concerned that the sentence was meted out in an invidiously discriminatory manner—a true equal protection problem.

By 1980, however, the liberal de facto moratorium in death sentences was collapsing (as the murder rate was steadily rising, by the way). The Supreme Court approved model death penalty statutes,[13] and the states slowly began to execute people.

In response, liberals forged new weapons, chief of which was delay through endless postconviction reviews. Prisoners began to make a mockery of the whole process by filing petition after petition for federal habeas corpus, usually succeeding in delaying executions while the courts agonized over plainly frivolous claims. The cases of Nunley and Taylor show how effective this ceaseless litigation has been. In fact, liberals so took advantage of the increasingly complex litigation process that as many as two-thirds of death sentences were set aside. Of course, the liberals who crowed about this achievement never mentioned that in almost *none* of these cases was there any dispute as to the guilt of the defendant.[14]

While tying the criminal justice system up in knots over endless death penalty procedural questions, liberals mounted one more frontal assault. As usual, they played the race card. Statistics, ah, statistics. Once more statistics were deployed to prove racial discrimination in capital sentencing. Proportionally more blacks than whites were sentenced to death for killing, more blacks were condemned for killing whites than whites for killing blacks, and interracial murderers were more likely to get a death sentence than murderers who stuck to their own race. This argument wended its way to the Supreme Court, and lost by one vote, in *McCleskey v. Kemp.* The *McCleskey* ruling temporarily sidetracked the liberals' war on the death penalty. But they didn't give up. (The illiberal liberals never, ever give up.)

Failing to get a broad declaration that the death penalty is invidiously discriminatory, liberals turned to a new strategy: selective exemption from the death penalty for specially favored groups. The first special group was the "mentally retarded." At first, the Supreme Court rejected this effort to create a special immunity from execution for this ill-defined class. But after Justice Anthony Kennedy became Blackmunized, and Justice Sandra Day O'Connor decided that what the *Washington Post* and *New York Times* said about her was more important than adherence to principle, the Supreme Court carved out the "mentally retarded" as a favored group exempt from execution.[15]

For centuries the touchstone of legal liability for crime and punishment has been sanity: Does the defendant know right from wrong? If so, then he's liable to conviction and sentence. If, as a result of mental disease or defect, he's not able to know right from wrong, or if, at any point in the process, he is unable to understand the proceedings, he cannot be convicted, sentenced, or executed. Now, however, sanity takes a back seat to retardation. Of course, the Supreme Court did not choose to define mental retardation, generously leaving that to the state courts and legislatures, with the prospect that the boundaries of the definition will be challenged repeatedly and result in further execution delays.

The Supreme Court next turned to limits based on age. In 2005, the Court decided the case of Christopher Simmons. This seventeen-year-old planned a burglary and murder with others even younger; he assured his confederates that they could get away with it *because* they were minors. Simmons picked a victim who had encountered him before, and who recognized him. Shirley Crook's fate was sealed at that point. Binding the poor woman, sheathing her face in duct tape, he took her to a bridge, "hog-tied" her, and threw her off the bridge to drown in the river below. Captured, tried, and convicted of murder in the first degree, he was sentenced by a jury to death.[16] The question the

Supreme Court considered in the Simmons case was whether our "maturing society" had carved out a special niche for murderers under the age of eighteen, immunizing them from the death penalty.

Juveniles, the Court said, are too immature to be subject to the death sentence, because they're not as morally culpable—that is, they're "less guilty." In the majority opinion, Justice Kennedy wrote, "The reality that juveniles still struggle to define their identity means it is less supportable to conclude that even a heinous crime committed by a juvenile is evidence of irretrievably depraved character." (Justice Kennedy is big on defining your identity; it was very important to him in finding a constitutional right to buggery in *Lawrence v. Texas,* and apparently defining your identity by throwing bound women off bridges is almost as important.) The susceptibility of juveniles to "immature and irresponsible behavior," Kennedy added, "means 'their irresponsible conduct is not as morally reprehensible as that of an adult.'"[17]

Was Christopher Simmons's behavior "immature and irresponsible"? The jury found, beyond a reasonable doubt, that he had deliberated on the death of Shirley Crook. (Let's not forget her name: Simmons gets enshrined in constitutional history, Shirley gets six feet of earth. Whom should the law protect and whose loss diminishes society more?) In Missouri, as in most states, deliberation means cool reflection upon the matter. Simmons planned the burglary and killing in advance, even the part about throwing the victim off the bridge. He bragged about it afterward. The fact that Shirley recognized him confirmed his plan to kill, clearly to get rid of the witness. Is that merely immature and irresponsible behavior, like throwing eggs at someone's house or drag racing on a deserted street? Justice Harry Blackmun Kennedy thinks it is. Then why not set aside the guilty verdict altogether?

Having carved out exemptions for the "retarded" and juveniles, liberals returned to the issue of blacks. After all, *McCleskey* was decided by a single vote—which means four liberals were prepared to rule the death penalty unconstitutional on the basis of flawed data. As Justice Clarence Thomas noted in the 1993 case *Graham v.*

Collins,[18] late-twentieth-century death penalty jurisprudence was motivated mainly by a belief that blacks were sentenced to death and executed disproportionately. Certainly this notion has been a recurring
theme of the postconviction litigation by Michael Taylor and Roderick
Nunley and their ilk. It was also the theme of Senator Ted Kennedy's
proposed legislation in 1994 that would have imposed quotas on
executions—just like in college admissions, except the executioner's
quota would have been a ceiling.[19]

If there is a huge disparity in the rate of execution of blacks for
murder, it is entirely appropriate under the equal protection clause to
look further, to see if the result of the specific trial was caused by discrimination. Were blacks excluded from the jury? Were the crimes
for which blacks were sentenced exclusively interracial? Did the trial
participants (lawyers, jurors, witnesses, judges) express any views
about the defendant's race at the time? The law has plenty of room for
proof of intentional discrimination. If it affected the sentence in a particular case, then throw that sentence out. That's what the Fourteenth
Amendment was and is all about.

But liberals aren't content with case-by-case proof of intentional discrimination. They prefer blanket condemnation of the criminal justice system—police, prosecutors, juries, and judges (that is, state
judges)—and, indeed, of the whole society. Such blanket condemna-
tions are typical of the illiberal liberals, who simply ignore the fact that
the evidence of statistical variation in the actual execution of blacks is
slim at best, and the variation in capital sentencing of blacks is little different. In fact, recent data in Missouri indicate that death sentences are
more likely to be meted out to whites than to blacks in that state—
a conclusion not at all to the liking of some politicians, who demand
more study.[20]

As the case of Michael Taylor shows, federal judicial interference in
state criminal proceedings has now expanded to allow use of federal
civil rights laws to seek injunctions against methods of execution.[21]
The liberals' latest gambit is to claim that all existing methods of
execution result in "lingering" and "unnecessarily painful" death. The
"evolving" standard of decency apparently demands something that

nobody knows how to do: inflict a wholly painless and instant death. Execution by lethal injection typically begins with sedation, and the death agony—if we can call it that—seldom lasts more than a couple of minutes. This is a far cry from death by hanging or electrocution. But even if a given prisoner does suffer pain, or "lingers" for a few minutes, so what? The Constitution says nothing about "painless" death. Hanging, electrocution, and gas chambers had all been approved by the courts, and lethal injection, no matter how ineptly handled, is a far cry from these methods of execution. And if we accept the current gimmickry that passes for legal reasoning in death penalty cases, there is obviously no "national consensus" against any particular form of execution, least of all lethal injection.

Ah yes, the "national consensus" argument. Many liberals have pointed to the reduced numbers of executions carried out in recent years as evidence of a supposed national consensus emerging in opposition to the death penalty. Of course, liberals themselves are responsible for the decrease in executions, since they have carved out special categories of murderers who are exempt from the death penalty and have tied up the legal system in eternal postconviction litigation. To cite the number of people actually executed as evidence of a new national consensus against execution in a particular class of cases is a little like using the results of an Iranian election to determine the level of freedom in that country: The exercise is rigged from the beginning.

Make no mistake, the liberal war on the death penalty is at bottom a war on criminal justice, a war begotten by liberal notions that ordinary Americans are too ignorant and bigoted to be trusted with decisions about the lives and liberties of criminals. Never mind that most crimes are and always have been committed by "the poor," against "the poor," today disproportionately composed of blacks, especially in metropolitan areas. And forget about individual responsibility for individual acts, or the idea that criminals should be held morally and legally accountable for their deeds, or that the innocent and law-abiding are demonstrably better off if criminals are incapacitated temporarily or permanently. None of this has any meaning for the liberals who control our judiciary, academe, and a good deal of the legal profession. What matters is *society's* failings, especially racial discrimination. The evolving standard of "decency" has no room for sternness, no room for moral condemnation, and definitely no room for the supreme penalty.

This is not an evolving standard of decency, but an evolving standard of idiocy. It runs in only one direction: toward leniency, toward abandonment of all moral standards and all standards of personal responsibility, toward regarding crime as a disease that is never, ever to be treated by quarantine or cauterization. This is a recipe for licentiousness and anarchy. It is also a recipe for the utter destruction of constitutional government. A Constitution that "evolves" has no meaning and offers no protection to anybody.[22]

FROM KILLERS TO COLESLAW

The mentality that causes federal judges to write execution protocols is the same mentality that has led them to take over prisons and jails as well. As if the war on the death penalty was not damaging enough to the criminal justice system, liberals have not hesitated to do for prisons what they have done for public schools: take control, by the same means and for the same reasons.

There was a time when being sent to prison amounted to "civil death." The felon was stripped of all civil rights, except the right to safe confinement. He was not to sue or be sued, and the running of prisons was left to the discretion of prison authorities.

As the tide of liberalism swelled in the wake of school desegregation decrees and legislative reapportionment decrees, the federal courts quickly became forums for "institutional reform" litigation of all kinds. Jails and prisons were early and easy targets, for were they not populated by the "poor," the "powerless," and minorities? In no time, federal judges were supervising parole practices, pretrial release procedures, and the whole gamut of prison life.[23]

In the 1970s, as government struggled to deal with the rising crime rates produced by the culture of leniency fostered by Lyndon Johnson's

Great Society,[24] the population of jails and prisons swelled out of proportion to the ability of state and local governments to provide more space. At first, the courts contented themselves with controlling the infliction of physical punishment on convicts in prisons. Soon, however, they spurred a whole new field of litigation by granting prisoners a "right of access" to the courts and rights to law libraries to make jailhouse lawyers more productive.[25] In short order, the federal courts went beyond all limits and began to investigate medical care, nutrition, recreation, and everything else.

The ostensible purpose of jail and prison litigation was to ensure humane treatment of prisoners. Its real purpose was to compel the release of thousands of prisoners, most of whom liberals thought should not be in custody anyway. Like school desegregation litigation, prison "reform" litigation soon was co-opted by bureaucrats who sensed an opportunity to break free of fiscal oversight by elected officials. After all, if the court ordered new food service, more guards, and even construction of new facilities, whose bureaucratic empire grew?

Prison reform litigation struck the city of St. Louis in 1972, when the city jail, a model of 1914 penology, was packed with prisoners, due to a swelling of the criminal docket in the city. The old jail had a design capacity of about two hundred prisoners, but was suddenly home to about four hundred. Representatives of the ACLU, taking a breather from Christmas bashing, sued, and a cap of 228 was fixed for the population of the city jail. There the matter would have rested, but in 1982 a fire struck another city jail facility known as the workhouse. The city foolishly ignored the court's limit at the city jail and temporarily relocated prisoners from the workhouse, ramping up the city jail's population well above 228. In no time at all, jailhouse lawyers were screaming, and the ACLU swung back into action. This is when I became involved in the case, as cocounsel for the City of St. Louis.[26]

The district judge in the case, recently installed in his seat by Jimmy Carter, had absorbed a concentrated course in illiberal liberalism in his long career as a lawyer. He decided that he was going to "solve the problem." In doing so, he took over supervision of the city workhouse, even though conditions at the workhouse had not been part of the original suit and even though a different federal judge had rejected another suit involving the workhouse.

Once the radical liberals get going, they never know when to stop. The St. Louis jail case quickly became a model of federal judicial intervention, even though the plaintiffs never produced any substantial evidence of unconstitutional conditions. Still, the city, like many others, entered into a "consent decree," which basically means, "we give up." The consent decree also imposed a population cap at the workhouse, limiting the city to a grand total of 778 prisoners at both the jail and the workhouse. Shortly after this consent order, the crime rate rocketed up, and the number of pending felony cases in the city of St. Louis followed.

Lawsuits over jail conditions give liberals the opportunity to attack something else that they don't like: the practice of keeping dangerous criminals in jail while they await trial. Here again, liberals do everything they can to ensure that these people are released to commit further depredations.

True, persons charged with crimes are presumed innocent. That is a courtroom presumption. Police officers, court staff, jailers, and judges act on that presumption outside the courtroom at their peril. Who gunned down the judge and others in Atlanta in 2005? A prisoner awaiting trial. Who escaped from the St. Louis workhouse, abducted a woman, and raped her around the clock for days? A prisoner awaiting trial. Persons charged with dangerous crimes are convicted more than 80 percent of the time even in San Francisco. They are dangerous persons. We trial judges try to protect the public by keeping them locked up. And we don't really care whether they're rich or poor. In fact, rich defendants are that much more likely to skip town, since they have the means to live elsewhere for an extended period.

But in the St. Louis case, the federal court pressured the city administration to insist that the state courts ease up bail bond conditions. In other words, to avoid criminal contempt for exceeding jail population limits, the city fathers had to demand that dangerous criminals be allowed to walk the streets. The state judges resisted, but the city released people anyway.

When I went on the bench, one of my earliest assignments was to supervise my court's central criminal docket. This included setting bail conditions for felons. I tried mightily to help my former client, the city, keep within the jail populations' limits mandated by the federal decrees. At some point, I realized that I was doing the public a disservice. Once, when my colleagues and I called a press conference to call attention to the jail crisis, we were asked if we were releasing dangerous people. We avoided the question as best we could, but the answer was "Yes!"

It also became apparent to me (as a judge) that the city officials were not too unhappy at having limits on the number of prisoners in custody. Prisoners cost money to feed, clothe, and provide medical care. Fewer prisoners meant lower jail costs. But the politicians didn't want to be seen as soft on criminals, so they simply left my court hanging.

Eventually, I decided that my court should not assume the responsibility of endangering the community by the release of dangerous felons. When the city once again released them anyway, I threatened the city with contempt of court, only to find myself threatened by the federal judge with contempt of his order. Needless to say, the federal judge was a liberal. Normally one of the sweetest-tempered of men, he turned positively vicious when his pet project of "solving the jail problem" was obstructed. No contempt orders ever got entered.

Later, when I was chief judge of my circuit, the same problem recurred. This time, however, we were ready. The Republican Congress had passed the Prison Litigation Reform Act in 1995, and my court hired lawyers to get the federal courts out of the business of running the jails and, indirectly, our state court criminal dockets. As a result, the federal court of appeals reversed the federal district judge and ordered him to comply with the Reform Act. The district judge, with whom I clashed both as counsel in the case and after I went on the bench, withdrew from the case as soon as the court of appeals refused to blindly accept his handling of the matter, and the succeeding district judge was likewise reversed when she failed to follow the Prison Litigation Reform Act. Today, thanks largely to the efforts of state judges, the federal courts no longer run our jails, and, to the credit of a subsequent mayor, a modern new jail has doubled prisoner capacity just in time to deal with the highest criminal dockets in modern history.

That long-term victory is encouraging, but consider all the needless litigation we had to endure and all the liberal rulings we had to overcome. The capstone of the St. Louis jail litigation was a hearing conducted by the federal judge on, among other things, food service. Here we had one of the most powerful figures in government, a federal judge, sitting in solemn state in an ornate courtroom, listening to evidence about the temperature of the coleslaw being served at the workhouse cafeteria.[27] Coleslaw? Was the Fourteenth Amendment adopted to ensure good coleslaw in jail?

CRIMINALS: ANOTHER FAVORED CLASS

The Fourteenth Amendment forbids depriving someone of liberty without due process of law. When a person is lawfully arrested and lawfully charged with a crime, or when a person is sentenced after being convicted of a crime, he has been deprived of his liberty *with* due process. Why should he retain any liberty at all, beyond the minimal demands of civilized treatment? Case after case after case has expanded the "rights" of prisoners at the expense of prison discipline. Now prison authorities must jump through procedural hoops to impose the simplest discipline on prisoners, and prisoners have "rights" to hearings before being transferred to high-security confinement.[28]

The dichotomy between the liberal attitude toward prisoners and the commonsense view (actually consistent with the Constitution as written) is starkly illustrated by the 2003 Supreme Court ruling in *Overton v. Bazzetta*.[29] There, the lower federal courts intervened to second-guess Michigan prison authorities in limiting visits to prisoners and in denying visits as a disciplinary matter, applying the liberal principle that in the realm of prison administration the federal courts must have the last word. The liberal "gang of four" (John Paul Stevens, David Souter, Ruth Bader Ginsburg, and Stephen Breyer) joined in sustaining the prison rules, but they seized the opportunity to crow about the "rejection" of the view that a prison inmate was a mere "slave."

This statement is perhaps the tip-off to why liberals insist that every prison regulation or action can be second-guessed by federal judges, whether it is the dosage of drugs in lethal injection, the transfer of prisoners to maximum-security facilities, prison visitation policies, or even the temperature of coleslaw. Formerly, the law saw prisoners as "slaves," and so in the modern, enlightened, "evolving" world of liberals, the same legal machinery that has been deployed to make certain favored groups more equal than others must also be directed toward giving criminals better treatment than victims.

Indeed, in the liberal worldview, criminals are yet another class to be favored. Minorities and the poor constitute a disproportionate number of criminals, so it is up to the courts, those great moral arbiters, to protect them. Don't worry about the innocent dead, violated, or maimed (just as you shouldn't worry about the innocent victims of abortion). They have no right to the satisfaction of seeing condign punishment visited upon their murderers, ravishers, or attackers. Nor do they have any right to a society that enforces norms and preserves order.

It is one thing to assure fairness to those charged with a crime, and quite another to elevate those *convicted* of crime into a special, protected class. The standard of decency that marks a "maturing" society should not be measured by how the society treats the guilty, but by how it treats the innocent. Under the tyranny of tolerance of the Brennans, Stevenses, and Souters of the world, that treatment is shabby indeed.

CHAPTER 8

LIFE, LIBERTY, BUT NOT PROPERTY

The protection of private property in the Fifth Amendment pre-supposes that it is wanted for public use, but provides that it shall not be taken for such use without compensation. A similar assumption is made in the decisions upon the Fourteenth Amendment. . . . When this seemingly absolute protection is found to be qualified by the police power, the natural tendency of human nature is to extend the qualification more and more until at last private property disappears. But that cannot be accomplished in this way under the Constitution of the United States. . . . We are in danger of forgetting that a strong public desire to improve the public condition is not enough to warrant achieving the desire by a shorter cut than the constitutional way of paying for the change.

—Justice Oliver Wendell Holmes Jr.,
Pennsylvania Coal Co. v. Mahon (1922)

THE CONSTITUTION GUARANTEES the right of property in several places. The Fourteenth Amendment expressly forbids states to deprive any person of life, liberty, *or property* without due process of law. The Fifth Amendment has the same language about due process and adds the further limitation "nor shall private property be taken for public use, without just compensation."

You would think that the express mention of private property in the Constitution would be of some significance. Shouldn't it be like freedom of speech or of the press? Perhaps it should be viewed as "fundamental." After all, under the common law, the concept of personal rights as a form of property was basic to the evolution of the idea that people in a very real sense *own* their freedom, and that freedom cannot be stripped away at the whim of government.

But no! The courts, especially since the ascent of the illiberal liberals, have treated property rights as constitutional stepchildren, having a status of something less than real constitutional rights. At bottom this contempt for property rights springs from the socialist mentality of most radical liberals: Their grand ideal is a collectivist, welfare state, perhaps just a shade this side of Marxism. They can't totally ignore property rights, since the language of the Constitution is hard to completely overlook, but they find it easy to "balance" and regulate those rights away, in a manner that they would not even consider in the realm of the First Amendment (except for "insensitive" or "intolerant" speech, as we'll see in Chapter 10). And judges do routinely ignore flagrant injustices perpetrated on property owners if those injustices advance liberal objectives.

The tyranny of tolerance strikes again.

THE "DIVERSE AND ALWAYS EVOLVING NEEDS OF SOCIETY" CLAUSE

The government takes your property in two ways (other than by taxation, that is). First there's the open and obvious way, by filing a condemnation lawsuit. But the government also resorts to indirect and sneaky methods—for example, by issuing regulations that destroy the property's value or your ability to use it the way you want to, or by simply grabbing the property and giving it to somebody else while insisting that you never really lost anything by the transaction.

Let's start with the direct taking of property. When written constitutions were adopted during and after the American Revolution (an integral part of what made the Revolution truly revolutionary, by the way), nearly all contained limits on the power of "eminent domain." The usual provisions were similar to those found in the Fifth Amendment: Property could be taken for public use, and only with just compensation.

The first battle was fought over "public use." The courts quickly decided that they got to make the call on what constituted public use. Though some courts in the nineteenth century insisted that public use meant just that—the government had to use the property itself— opposing forces soon prevailed. The courts promptly rewrote public use to mean "public purpose." This was in large part to help the rail-roads and the textile mill industries.[1]

From there, the courts happily allowed the legislative branch almost full power to decide what a "public purpose" is.[2] In the 1950s, urban re-development, or slum clearance, became the biggest issue in eminent domain or condemnation law. Supreme Court Justice William O. Douglas, liberal par excellence, got his hands on the issue in *Berman v. Parker*.[3] In ringing tones he exalted the cause of urban redevelopment: "[T]he concept of the public welfare is broad and inclusive. The values it represents are spiritual as well as physical, aesthetic as well as mone-tary. It is within the power of the legislature to determine that the com-munity should be beautiful as well as healthy, spacious as well as clean, well-balanced as well as carefully patrolled."[4]

Notice how public use became public purpose became public wel-fare? At least in the *Berman* case the condemnor was a government entity, and the property condemned was indisputably blighted and un-productive at best. An argument could be made that the public in fact would "use" the property by clearing it first, to make it suitable for re-development by private owners. But Douglas's characteristically sweep-ing language gave government virtually a blank check to determine when it could take private property for almost any purpose it deemed to justify the taking.

Although it was recognized virtually from the time of the adoption of the Constitution that government could not, with or without compen-sation, simply take A's property and give it to B[5] (land redistribution schemes in the old Communist countries come to mind), *Berman* set off more and more ambitious government forays into expropriation. The climax came in the 1960s, when the state of Hawaii decided that too few landowners controlled too much land. So the legislature created "land reform," which quite simply allowed title in real property to be taken from lessors and transferred to lessees "in order to reduce the concentration of land ownership." Come again? Isn't that the state taking A's land and giving it to B? Of course. But the U.S. Supreme Court let it stand, when it finally ruled on the case of *Hawaii Housing Authority v. Midkiff* in 1984.[6] Here we see the remarkable—and troubling—confluence of liberal joy in destroying property rights and "conservative" deference to legislative judgments.

Amazingly, the notoriously liberal Ninth Circuit Court of Appeals, in an opinion by a Jimmy Carter appointee, condemned the "land reform" scheme that the Supreme Court upheld in *Midkiff*. The court of appeals cited James Madison's views on the need for a bill of rights to protect a minority (property owners) from a majority seeking to remedy unequal property distribution through legislative action. Madison recognized that in a free country, with a free economy, there would be inequalities in ownership, and that the Constitution must prevent violations of property rights. Alexander Hamilton echoed Madison's view that protection of property rights was a crucial part of the new Constitution. The Ninth Circuit, unlike the Supreme Court, gave effect to the plain meaning and intent of the Constitution in condemning the Hawaiian land redistribution scheme.[7]

After *Midkiff*, it could hardly be surprising that the Supreme Court would uphold condemnation of private property for the sole purpose of putting it to a "better" use ("better" in the view of the government). What was surprising was that the Court that was unanimous in *Midkiff* was divided 5–4 on the issue. Even more surprising was that the latest case, *Kelo v. City of New London*, seems to have struck of chord of opposition in the nation at large. "Hands off my land" suddenly seems to be a battle cry—far stronger, it seems, than the outcry when the Supreme Court arrogated to itself the power to tax.

Kelo v. City of New London, decided in 2005, involved condemnation not to remove blight, but for the purpose of "economic development." Justice John Paul Stevens and the other liberals—Ruth Bader Ginsburg, Stephen Breyer, and David Souter—had no difficulty in upholding the condemnation as for a "public purpose." In this area, as in no other, Justice Stevens was slavish in his deference to the judgment of the city council. Justice Blackmun, I mean, Kennedy, went into "rational basis" mode, too, finding that property owners deserve less constitutional protection than persons engaging in deviant sex.

In his dissent, Justice Clarence Thomas, as is his wont, demanded that the courts adhere to the plain meaning of the Constitution. Forget the gloss the courts had placed on the Fifth Amendment over the years; public use does not equal public purpose. Justice Thomas wrote, "When faced with a clash of constitutional principle and a line of unreasoned cases wholly divorced from the text, history, and structure of our founding document, we should not hesitate to resolve the tension in favor of the Constitution's original meaning."[8] In the hands of the Supreme Court, Thomas said, the public use clause had become the "diverse and always evolving needs of society" clause.

"Diverse and always evolving needs of society"? Why, those were the very words Justice Stevens used in his opinion to justify the majority's ruling. The Stevens standard here is reminiscent of the Court's malleable "evolving standards of decency" yardstick on the Eighth Amendment and capital punishment.

YOUR MONEY DIVERTED TO A SLUSH FUND

As shocking as the *Kelo* ruling was, at the very least the Supreme Court still enforced one part of the Constitution—namely, by requiring the government to pay for what it takes. But when it comes to the sneaky ways government takes your property, the liberal courts have allowed your property to be taken without the government paying for it.

With some of the liberals' pet projects—notably, legal aid and the environment—we find plenty of examples of what lawyers call "regulatory takings." When the government destroys the value of your property, but doesn't physically occupy it or take the title away, you have been "regulated." Sometimes we call this "inverse condemnation": The government grabs the property first and forces you to sue to receive compensation. Such "regulatory takings" advance the liberal agenda.

The Legal Services Corporation, a federal agency created during the Nixon administration in the mold of Lyndon Johnson's Great Society, provides taxpayer-subsidized legal services for "the poor." Sure, the poor need advice in landlord-tenant matters, domestic relations, and debtor-creditor relations. But is that what the Legal Services Corporation and its numerous subsidiaries (which I will describe as Legal Aid) actually do? Sometimes. But a great deal of their time is taken up in litigating against the taxpayers on behalf of those who are more equal than others. Should the government subsidize lawsuits against taxpayers? According to the Supreme Court, yes: In 2001 the Court declared unconstitutional the limits that Congress tried to place on the Legal Aid lobby's ability to litigate against the taxpayers.[9]

Faced with comparatively stingy GOP Congresses after 1994, the Legal Aid lobby came up with new gimmicks to increase its funding, the most popular of which has been to take the interest from lawyers' trust accounts. Lawyers have an ethical duty to take care of their clients' money, treating it as a trust fund. Many states require, and many lawyers voluntarily ensure, that clients' funds are kept in "trust accounts," accounts that pay interest and that are segregated from the lawyer's personal funds. The Legal Aid lobby decided that the interest on lawyers' trust accounts didn't really belong to anybody and could make a nice slush fund for Legal Aid. With the American Bar Association leading the charge, many states hit lawyers with a wave of "IOLTA" (interest on lawyer trust accounts) rules that require lawyers to place client funds in interest-bearing trust accounts and pay the interest . . . to a Legal Aid fund.

Wait a minute! The lawyer's client is the owner of the principal that generates the interest. If I have a bank account that pays interest on my money, doesn't the interest belong to me as the owner of the principal? Of course—except when the courts, at the behest of liberals, say it doesn't. That's exactly what many state courts did. Some paid lip service to the property rights of the clients and came up with "consent" devices to pretend that the clients agreed to the taking of their money.

Finally, the Washington Legal Foundation went to bat for the property owners. In 1998, in *Phillips v. Washington Legal Foundation*,[10] the Supreme Court held (liberals dissenting) that the interest on client funds really did belong to the clients and that a Texas Legal Aid slush fund rule that effectively expropriated the clients' property was an unconstitutional taking.

That was not the end of the story, though.

Legal Aid, like radical liberals generally, never, ever gives up. Some states devised new ways to steal the interest, and in 2003 the Supreme Court gave the rubber stamp to this liberal mechanism for seizing property. In *Brown v. Legal Foundation of Washington*,[11] the Court held that if the amount of interest money due an individual client was less than the "transaction cost" of actually paying it over to the owner, then there really wasn't a taking in the constitutional sense, and government could simply keep the money and give it to Legal Aid.

The *Brown* decision, written by the ineffable Stevens, illustrates the fundamental hypocrisy of illiberal liberals. Outside the property context, they bray that there is no such thing as a de minimis constitutional violation.[12] Any constitutional violation requires redress. Oops, well, any violation that involves our favorites like pornography, abortion, sodomy, or criminals, but property—well, that's not really a constitutional right, is it?

Brown's perversion of the Constitution, which admittedly involves taking only a little money from each victim, pales in comparison to the highway robbery committed in the name of the environment. The power given to government bureaucrats in this regard makes the British writs of assistance (or general search warrants) that the Americans rebelled against in the Revolution seem trivial.

INSECTS AND MICE ARE MORE EQUAL THAN PEOPLE

By now, everybody should know of the travesty called the Endangered Species Act, another Nixon legacy, borne of his desire to buy off the liberals in one area in the hope that they'd leave him alone in other areas. Worked like a charm, didn't it?

The Endangered Species Act is another example of the liberal method of using the judiciary to advance policies agreeable to liberals, without letting little things like the Constitution or established principles of statutory construction get in the way.

Under the terms of the act, by merely listing a bug as an "endangered species," the federal government strips states, cities, and private citizens of the ability to do anything with their own land. In 1990, the government did just that by declaring the northern spotted owl "threatened." Once that happened, millions of acres of private property in the Pacific Northwest became off-limits to logging, because any northern spotted owl nest is entitled to be insulated by thousands of acres. Small landowners, logging companies, and families dependent on logging filed suit, contending that administrative regulations under the Endangered Species Act went too far in defining what will "harm" a threatened or endangered species. The federal court of appeals in Washington, D.C., agreed.

Ah, but any optimism that the courts would continue to uphold the rights of landowners soon proved misplaced. In 1995 the Supreme Court reversed the court of appeals. In *Babbitt v. Sweet Home Chapter of Communities for a Greater Oregon*,[13] the usual liberal lineup found no problems with the government regulation's defining "harm" in a way that covered anything remotely affecting a species habitat.

Since *Babbitt v. Sweet Home* the government has done little to acknowledge the rights of private property owners. There was a glimmer of hope in 2005, when the courageous Republican congressman John Pombo pushed through the House of Representatives a much-needed reform of the Endangered Species Act. Congressman Pombo's bill, entitled the Threatened and Endangered Species Recovery Act of 2005, would impose more stringent standards on the listing of "endangered" species and would provide modest remedies for property owners whose land is seized for the sake of protecting vermin.[14] Alas, the bill languished in a Senate committee, seemingly with little chance of passage. In the meantime, property owners in Colorado find themselves struggling to free themselves from something called "Preble's mouse," a rodent the Interior Department declared to be endangered on the basis of false data.[15]

Doesn't the impact of the Endangered Species Act on your property entitle you to compensation? Don't bet on it. This is another "regulatory" taking. If your land has any value left, you have no gripe. Never mind that you have been deprived of your right to use your land in a productive way. Your property has simply been conscripted to national zoological use.[16] The Endangered Species Act has been the vehicle for forcing counties to relocate needed hospital facilities, and for prohibiting other development on private property—all without compensation. Bugs are more equal than people.[17]

Similar draconian regulations have been issued in regard to wetlands. Once you've got a wetland, you've got no right to use your property. The wetland must be preserved at your expense. And almost anything can be a wetland. The Supreme Court, departing from its Endangered Species Act mold, has tried to limit the reach of regulation of wetlands under the Clean Water Act. In 2001, the Court held that the Clean Water Act did not give the Army Corps of Engineers the authority to regulate nonnavigable ponds, even if the ponds were used by migratory birds.[18] The liberals dissented, insisting as usual that the sky was falling, and that Congress can regulate anything it wants to (except abortion and obscenity and a lot of other things not mentioned in the Constitution).

The Supreme Court had another opportunity to vindicate private property rights in the face of overreaching "wetlands" regulation in 2006. In *Rapanos v. United States*,[19] a property owner, exhibiting a spirit akin to the Sons of Liberty, defied the Army Corps of Engineers by filling in "wetlands" that were miles from any navigable waterways and were at most a moist patch of earth. The bureaucracy descended upon Rapanos with its full fury, leveling civil penalties and adding a criminal prosecution for good measure. Four justices—John Roberts, Antonin Scalia, Clarence Thomas, and Samuel Alito—rejected the notion that Congress and the Corps of Engineers can declare any wet piece of ground to be "waters of the United States." Unfortunately, Justice Kennedy again was unable to take a forthright stand. Instead, he babbled about the government's needing to establish a "significant nexus" between a supposed "wetland" and navigable waterways. With such a mushy standard, the Corps of Engineers will have no difficulty in manufacturing a connection between Rapanos's moist patch of earth and any navigable waters anywhere within a hundred miles. Of course, the true blue liberals on the Court dissented, inviting the Corps to find a "nexus" anywhere it could.

Other than the puny steps taken to rein in the Corps of Engineers, the Supreme Court has basically dodged the issue of compelling government to pay compensation for property it takes, or it has imposed more and more complex procedural hoops for property owners to jump through before the government can be forced to pay for destroying the owners' rights.[20]

THE GOVERNMENT GRABS PROPERTY, THE LIBERALS GRAB POWER

Under the tyranny of tolerance, just as some classes of citizens are more equal than others, some constitutional rights are more important than others. Property rights, unless we're talking about welfare benefits,[21] take second place in the liberal scheme of constitutional law.

Private property and its associated rights more often than not present obstacles to liberal schemes to achieve "social justice." The radical liberals will always defer to government efforts to destroy private property, as property really shouldn't count as a constitutional right anyway. Private property rights also smack of economic freedom. No good can come of protecting economic freedom. That sort of thinking leads to the invalidation of "progressive" legislation.

The attitude toward property also fits well with the liberal notion of the role of the courts. The courts do not protect rights actually set out in the Constitution, but rather they *create* constitutional rights to advance the liberal agenda. The Fifth Amendment's just compensation clause usually stands in the way of the liberal agenda, and so it must be nullified. Likewise, the idea of blind deference to the legislature in economic matters sits well with liberals, as it makes possible all manner of "progressive" schemes, such as giving bugs priority over property owners, or taking money from litigants and giving it to Legal Aid lawyers to sue the taxpayers from whom the money was taken in the first place. Indeed, the idea of giving rats and bugs, and trees and owls, the standing to sue in court is part and parcel of the jurisprudence of tolerance: The rights of taxpaying citizens take second place to the tolerant society of our judicial philosopher kings.

In 1996, a lawsuit came before me challenging a decision by the Missouri Department of Natural Resources to permit the trapping of river otters. The evidence showed that river otters had been on the edge of extinction in Missouri, but the simple device of forbidding hunting and trapping the creatures had resulted in a rapid multiplication of otters—to the point that their nests were obstructing streams and the otters were making a nuisance of themselves by feasting at private fish hatcheries. The plan called for a limited number of permits and a limited bag, but the environmentalists screamed like wounded panthers. I found that the trapping permits were well within the discretion of the Missouri authorities.[22] In the course of the opinion, I noted that the real parties in interest were the landowners and the otters, and that the latter did not have standing. I am sure that this aside made me few friends in the Sierra Club, but it was true.

As Justice Thomas makes clear, the government's ability to grab private property should be limited to situations in which the government itself will use and occupy the property, or at least situations in which the property will be put to a use that is itself "public," such as by creating rights of way for common carriers.[23] But such limitations hew too closely to the plain meaning of the language of the Constitution itself, and if there's one thing the illiberal liberals can't abide, it's enforcing the plain meaning of the Constitution. To do so implies that the Constitution creates fixed, permanent rules that the government must always follow.

We can't have that, can we? Because if we do, then we can't have brilliant government programs designed to put private land to better use (that is, use dictated by government); we can't have bike trails and other amenities, unless the government pays for them. And if the government must pay for property rights it takes to protect bugs or owls or wetlands, why, it might think twice about enacting such regulations in the first place. Worse yet, government money might need to go to property owners instead of being spent on better things, like welfare benefits. But above all, if we enforce the Constitution as written, we can't have new constitutional rights created by the judiciary, like sodomy and abortion.

CHAPTER 9

THE ANTI-CHRISTIAN LITIGATION UNION

Alas, Virginia, there is a Santa Claus.

He exists as certainly as hate and racism and Eurocentrism exist. He is a clever marketing tool of the Christian Right. Christianity, if you will, with a friendly face. How much better would be the world if there were no Santa Claus—almost as good as if there were no Christmas. There would be no childlike faith then, no creche displays on public property, no cumbersome distinctions between true and false. . . .

No Santa Claus? Only a child might say so. A thousand years from now, Virginia, nay 10 times 10,000 years from now, he will remain among the gravest threats to our Constitution and the separation of church and state, as a panel of legal experts from Harvard and Yale are ready to testify before Congress at a moment's notice.

—The *Wall Street Journal,* essaying a satirical modernization
of the famous 1897 *New York Sun* editorial
"Yes, Virginia, There Is a Santa Claus"

EARLY IN 1999, POPE JOHN PAUL II was coming to St. Louis. Planning for the visit began in late 1998, when I was the chief judge (we call it "presiding judge") of my judicial circuit, which encompasses the city of St. Louis. The city fathers were mightily concerned about a repeat in St. Louis of the gridlock caused by hordes of pilgrims who descended on Colorado when John Paul had visited there several years earlier. Police, bureaucrats, and civic leaders clamored about the need to close down the courthouses downtown and, reluctantly, I agreed. But while responsible people were concerning themselves with serious issues of safety and security, I later learned that others were concerning themselves with something much more important: the "cross" on our Civil Courts Building.

The St. Louis Civil Courts Building is a majestic, twenty-six-story building situated on a downtown mall that runs from the St. Louis Gateway Arch westward for several miles. At the time of the pope's visit, we were completing a renovation of the building, and new lighting had been installed. The building had large public lobbies in the middle of every floor with huge windows at each end. The lights were always left on in these lobbies, mainly as a matter of security and safety. On the eighth floor of the building (which is actually the sixteenth story due to the double height of the courtroom floors), offices ran across the width of the building. The lights in the offices, which housed the Sheriff's Department, were always left on at night also, partly to accommodate the cleaning crews, but mostly through simple inattention. The effect of the line of lighted offices across the eighth floor, intersecting the vertical line of the lighted public lobbies, created the appearance of a cross. This cross pattern had existed for more than a year, on one side of the building only.

Well, guess what? As the pope's visit drew nigh, the alert minions of the American Civil Liberties Union (ACLU) noticed the cross of lights on the Civil Courts Building and had a fit of separation of church and state anxiety. How terrible! The pope coming to St. Louis, and something resembling a Latin cross besmirching our court building!

The ACLU called the sheriff and demanded that he douse the lights on the eighth floor. The sheriff, a placid, accommodating fellow, did as he was told. Had I been consulted, the organization's ridiculous demand would have gotten a rather different reception.

This wasn't the first time the ACLU had gone after our court. In another incident, a clerk's employee was ordered to remove a small

Nativity scene at her workstation at Christmastime, as that, too, was deemed unconstitutional by the ACLU. That incident, together with the case of the accidental cross, drove home for me how the acronym ACLU really seems to stand for Anti-Christian Litigation Union. The ACLU's commitment to free expression comes to a screeching halt at the point when that expression takes the form of religious belief.

What enables the ACLU to stamp out religious expression in public so effectively, even though the Constitution expressly forbids government interference with the free exercise of religion? Why does the law reflect this curious attitude that religious expression can be singled out for extirpation from public property and government-related activities?

THE LITIGATION SHOCK TROOPS

In 1896, in the case of *Reynolds v. United States,* the Supreme Court commented that "we are a Christian nation," in a case upholding Congress's power to forbid polygamy by law, notwithstanding Mormon religious beliefs on the subject.[1] A century later, Justice Sandra Day O'Connor was castigated merely for quoting the *Reynolds* opinion in a letter to a schoolchild who had solicited some comments on the Supreme Court and religion.

We have now reached a point where judges shy away from anything that smacks of "endorsement" of religion. As Justice O'Connor herself has declared, "Endorsement . . . sends a message to nonadherents that they are outsiders, not full members of the political community, and an accompanying message to adherents that they are insiders, favored members of the political community."[2]

What has happened over the past century? The tyranny of tolerance has emerged.

"Endorsement" of religion "excludes" people and is not the hallmark of a "tolerant" society. And we must be tolerant above all—just not tolerant of public or governmental recognitions of the faith (or even faiths) of our people.

Here we have the tyranny of tolerance at its most hypocritical and oppressive. The Boy Scouts, Christian religious groups, the Ten Commandments, Nativity scenes, voluntary prayer at high school events, even moments of silence—all have been expelled from the public square in the name of tolerance. Every Christmas season brings its quota of lawsuits by the ACLU to drive Christmas out of public life, except to the extent that it manifests itself by "secular" symbols like Santa Claus and reindeer (and, of course, the newly dubbed "holiday" tree).

How did this happen? How did the First Amendment, ratified as a limitation on the power of government to suppress religion, become the means of suppression and exclusion of religion? Once again, the answer is found in the alliance of the courts and liberals. It is no coincidence that God was placed in the dock shortly after the New Deal hijacked the courts.[3] Nor is it a coincidence that the ACLU, supposedly founded to protect against the suppression of political dissent, has almost always been in the vanguard of attacks on religion. The shock troops of the Anti-Christian Litigation Union have found a congenial (and lucrative) career in persecuting, er, prosecuting lawsuits against federal, state, and local governments, and many private organizations, in the name of separation of church and state.

INTOLERANCE FOR RELIGIOUS EXPRESSION

The ACLU was founded in 1920 by persons best described as Communist sympathizers. The organization boasts that it "has led the way in creating a body of law that has made the principles of equal rights, freedom of expression, due process and fundamental fairness come alive. . . . The ACLU was the first public interest law firm of its kind, and immediately began the work of transforming the ideals contained in the Bill of Rights into living, breathing realities."[4] Significantly, the ACLU doesn't boast much about freedom of religion. Perhaps that is because the ACLU has little use for religion, and none at all for religious expression in the public square.[5]

Case after case that the ACLU has prosecuted (or threatened to prosecute) reflects the organization's hostility to religion and especially to Christianity.[6] The organization's overwhelming success in these cases reflects the antireligious sentiments of its judicial allies.[7]

The city of Los Angeles adopted a city seal in 1957 that included images of the Hollywood Bowl and a nearby hillside cross that had long been a Los Angeles landmark. The seal was used without remark until 2004, when the local ACLU hit men sent a typical extortion demand: Remove the cross or face a federal lawsuit. Doubtless this demand was spawned by the publicity attendant upon a federal court case (discussed later) holding the Pledge of Allegiance unconstitutional due to its reference to God. The county board of supervisors, like the St. Louis sheriff, obediently knuckled under to the ACLU and changed the seal.[8]

The city of Republic, Missouri, was not quite so subservient. It adopted a city seal in the 1990s that featured a fish symbol. The city council admittedly wanted the seal to reflect their community's Christian heritage. The fools! The ACLU struck almost immediately, suing on behalf of a self-proclaimed "wiccan" or witch, and the federal courts swiftly declared the seal unconstitutional. (The same judge who imposed taxes on the people of Kansas City had no difficulty in condemning this Christian symbol.) The city was left with no seal and a hefty bill for the ACLU's attorney's fees.[9]

More recently, the city of San Diego became locked in a struggle with the ACLU over the famous Mount Soledad cross, originally erected nearly a century ago and dedicated as part of a war memorial in the 1950s.[10] In the 1990s, the forces of tolerance decided the cross must go. Relying on the California constitution, the federal courts decreed that it must. The citizens of San Diego resisted, voting overwhelmingly to allow transfer of the monument to the federal government. The state court branch of the tyranny then jumped into the fray, forbidding the transfer. In 2006, Congress passed a resolution indicating its willingness to accept the transfer, and Justice Anthony Kennedy granted a stay of the lower federal court's orders mandating destruction of the cross and levying heavy fines on San Diego if it failed to do so. The stage may be set for another Supreme Court pass at the issue of religious monuments on public land.[11]

Although prayers or invocations at the commencement of legislative sessions (both state and congressional) have been upheld by the Supreme Court (over dissents from liberal justices, of course),[12] the ACLU regularly hammers public school boards and municipal bodies if God appears anywhere in their proceedings. Why is there a difference? Well, because school boards are part of public school systems, and religion has no place in public schools, lest impressionable children be subjected to such horrendous influences. The Supreme Court said as much in *Stone v. Graham,* in 1980.[13] So when a school board in a small Louisiana county (called a "parish") insisted on rather florid invocations to Jesus to open and close its meetings, it found itself prostrate before a federal judge, urged on by, guess who?[14]

The ACLU's intolerance for religious expression is cast in sharp relief by its concerted campaign to exclude the Boy Scouts from the most indirect and meager forms of government support.

The Boy Scouts dared to insist on moral principles in admitting members and scoutmasters. They refused to accept homosexuals. When this practice was outlawed by New Jersey, the Boy Scouts sought refuge in the First Amendment—like other oppressed groups before them, such as the Amish, the Jehovah's Witnesses, and Communists. The Supreme Court accepted their proposition that the state could not compel them to admit members who did not or could not subscribe to the Scouts' moral code. Despite this victory, the Scouts had made two mistakes that the ACLU quickly seized on: First, they chose to adhere to moral principles that condemn homosexual conduct; second, they invoked God as one branch of their argument that the state could not coerce them to abandon their moral principles.

Aha! The Boy Scouts believe in God. Therefore, they are a religious organization. They must be driven out of public life. Does a school district sponsor a Boy Scout troop? Establishment of religion! Off with their heads! Does the military sponsor Scouts? Establishment of religion! Drive the Scouts off military bases!

For a hundred years, the Boy Scouts and the government had enjoyed a relationship of mutual respect and support. Suddenly, within a very short time of the Supreme Court's decision in *Boy Scouts of*

America v. Dale, the ACLU had instituted a campaign of legal terrorism, one backed by the federal courts.[15] The federal judiciary, controlled by liberals, treated the Scouts worse than the Ku Klux Klan: The Klan, unlike Boy Scouts, gets to erect crosses on public property.[16]

There's tolerance for you. Dare to stand up for moral principle and we will not only drive you out of public life, but we will bankrupt you with heavy attorney's fee awards.

If the ACLU gets exercised about crosses depicted in city seals, imagine how it responds when actual crosses show up on public property. The organization filed a lawsuit on behalf of an activist who, two to four times a year, had to bear the horrible agony of seeing a steel-pipe cross that was erected on a small rise in the Mojave Desert known as Sunrise Rock. A small group of World War I veterans put up the cross in 1934 as a monument to the men who fell in that war. Though the cross was not maintained with a penny of public funds, in 2004 a federal judge found it to be unconstitutional: It was on public land—though land that the government had not made public until 1994. Not only must the cross come down, said the judge, but the government couldn't give the land away to people who would maintain the cross—that would be an establishment of religion, too. And, by the way, the ACLU got at least $63,000 in attorney's fees for excising this religious cancer from the desert.[17] Justice Clarence Thomas later alluded to the Sunrise Rock cross, remarking, "If a cross in the middle of a desert establishes a religion, then no religious observance is safe from challenge."[18]

For decades, if not centuries, crosses and monuments to the Ten Commandments have been erected and maintained on government property, almost always because a private party has donated the monument or otherwise was responsible for erecting it. The crosses and monuments cost the taxpayers little or nothing. They send no message of "exclusion." They are no more exclusive than a statue of Bertrand Russell or some other prominent atheist would be. They constitute at most a recognition or acknowledgment that the great majority of Americans, and nearly all of its founders, were and are people of faith.

But in the twenty-first century, all crosses and monuments to the

Ten Commandments became targets for the ACLU. The catalog of cases brought by the ACLU to rid public property of these subversive symbols is mind-boggling. Even Justice John Paul Stevens has alluded to the "deluge of cases" flooding lower courts, but of course he sees that deluge as evidence of "the discord these displays have engendered."[19]

Not only has the ACLU won nearly all of the cases, but the taxpayers have had to pay the ACLU enormous sums for attorney's fees—even when the attorneys involved donated their time! So an attack on a merely theoretical taxpayer subsidy of religion actually is a form of extracting a subsidy for carrying on the campaign against religion.

Where has the liberal persecution of religion led? It has led to the Pledge of Allegiance being declared unconstitutional by a federal appeals court, in response to a claim raised by a plaintiff who simply had no right to sue in the first place; and it has led to wholesale destruction, quite literally, of crosses and monuments incorporating the Ten Commandments.

Take the Pledge of Allegiance case. Michael Newdow, the plaintiff, was the noncustodial divorced father of a child in California public schools. Surprisingly, even in California, public school students recite the Pledge daily. Since 1954, by act of Congress, the Pledge has included the phrase "one nation, under God." Neither the child nor her mother, the custodial parent, had a problem with this. Newdow, a self-professed atheist, was outraged that his child should recite this paean to the Almighty. Of course, since 1943 no child can be compelled to recite the Pledge, but this didn't stop Newdow. He sued, and he won. (Oddly, the ACLU seems to have sat this one out.) The liberals on the federal court of appeals for the Ninth Circuit, covering California, insisted that Newdow had the right to sue and that the reference to God in the Pledge was unconstitutional as an establishment of religion.

On review, the Supreme Court evaded the constitutional issue by holding that Newdow lacked "standing" to sue—that is, he was not really injured by his daughter's exposure to the Pledge. All the liberals on the Court agreed that there was no standing. Chief Justice William Rehnquist and Justice Clarence Thomas said that there was standing, and that the Court should reach the merits and uphold the Pledge.

Perhaps sensing the outrage that would sweep the nation and potentially derail the tyranny of tolerance if they struck down the Pledge, the liberals plus the sainted "moderate" Justice Anthony Kennedy ducked the issue.[20]

The Supreme Court may have shown Newdow the door, but the ruling did not stop him from going back at it, as attorney for others; in fact, another federal judge has enjoined recitation of the Pledge, but stayed the ruling pending appeal. Nor did the Supreme Court ruling stop the ACLU and its allies from taking up the attack. The issue has been raised anew in other lawsuits, presumably by parents with legal standing. The House of Representatives has acted to prevent further judicial attacks on the Pledge, but this effort is no more likely to stop the liberal judges than did the statute on flag-burning or the statute aimed at preventing federal court jurisdiction over Guantánamo Bay terrorist prisoners.[21]

THE FICTITIOUS "WALL OF SEPARATION"

Underpinning the ACLU's relentless assault on religion is the liberal aim of creating a "wall of separation" between government and religion. That phrase first appeared in a legal context in a 1947 Supreme Court ruling, *Everson v. Board of Education*—the first case to try to define "establishment of religion."[22] Ever since, liberals have seized on the "wall of separation" dictum as (pardon the expression) holy writ.

There are a few problems with the liberal reliance on the "wall of separation" language. First of all, the Constitution does not mention anything about a strict separation between government and religion. In *Everson,* the Supreme Court cited Thomas Jefferson: "In the words of Jefferson, the clause against establishment of religion by law was intended to erect 'a wall of separation between Church and State.'" But Jefferson's comment came in a private letter, and as James Hutson of the Library of Congress has noted, in the letter Jefferson was *not* making "a dispassionate theoretical pronouncement on the relations between government and religion."[23] In any case, by now we know very well that Jefferson's ideas of what the Constitution and Bill of Rights meant are seldom reflected in the text. In fact, there is no sound reason to believe that James Madison (the draftsman of the First Amendment), the First Congress, or the ratifying states had any idea that forbidding federal laws "respecting an establishment of religion" meant anything like the "wall of separation" demanded by liberals.

The illiberal liberals, and even honest scholars, argue that the meaning of "an establishment of religion" was unclear in 1791. This is unsound historically and legally. What was an "establishment of religion" in 1791? We know what it was, because it existed in England and in many of the states. Do you want to know the elements of an "established" church? Look at the laws of Virginia and Massachusetts. What do you find? You find three things: legislative approval of doctrine, financial support of the church as a church, and enforced obedience to some or all church mandates.[24] This is almost exactly what Justice Thomas found when, in the Pledge of Allegiance case, he reviewed the law and history of religious establishment: The hallmarks of "an establishment of religion" are coercion of belief or participation, and direct government funding of the church as a body corporate.[25]

Coercion, it must be noted, occurs when the government punishes individuals for failing to follow the dictates of the established religion; it is not "peer pressure" or some other indirect penalty that has nothing to do with the force of law.[26] Indeed, if proof of coercion were a necessary element of a claimed violation of the establishment clause, the vast majority of cases brought by the ACLU would not survive what lawyers call a motion to dismiss. A motion to dismiss says, in effect, *So what? Where's your injury? You have shown no right or duty, so you're out of court.*

Justice Thomas, reviled by liberals, had it right when he said in the Pledge of Allegiance case that Nativity scenes, voluntary school prayer, ceremonial prayer or invocations, crosses, monuments to the Ten Commandments, and the Pledge of Allegiance do not constitute "an establishment" of religion. With such displays and recognitions of religion, the government does not compel belief or action by anyone, nor does it lend financial support to a church as a church. There is no message of "exclusion," no creation of a special insiders' clique. The displays simply acknowledge the sometimes transcendent role that religion has played in our nation's history, and its importance to the vast majority of our people.[27] This is a country, after all, where every president since George Washington (including even the Great Prevaricator) has invoked God on a regular basis. It is a country whose Congress has always had a chaplain and that has always provided for chaplains in the armed services. It is a country where the Ten Commandments are emblazoned in the courtroom of the highest court in the land—a court that opens each session with a marshal intoning, "God save the United States and this Honorable Court."

Such government recognition of religion is of no constitutional significance, except in the minds of those who say they equate law and liberty with "tolerance,"[28] but who really value only the sort of tolerance that suppresses the beliefs of the majority at all costs.

"RELIGIOUSLY BASED DIVISIVENESS"

Even Justice Stephen Breyer has recognized the danger of attempting to purge religion from public life. In 2005, voting to allow a Ten Commandments monument at the Texas capitol, he wrote:

> [T]o reach a contrary conclusion here, based primarily upon the religious nature of the tablets' text would, I fear, lead the law to exhibit a hostility toward religion that has no place in our Establishment Clause traditions. Such a holding might well encourage disputes concerning the removal of longstanding depictions of the Ten Commandments from public buildings across the Nation. And it could thereby create the very kind of religiously based divisiveness that the Establishment Clause seeks to avoid.[29]

Don't look now, Justice Breyer, but the federal judiciary's hostility to religion *has* provoked divisiveness. Thus, students who desire to conduct prayer meetings or similar religious-based activities on public property must fight for the right—and, unlike in the ACLU cases, they do not inevitably win.[30] Student religious clubs have been denied equal access to school facilities to conduct their activities. Persons of faith at the United States Air Force Academy have been the target of an investigation that would be labeled McCarthyite, if religion (evangelical Christian religion) were not the focus.[31]

Of course, to liberals, it's the faithful themselves who are responsible for the divisiveness. When Justice Stevens referred to the "deluge" of cases, he did not mention that the ACLU has contrived most, if not all, of this litigation by rounding up wiccans and assorted gadfly atheists to sow such "divisiveness." The identity of the plaintiffs in such cases is a testament to how little discord there really is.

In one of the Ten Commandments cases the Supreme Court decided in 2005, Justice David Souter smugly referred to the St. Bartholomew's Day Massacre in sixteenth-century France and the Massachusetts Bay Colony's persecution of heretics in the seventeenth century, then added that "the divisiveness of religion in current public life is inescapable."[32] What twaddle! The idea that the fish symbol on the city seal of Republic, Missouri, is comparable to religious wars from centuries ago would be perfectly ludicrous if it were not symptomatic of a powerful antireligious sentiment pervading the legal and judicial elite. If there is "divisiveness" attributable to religion in twenty-first-century America, it is almost entirely the product of the ACLU and associated antireligious organizations using the federal courts to suppress public religious expression, in and out of government. And don't forget the Supreme Court's determination to exalt sexual deviancy and obscenity in the face of the moral and religious beliefs of the overwhelming majority of people in this country.

The Supreme Court has tied itself in knots in trying to come up with a "neutral" position on religion in the public square. The Ten Commandments cases decided by the Court in 2005 revealed the tortured logic: The Court approved the monument at the Texas capitol but barred displays at two Kentucky courthouses. In the Pledge of Allegiance case, Justice Thomas rightly noted that the Court's "jurisprudential confusion" over how to interpret the establishment clause "has led to results that can only be described as silly."[33]

But in fighting to maintain "neutrality" on religion, the liberal jurists have done something far worse than silly. They have interpreted the establishment clause to mean that the government cannot "endorse" any religion or all religion without threatening liberty. As noted, even the so-called moderate Justice O'Connor obsessed about government "endorsement" of religion[34]—*We cannot have that, because that sends a message of exclusion. That's intolerant.* She came up with a rationale ("ceremonial deism") that would authorize government recognition of God or religion only on the basis that, over time, the context of the recognition has lost all overtly religious significance and is on par with a St. Patrick's Day or Columbus Day parade.

This sort of analysis is seriously flawed. Endorsement of religion is simply not the same thing as establishment of religion. Think of it this way: The establishment clause does not establish atheism. At least, it cannot be construed to do so. But in the hands of the ACLU and the liberal judiciary, the establishment clause virtually demands that the government be atheistic.

This is not tolerance; this is not neutrality; this is implacable hostility toward religion and the country's Judeo-Christian heritage. By insisting that the government must be "neutral," the Supreme Court has appealed to what Justice Antonin Scalia called the "demonstrably false principle that the government cannot favor religion over irreligion."[35] The relentless liberal persecution of religion in the public square has done more than maintain a "wall of separation"; it has tumbled the wall over onto people of faith.

Religion is not a communicable disease, to be quarantined. It is the wellspring of law and moral values in American civilization. The government can and should recognize this fact. If such recognition means permitting voluntary prayer, referring to God in the Pledge of Allegiance, allowing crosses on public property (even when not erected by the KKK), and monuments to the Ten Commandments in courthouses, the courts need not interfere. The atheist who resents the Nativity scene at Christmas is no more disqualified from the privileges and immunities of a citizen than is the Muslim who resents seeing a menorah.

Isn't that the real tolerance contemplated by the First Amendment? Americans may espouse any religion or no religion; their representatives may recognize the community significance of any religion or no religion, so long as that recognition carries no penalty or public subsidy. If Allegheny County wants to put up a Nativity scene in the rotunda of the county government building at Christmas, let it! If New York wants to display a menorah at Hanukkah, let it! Atheists can rejoice that for the other three hundred odd days of the year, government ignores God and religion.

"A VOICE CRYING IN THE WILDERNESS"

Some years ago, a federal judge, W. Brevard Hand (a Reagan appointee) found himself confronted with a "moment of silence" case, involving an effort to allow public school students to pray or meditate if they want to. Judge Hand upheld the moment of silence, issuing an urgent plea in the process. Describing himself as "a voice crying in the wilderness," he attempted to raise the alarm about the establishment of "secular humanism" as the official religion of the United States, to the exclusion of God in whatever form He is recognized.[36]

Too few of us listened. But Judge Hand was right: The courts are imposing a new form of state-sponsored religion in this country. He called it secular humanism; I call it the tyranny of tolerance.

CHAPTER 10

FREE SPEECH FOR ME BUT NOT FOR THEE

In its demand for total exclusion of military recruiters from their campuses, "fair play" is not a phrase in the law schools' lexicon.
—Judge Ruggero J. Aldisert, U.S. Court of Appeals for
the Third Circuit, dissenting in
Forum for Academic and Institutional Rights v. Rumsfeld (2004)

What is before us, after all, is a speech regulation directed against the opponents of abortion, and it therefore enjoys the benefit of the "ad hoc nullification machine" that the Court has set in motion to push aside whatever doctrines of constitutional law stand in the way of that highly favored practice. . . . Having deprived abortion opponents of the political right to persuade the electorate that abortion should be restricted by law, the Court today continues and expands its assault upon their individual right to persuade women contemplating abortion that what they are doing is wrong.
—Justice Antonin Scalia, dissenting in *Hill v. Colorado* (2000)

FOR MOST OF OUR HISTORY, American law recognized only three exceptions to freedom of speech: defamation, obscenity, and "fighting words," which are face-to-face insults intended to and likely to provoke a violent response—not "discomfort," not distaste, but violence.[1] So the courts have recognized that it's okay to wear a jacket in a courthouse that proclaims "[BLEEP] the draft."[2] It's okay to tell a police officer, "[BLEEP] you."[3] It's okay to wear black armbands in high school to protest a war.[4] It's okay to burn crosses.[5] It's okay to burn the American flag.[6] It's okay to express approval of attempts to kill the president.[7] It's okay to publish "virtual" child pornography via the Internet.[8] All of these things, distasteful as they might be, are part of a constitutional right, a right of free speech that, in essence, everybody—liberals, conservatives, libertarians, everybody—agrees is at the heart of constitutional liberty. Why? Because, as the Founding Fathers knew from personal experience, tyrannical governments retain power by suppressing dissent, public or private. Open and robust public debate is crucial to our freedom, and the government has no authority to suppress such debate, and certainly can't control what is said in private.

Or at least that's how we understood matters until recently. Then the tyranny of tolerance came along.

Like all tyrannies, the tyranny of tolerance must suppress speech that disagrees with its premises. Like all tyrannies, the tyranny of tolerance cannot tolerate dissent. In enforcing the tyranny of tolerance, liberals have resorted to speech codes and "antiharassment" laws. Much as the post–Civil War South resorted to "black codes" to enforce its concept of proper behavior by blacks, the illiberal liberals impose speech codes to enforce their concept of politically and socially correct behavior.[9] Ultimately they aim to change not just behavior but thoughts and attitudes as well. One court succinctly expressed the liberal goal of using laws to enforce "tolerance" when it stated (ungrammatically), "By informing people that the expression of racist or sexist attitudes in public is unacceptable, people may eventually learn that such views are undesirable in private, as well." The government thus can use its laws to "advance the goal of eliminating prejudices and biases in our society."[10]

The liberals' strategy for advancing the goal of eliminating prejudices and biases in the name of tolerance takes a highly intolerant—indeed, totalitarian—approach. *If you disagree with us, your speech is not worthy of protection, and you are to be excluded from schools, employment, and the public square itself.*

LIBERALS AND SPEECH CODES

One would think that speech codes, either officially adopted and enforced by government, or adopted by private entities under compulsion from the government, would run up against the same judicial shoals on which obscenity and flag-burning laws have foundered. One would be wrong.

Speech codes allow liberals to have it both ways. On the one hand, as the champions of tolerance, liberals declare that it is perfectly legitimate to combat intolerance by suppressing its expression, and that if you object to the suppression of intolerant speech, why, you must be intolerant, and unworthy of constitutional protection in the first place. On the other hand, if all you want to do is desecrate religion by immersing a cross in urine, or promote pornography, or denigrate our nation by burning the flag, why, you must certainly be protected (if not rewarded with government money), because of course we must tolerate dissent!

Speech codes target groups that are most capable of leading vigorous debate and dissent against the tyranny of tolerance. Lawyers and judges are among the main targets. Speech codes applying to them generally forbid "manifesting bias" on the basis of race, sex, "sexual orientation" (very important), disability, etc., etc. What is "manifesting bias"? The codes never attempt to define it, since that might narrow the scope of the codes. But I can point to one example: My opinion on sexual harassment was the subject of a disciplinary investigation because I denounced the "cloud cuckooland of radical feminism," and expressed the view that Catharine MacKinnon was a vapid maunderer. This apparently "manifested bias" against women. I am not alone. Lawyers and judges throughout the country have been the subject of disciplinary investigations and sanctions for statements that the tolerance police considered to be forbidden.[11]

The universities are subject to even more notorious speech codes and "nondiscrimination" policies. As a result, these supposed bastions of free thinking enforce a single, uniform point of view on all students and faculty on a variety of subjects having nothing whatever to do with invidious discrimination.[12]

The speech codes and "nondiscrimination" policies of universities have had one especially important consequence: cutting military recruiters off from a source of recruits. America's elite educational institutions have long denigrated the military, and, during the Vietnam War, many colleges and universities drove the military off campus by kicking out the Reserve Officer Training Corps (ROTC).[13] Then, in a movement that accelerated during the 1990s, law schools self-righteously denounced the policy that prohibited practicing homosexuals from serving in the armed forces—a policy enacted by Congress and in force for decades, if not centuries.

Congress sensibly noted that the universities derive a good bit of money from the federal government, especially the Department of Defense, and decided, by open and democratic vote, that universities should not take federal money with one hand and slap the face of the military with the other. If they wanted the dough, they had to take the doughboys. This law, passed in 1996, was known as the Solomon Amendment.[14]

The Clinton administration (surprise!) did not vigorously enforce the Solomon Amendment, notwithstanding the overwhelming majorities by which it was adopted in Congress. Instead, as liberals advanced the homosexual agenda and denounced the military's "don't ask, don't tell" policy on homosexuality, the Clintonites compelled the armed forces to settle for "separate but equal" on campuses. The universities could pretend to provide opportunities for the military to recruit on campus, but they could deny the military any use of placement and career counseling services, and even of interview rooms in placement departments. The Clintonites not only accepted this second-class citizenship for the armed forces, but applauded it.[15] When Congress refined the Solomon Amendment to cover all forms of federal aid, not just Defense Department money,[16] the revision had no real effect, as the Clinton administration had already acquiesced in separate but equal.

After 9/11 and the commencement of the war on terror, the Bush administration took another look and decided that separate but equal was in fact unequal. Donald Rumsfeld's Defense Department demanded equal access in all respects: The military was to be treated in all ways as any other prospective employer. If the universities wanted to denounce the military, or disclaim any support for the military, that was their right, but it could not be done by segregating the military and preventing it from recruiting on campus.[17]

It wasn't long before the liberal law schools organized a response to the Bush administration's determination to enforce the Solomon Amendment. Oddly enough, they didn't have the nerve to sue in their own names, or in the names of their universities. One would think that, to have standing to attack the Solomon Amendment, you must be an actual or prospective recipient of the federal money. Well, no. You organize something called Forum for Academic and Institutional Rights (FAIR), composed of a bunch of liberal law professors, and, naturally, *you go to federal court.*

FAIR insisted that the Solomon Amendment violated First Amendment rights by requiring universities to allow equal access to military recruiters (in other words, by forbidding *discrimination against the military*). The liberals claimed that Congress forced the universities to associate with people they didn't want to associate with and to implicitly endorse discrimination on the basis of "sexual orientation."

The federal district judge who drew *Forum v. Rumsfeld* wasn't buying it.[18] But the federal court of appeals for the Third Circuit, led by a Clinton appointee of course, was.

Some years ago, in cases involving the Rotary Club and the Jaycees, the Supreme Court held that states and municipalities could force private clubs and organizations to accept women members whether they liked it or not. The Court insisted that a mandate to admit members you don't want did not violate the First Amendment right of "association," at least if we're talking about women.[19] In the Solomon Amendment litigation, liberals needed to get around these cases, which clearly held (to the applause of liberals) that the government can require "places of public accommodation" to admit people that the proprietors or other members object to if there's a good reason to compel such access. National security is almost uniformly said to be a "compelling state interest," and sometimes even has been held to justify restrictions on First Amendment freedoms.[20] One would think that military recruiting and national security are inseparable. So how did liberals and their judicial allies get around this issue? The Boy Scouts!

In *Boy Scouts of America v. Dale*,[21] New Jersey tried to force the Boy Scouts to accept homosexual Scout leaders, against the Scouts' will. New Jersey relied on the same "public accommodations" law reasoning as announced in the *Jaycees* and *Rotary Club* cases, condemning discrimination on the basis of sexual orientation. The Supreme Court, voting 5–4 (liberals dissenting), held that the First Amendment protected the Boy Scouts, because the Boy Scouts legitimately wished to teach that homosexual behavior was immoral, and forced membership of practicing homosexual Scout leaders would directly conflict with this objective. Of course, as noted in the previous chapter, liberals then turned around and used this decision to drive the Scouts off of public property and out of public life by (falsely) characterizing the Scouts as a religious organization.[22] Religion and the military—no room for them in the liberal realm of tolerance.

In the law schools case, the federal court of appeals thought that *Boy Scouts v. Dale* authorized the law schools to exclude military recruiters. The law schools are "expressive associations," the court said, and can't be forced to send messages they don't want to send. According to this ruling, by forcing universities and law schools to give military recruiters equal access on campus, on pain of loss of federal funds, Congress is forcing the schools to surrender a constitutional right as a condition of receiving a public benefit, and Congress can't do that.[23]

Well.

In the first place, the law schools are not "expressive associations" like the Boy Scouts. They are not even membership groups like the

Jaycees or the Rotarians. If the law schools are "expressive associations," their message is nothing more than teaching law, including *Boy Scouts v. Dale*. Indeed, under their own concept of unbridled academic freedom, they can hardly be said to have a unified, central message at all. If we can parse their "message," as Justice John Paul Stevens felt able to do in his dissent in *Boy Scouts*,[24] we find that the message is that anything goes. If that is so, then adding the military to the mix merely gives liberal professors and students somebody to picket against on the campus.

In reality, law schools are educational institutions having more in common with business enterprises than with the Boy Scouts. If the Jaycees and the Rotarians can be forced by law to admit women, and if Bob Jones University can be stripped of its tax-exempt status for excluding blacks, law schools and universities can be forced to make placement office space and services available to the military on a transient, nondiscriminatory basis. The universities are not being required to admit military recruiters to any form of membership or affiliation with the law schools. They are simply commanded to treat the military just like any other prospective employer that is allowed to recruit on campus. The universities, not Congress, are engaged in viewpoint discrimination. Indeed, as federally funded entities, they might well be considered state actors anyway.[25] Regardless, if they don't end their discrimination against the military, then they shouldn't get federal money.

The Supreme Court granted review of the *Forum v. Rumsfeld* case in the fall of 2005. The decision came down in March 2006. I confess to surprise—nay, astonishment—that the Supreme Court *unanimously* reversed the Third Circuit.[26] Not even Stevens, David Souter, and Ruth Bader Ginsburg could bring themselves to join the hypocrisy of the law schools. In a remarkably lucid opinion, considering that the Court was dealing with a First Amendment jurisprudence that seldom generates lucidity, Chief Justice John Roberts made short work of the law schools' absurd arguments, noting at one point that their arguments "trivialized" the freedom protected by the First Amendment. In a scathing summary of the Court's holding, Chief Justice Roberts wrote:

In this case, FAIR has attempted to stretch a number of First Amendment doctrines well beyond the sort of activities these doctrines protect. The law schools object to having to treat military recruiters just like other recruiters, but that regulation of conduct does not violate the First Amendment. To the extent that the Solomon Amendment incidentally affects expression, the law schools' effort to cast themselves as just like the school-children in *Barnette* [the "flag salute" case], the parade organiz-ers in *Hurley* [exclusion of homosexual groups by private veterans' organization], and the Boy Scouts in *Dale* plainly overstates the expressive nature of their activity and the impact of the Solomon Amendment on it, while exaggerating the reach of our First Amendment precedents.[27]

As the law school case reveals, liberals have decided that any "dis-crimination" against homosexuals is "intolerant" and therefore illegit-imate under any and all circumstances, and it doesn't matter what Congress, the president, or the American people think. The illiberal liberals *know* and they are always right. The tyranny of tolerance has no tolerance for opposing viewpoints.

The last time I looked, the members of the military were out there dying for all of us, regardless of race or sex or sexual deviancy. The law schools and their favored groups all get the benefit of the sacrifices of the armed forces, and all that is asked in return is that the law schools not spit in the face of the military while taking the military's money.

Though the Supreme Court has now shot down the law schools' lu-dicrous First Amendment claims, we shouldn't expect to see the liberal hostility to the military subside. Amazingly, *after* the war on terror began, the law faculty at Washington University in St. Louis—a group of flaming liberals—voted not only to keep the military out of their sacred temple of tolerance, but to deny loan benefits to *their own students* who entered the military.[28] The dean overruled the faculty, but did the faculty suffer any retribution for this monstrous affront to their own students, who had elected to put their lives in jeopardy so liberal college professors could pontificate about sexual orientation? Of course not.

SUPPRESSING THE RIGHTS OF ANTIABORTION PROTESTERS

For decades, the Supreme Court held that the public ways were public forums, and people could speak there or distribute literature without restriction. Thus, government regulations controlling or forbidding speaking or handbilling on public streets were never upheld, unless the government could demonstrate a "clear and present danger" of disorder.[29]

Then came abortion protests. Utilizing tactics used by Vietnam-era war protesters (or labor unions, for that matter), the abortion protesters sought to block access to abortion clinics, to publicize the bloody and sordid aspects of abortions, and to try to persuade women not to pursue abortions by confronting them at the threshold of the abortion clinic.

Following the rise of mass abortion protests, the reaction of liberals was astounding—at least if you believed their rhetoric about the sanctity of the First Amendment. Federal and state laws were passed to restrict the rights of abortion protesters, and court injunctions were handed down imposing additional restrictions.[30] The abortion protesters, like the civil rights protesters before them, resorted to the courts for relief and vindication of their rights of speech and assembly. They resorted in vain. In case after case, the Supreme Court has yet to strike down a regulation limiting picketing or speech by abortion protesters.[31]

In one particularly egregious case of speech suppression, an antiabortion protest group published "wanted" posters identifying the principal abortion doctors in various parts of the country. The posters did not advocate violence against the abortionists, although they certainly condemned their conduct as murder. Unfortunately, some of the persons involved in the organization chose to go beyond speech to action, killing some of the doctors featured in the posters. The abortion industry sued the group that sponsored the website publishing the posters, as well as others involved, and obtained a huge verdict for actual and punitive damages.

The abortionists also obtained an injunction forbidding the publication of the wanted posters.[32] Such an injunction, approved by the notoriously liberal federal court of appeals for the Ninth Circuit, flew in the face of centuries of Anglo-American law, which recognized that "prior restraints" on speech were illegal. That is to say, the government could not forbid publication of anything in advance, and the writer or publisher could be liable only after the fact for damages.[33] This principle of no prior restraints led the Supreme Court to condemn an injunction against publishing classified military papers in the *Pentagon Papers* case in the 1970s.[34] But the federal court in this case would let nothing stand in the way of the tyranny of tolerance.[35] Abortion is to be promoted; opponents are bigots and misogynists whose views are to be censored and preferably suppressed altogether.

Of course, the liberal jurisprudence on speech is entirely hypocritical. Remember, it's protected conduct for a police department employee to express approval of an attempt to kill the president, but it's illegal for an antiabortion group to use "wanted posters" to express its view that abortionists are murderers. It seems antiabortion protesters just are not entitled to the same constitutional protection that other, favored groups are. Look at how the Supreme Court has treated the NAACP. In one case, the Court held that the NAACP could not be held liable even for patently illegal actions committed by individual members of the organization, even though the illegal acts were committed in the course of carrying out an economic boycott the NAACP had mounted. Furthermore, the Court ruled that impassioned speeches that conveyed implied threats of force or violence could not be the basis of liability. Good ol' John Paul Stevens said that "mere *advocacy* of the use of force or violence does not remove speech from the protection of the First Amendment."[36]

Again, some are more equal than others.

THE "HOSTILE AND OPPRESSIVE WORK ENVIRONMENT"

Like speech codes, "hate crime" legislation, and compulsory association laws and regulations, workplace harassment law enforces obedience to the liberals' notions of tolerance.

The Civil Rights Act of 1964 included a section—Title VII—that forbids employment discrimination on the basis of "race, color, religion, sex, or national origin." But it quickly became apparent that intransigent employers could connive at or acquiesce in egregious conduct by employees that would effectively drive blacks out of the workplace. To get around the general principle of law that an employer is liable for the acts of his employees only in the course and scope of employment,[37] federal courts held employers liable for harassment that drove blacks away from employment, even if the employer did not authorize the harassment. Thus was born the doctrine of the "hostile and oppressive work environment." Employers could be liable for simply permitting an environment that was so pervasively hostile to minorities that it effectively altered the terms and conditions of employment. When this rationale was extended to sex discrimination claims,[38] "sexual harassment" became the favorite cry of the femifascists whenever they wished to assert supremacy in the workplace.

As the rules of workplace harassment evolved, no one thought about the obvious issue that what employees *said* might just involve something called free speech. Legal actions that would be deemed patently unconstitutional in any other context are perfectly fine in the workplace harassment context. So if a man posts a nude photo of a woman in the workplace, his employer must discipline him for "harassment."[39] If an employee dares to express disagreement with employer policies promoting homosexual sodomy, he can and should lose his job, since he is "intolerant" and "insensitive."[40] If an employee seeks to proselytize his religion at the workplace, he, too, must lose his job, as he is making others "uncomfortable," or his espousal of religious belief is "offensive."

The Supreme Court used to insist that speech could not be suppressed because of its effect on the audience, unless it was incitement to immediate civil disorder. The Court recognized that free speech by definition includes speech that hearers may deem offensive or disagreeable. That's what free speech is all about, or so we are told when the flag is being burned.

The amusing thing about workplace harassment law is that it is a form of special protective legislation for selected groups, especially women. Women are more equal than men, so certain actions or words spoken by men must be suppressed, because (some) women disapprove of them and find them offensive.

It is ironic that liberals are responsible for a return to Victorian propriety in sexual relations in the workplace. Perhaps we should be thankful that liberals demand propriety of any sort, anywhere. But the problem is that Victorian proprieties seldom had the force of law. If one violated the proprieties, the employer might well fire him, but the employer was under no compulsion to do so. The liberal code of tolerance is not a custom or convention: It is a form of law, enforced by the courts through employment discrimination law.[41]

This oppression is really quite clever, in its way. The government has no direct role in suppressing speech. It simply holds the employer liable if he does not. So what's the risk-averse employer going to do? He's going to go overboard.

Wait a minute, you say, do you want your daughter exposed to lechers at work on a daily basis? No, but neither do I want my son to lose his job because he rashly compliments a female coworker on her appearance. It's not just outrageous speech that is suppressed. Read sexual harassment policies created by employers to avoid Title VII liability for sexual harassment. Almost anything a man says to a woman that she considers objectionable or "unwelcome" is grounds for dismissal. Why should that be? Remember the case of the comment about "making love to the Grand Canyon"? That issue reached the United States Supreme Court.[42] The Court held that the single remark was not actionable, but that's cold comfort to an employer who has spent many thousands in attorney's fees on account of a single thoughtless remark.

And why doesn't a man have a *right* to make advances to a

woman?[43] Indeed, suppose he prefaces the advance with a preamble like, "As a gesture of protest against the arbitrary restrictions of Title VII on free speech, I want to ask you to sleep with me." Is that protected or unprotected speech?

Oh, by the way, we're not just talking about sexual advances here. "Harassing" speech in the Title VII context includes speech related to religion, age, national origin, and disability. Under many state and local laws, you get "sexual orientation," marital status, economic status, and medical condition.[44] In any other context (criminal law or public employment law generally), these sorts of regulations would be considered void on their face.

The main vice of employment harassment law is the same vice in any vague and overbroad restriction of speech: The legitimate is tossed out with the illegitimate. The listener gets to control the content. Worse, in all too many employment discrimination cases, the courts have not contented themselves with awarding damages but have also imposed injunctions designed to censor workplace speech in the future. Prior restraint, anyone?

Consider the case of an Avis rental car manager who was accused of making racist remarks to Hispanic employees.[45] A jury found illegal discrimination under California law and awarded damages. For good measure, the trial judge then entered an injunction forbidding the manager to utter *any* remark "deemed offensive" by Hispanic employees in the future. Obviously, if this injunction was violated, the manager could go to jail for contempt. As later modified by the California appellate courts, the injunction listed specific forbidden words and was limited to using them at the workplace, but even a single use of one of the prohibited words could mean jail. Did the U.S. Supreme Court seem concerned? Nobody but Justice Clarence Thomas thought the matter worthy of review.

Many other courts have entered orders censoring speech in the workplace, such as by forbidding display of nude photographic calendars or pinups and similar behavior. The courts in effect are the telescreens in this liberal version of Big Brother. To what end? Why, eliminating prejudices and biases, of course. Isn't that a good enough reason?

TO THE SENSITIVITY GULAG!

Now do you see what I'm driving at about the tyranny of tolerance? Moving from race to sex, from sex to "sexual orientation," and from there to age, religion, national origin, disability, "economic status," and any other formulation of another group of hyphenated Americans, the illiberal liberals have used the law and the judiciary to impose their creed of "tolerance" on the American people. They brook no dissent. That's the beauty of it.

You're a judge or lawyer who wants to denounce affirmative action or the ludicrous concept of "reparations." That's "manifesting bias," isn't it?

You're a judge or lawyer who thinks that criminalizing sodomy is a good thing. Dare you say anything?

You're a judge who thinks radical feminism, or femifascism, has no place in American law. Dare you write anything? I did, and the next thing I knew my job was in jeopardy.

You're a student who wants to argue in class that childbearing is more important for women than careers. Not only are you not allowed to say anything about that, you're not even allowed to think it!

And, if you're a man, just try and say something mildly lascivious to a woman in the workplace, in a court, or on campus. To the sensitivity gulag!

The tyranny of tolerance is far more effective than the book burners of Nazi Germany. Liberals have found a way to choke off speech *in advance,* so we needn't worry about book burning, as there won't be any written to burn.

Liberals have done nothing less than stifle public debate on the most serious social issues of our time. People who genuinely disagree with policies favoring homosexuals, the handicapped, or other categories of persons favored by liberals are severely hampered in their ability to get their message across to the public by the traditional means of picketing, handbilling, or even just talking with coworkers. Men who hold traditional views about the roles of men and women in society are forbidden to discuss these views. Men who desire to make sexual advances to women (surely that's part of the right of reproductive privacy created by the Supreme Court, isn't it?) dare make no such advances in the workplace, on campus, or perhaps anywhere. Persons who hold views about the fundamental evil of abortion are censored in the manner in which these views can be expressed, and, indeed, are restricted as to how and where these views can be presented. The standard is no longer free and open debate, but debate (if it can be called debate) that is free of "offensive" content. (If I violently disagree with somebody, the opposing views are almost always going to be "offensive." If that is the touchstone to measure the lawfulness of restrictions on speech, debate is over—and that's the way liberals want it.)

I have to admit that, particularly in light of my own brush with the PC police, I have gained far more respect for Justice Hugo Black's "absolutist" view of the First Amendment.[46] There is precious little anyone can do to change government policies, or social conditions, if one is afraid to talk about them. Liberals know that, and they use the weapon of censorship deftly, aided by the courts. So we have it that the judiciary—which protects Communists, pornographers, civil rights boycotters, antiwar demonstrators, and street gang members[47] with great zeal—cannot find it in the Constitution to protect those who condemn homosexual sodomy, abortion, or the femifascists, or who simply want to compliment a woman about her nice legs. And even though liberals applaud courts for compelling private membership groups to accept members they don't want, they condemn Congress when it simply tries to ensure that federally funded colleges and law schools treat the military with respect and fairness.

Tolerance? Or tyranny in the name of tolerance?

CHAPTER 11

THE CULT OF DISABILITY

Complaints about this case are not "properly directed to Congress". . . They are properly directed to this Court's Kafkaesque determination that professional sports organizations, and the fields they rent for their exhibitions, are "places of public accommodation" to the competing athletes, and the athletes themselves "customers" of the organization that pays them; its Alice in Wonderland determination that there are such things as judicially determinable "essential" and "nonessential" rules of a made-up game; and its Animal Farm determination that fairness and the ADA [Americans with Disabilities Act] mean that everyone gets to play by individualized rules which will assure that no one's lack of ability (or at least no one's lack of ability so pronounced that it amounts to a disability) will be a handicap. The year was 2001, and "everybody was finally equal."
—Justice Antonin Scalia, dissenting in
PGA Tour, Inc. v. Martin (quoting Kurt Vonnegut)

FROM THE EXALTATION OF SEXUAL DEVIANCY, the tyranny of tolerance finds it an easy ascent to the next height: making the blind see and the lame walk. In other words, mandating that the inherently unequal shall be made equal, if not more than equal. This exercise in human reengineering involves turning the equal protection clause on its head. Do you want to put a group home for the mentally retarded or a halfway house for drug-addicted felons in residential neighborhoods? Well, of course you can! They're the same as any other single family home, aren't they? Only the intolerant and insensitive would say otherwise, as federal judges held in cases from Texas and St. Louis, and elsewhere. Have an HIV-infected paramedic give mouth-to-mouth resuscitation? Sure, the patient has no rights, only the HIV-infected paramedic does. Here, of course, the liberals were aided by Congress, but as with most "civil rights" legislation, where Congress gives an inch, the liberal judiciary takes a mile.

At the beginning of Chapter 2, I described my daughter's puzzlement at playing tennis against a wheelchair-bound opponent. This happened several years before the Supreme Court decreed that the Americans with Disabilities Act (ADA) compelled the PGA to permit a physically handicapped player to use a golf cart during tournaments, when everybody else had to walk.[1] As I watched my daughter's match, it gradually dawned on me that something was not right. My daughter never, ever went to the net. Her opponent was returning serves on the second bounce. I know very little about tennis, but it was fairly clear that my daughter was missing chance after chance to put the game away. Then, I realized (yes, rather slow on the uptake that night) that my daughter and her opponent were not playing by standard rules. Clearly, my daughter was *forbidden* to go to the net, and, just as clearly, her opponent got the benefit of the extra bounce.

My daughter lost her match. Although I marveled at her opponent's determination, and although I was glad to help the girl get her wheelchair over a rough spot on the path leading away from the court, I knew that my daughter was embarrassed and vexed to the point of tears. As she endured the stares and pitying smiles of some of her teammates, I could not help thinking that her opponent's self-esteem surely had been enhanced that evening, but what about that of my daughter? Oh, yes, my daughter walked away from the court, and her opponent had to be helped, and that difference probably would never be erased. So surely it is petty and *intolerant* or, equally evil in the liberal world, *insensitive* and *mean-spirited* to begrudge the "accommodation" given to the girl in the wheelchair. Petty and insensitive it might be, but this vignette gave me new insight into the tyranny of tolerance. When my daughter cried out afterward, "Why? Why were the rules different?" I had only one answer: Score one more point for the special-treatment lobby, one more sacrifice of one person's right to equal treatment in the name of equality for a special class.

As I approach the age when wheelchairs and walkers seem likelier to be used than skis or bicycles, I am by no means "insensitive" to some of the advantages of federally mandated "accommodations" for the disabled, from ramps and elevators to handholds in bathrooms. But what has brought us to the point that young girls must be sent away in defeat in athletic competitions in order to make some more equal than others? The cult of the disabled, and the growing favoritism that the law now displays toward people falling within that incredibly elastic term, illustrates, perhaps better than anything else, the "more than equal" protection philosophy that liberals have imposed on our nation. Courts, Congress, and state and local legislatures have fallen all over themselves to cater to the cult of the disabled. It is a testament to the power of the illiberal liberals and their tyranny of tolerance that even nominally conservative elected officials are unable or unwilling even to *appear* to question the premises of such special-privileges legislation.

EQUAL PROTECTION, OR "ACCOMMODATION"

Remember the Supreme Court case involving the city of Cleburne, Texas, and a group home for the mentally retarded?[2] This case epitomizes the tyranny of tolerance when it comes to treatment of the handicapped. A federal district judge had found that the city could require the group home to apply for a special-use permit as the city's ordinance took into account the legal liabilities of the group home's operator, and the safety and fears of the residents of the adjoining neighborhood. But not a single Supreme Court justice could be persuaded to agree; the Court said that requiring the group home to apply for a permit rested on "irrational prejudice."

Oh? The city ordinance did not exclude the mentally retarded from living in the community: It simply limited the ability of organizations to plop "group homes" down in the middle of a neighborhood that might present a hazard to the home's occupants or to which unsupervised retarded persons could themselves present a hazard. The Court acknowledged that the residents in the group home needed to "be under the constant supervision" of professional staff, and that such group homes were "covered by extensive regulations and guidelines" established by state and federal agencies.[3] Was it irrational to require a special permit for such a special use, so long as there was a fair hearing and a reasonable determination as to whether the group home in fact would be a good fit in the area? According to the tyrants of tolerance, yes.

The idea the Court expressed in *Cleburne*—that it is irrational and invidious to treat the mentally retarded differently—has been the basis for all sorts of new constitutional and statutory interpretation, and new legislation as well. Indeed, the very basis of the ADA, insofar as it imposes many of its mandates on state and local governments, is that it merely enforces the equal protection clause. The good Justice Ruth Bader Ginsburg explained this idea in *Tennessee v. Lane,*[4] a case involving a courthouse and a wheelchair, in which she maintained that Congress can command "reasonable accommodation to secure access and avoid exclusion" because it is guaranteeing " 'a baseline of equal citizenship.' "[5] The Court majority branded legislation that treated disabled people differently as "indiscriminate." The problem, of course, is that the Fourteenth Amendment calls for *equal protection,* not "accommodation" or "more than equal" protection. The liberal majority seems to treat its special class—"the disabled"—rather indiscriminately, regardless of the fact that "disabilities" run the gamut from infectious diseases to blindness.

THE TOLERANCE BANDWAGON

Do you want a schoolteacher in your child's classroom with a raging case of tuberculosis, or any other serious contagious disease? What, you don't? You irrational bigot! You intolerant swine! You are guilty of the capital sin of *discrimination*! Congress has passed laws that curb your desire to isolate and discriminate against such "handicapped individuals" (or must we say "disabled" or "bacterially challenged"?). And the Supreme Court has made sure that those laws apply to persons with contagious diseases. So if you think you or your child has a right to remain free from exposure to serious contagious diseases, think again. No, according to Justice William Brennan, your concern for the health and safety of your child is just "ignorance" or a "prejudiced attitude."[6]

Do you think that people in need of CPR and mouth-to-mouth resuscitation have a right to be sure that emergency medical personnel are free of contagious diseases, like HIV? Tell that to liberal federal judges. It will get you branded as irrational and bigoted. Employers get sued in federal court if they put the interests of the helpless patient above those of employees with contagious diseases (especially HIV, which enjoys that added éclat of being predominantly a disease of a favored group, homosexuals).[7] Sure, the risk of HIV contagion by means of mouth-to-mouth resuscitation may be small, and perhaps certain special equipment can further reduce even that small risk, but is the public's very real fear simply bigoted and irrational? Is it rational to want to avoid contagion, even if the risk is small? If this fear is irrational, why do liberals scream about trace amounts of arsenic in our drinking water? Aren't the risks small?

As such instances indicate, liberals have dramatically stretched the meaning of the term "disabled." We even saw this in the *Cleburne* case, as the ordinance dared to single out alcoholics, the insane, and drug addicts, as well as the "feeble-minded." It didn't take long for the courts, with the aid of liberal legislation,[8] to jump on the "tolerance" and "equality" bandwagon on behalf of these other groups, and on behalf of convicted felons as well.

Two decades ago, somebody dreamed up the Oxford House, a group home for recovering addicts or alcoholics, most of whom would be convicted felons. As so often happens with such new approaches to treating old problems, a few early cases of apparent success led to the usual welfare state syndrome: The feds started throwing money at the proprietors of Oxford House. Soon a cottage industry sprang up to create and serve Oxford Houses—and to make sure that citizens couldn't block them from being set up in their communities. Soon Oxford Houses and lawsuits to suppress opposition to Oxford Houses sprang up like mushrooms all over the country.[9]

I happened to live in a very nice neighborhood in the city of St. Louis (and take note, liberals, it was a "diverse" neighborhood) in 1987, when our neighborhood association was notified that a home on the edge of our neighborhood was to be leased for an Oxford House. We were all invited to a meeting with persons representing the Oxford House. As it turned out, the paradigm of the liberal, the head of the St. Louis branch of the Anti-Christian Litigation Union was there with some of her minions, plus agents of the state Board of Probation and Parole (which was funding the House), as well as several House residents. At the meeting, the ACLU made it clear that if the neighborhood tried to keep Oxford House out, it would provoke swift and expensive retaliatory litigation. In short, we were told that the Oxford House was coming and that we better keep quiet about it. Stalin would have been proud.

Fortunately, the city of St. Louis required that *all* "group homes" or boardinghouses be limited in the number of occupants. Our Oxford group insisted that it could not operate effectively (profitably? remember, federal and state aid was involved) if it complied with the ordinance. The city, God bless it, insisted on compliance. So the ACLU types naturally sued the city. The district judge, a bona fide liberal, naturally sided with the Oxford House, and imposed enormous attorney's fees on the city.[10] But the ACLU had met its match in the city's very able legal team. The district court was reversed by the court of appeals—a majority of whom were Reagan appointees by that time. The Oxford House had to comply with the occupancy limits, and what do you know? It still operated, at least for a considerable time.

My neighbors and I were lucky. The city government stepped in on its own initiative. Some good citizens of Berkeley, California, were less fortunate. They thought they had First Amendment rights to speak out against government actions and petition for redress of grievances, so they sought administrative action to block the Oxford House in their neighborhood. This time the Oxford House didn't need the ACLU. The Clinton Department of Health and Human Services stepped in to beat up on the intolerant Berkeley folks. (Hard to believe anybody in Berkeley is intolerant, isn't it?) The weapon of choice was the Fair Housing Act, which authorizes *administrative* action against people who "discriminate" in housing. No courts, no juries, just tolerant and sensitive bureaucrats, who made life hell for the Berkeley dissenters for several years. Surprisingly, the federal courts ultimately protected the dissenters, enjoining the administrative persecution and eventually awarding the Berkeley homeowners substantial damages and attorney's fees.[11]

DISCRIMINATION AND PREFERENCES

We all admire people who overcome adversity to do what they want to do. I admired the girl in the wheelchair who beat my daughter at tennis, and I still do. But how much more glorious for both if they had been playing by the same rules, and the girl in the wheelchair demonstrated that she could compete, even if she could not win. The cult of disability, as part and parcel of the tyranny of tolerance, thrives on the liberal "more equal than others" mentality. Yet it is a hollow thing, inducing delusions of equality where none exists. It ties in neatly with the notion of "affirmative action," that there are "benign" ways to discriminate *in favor* of selected groups. Overlooked in the intoxication of tolerance is that you can't discriminate in favor of somebody without discriminating *against* somebody else. By all means give the handicapped *equal* protection. But the illiberal liberals won't settle for that, and that's what the tyranny is all about.

CHAPTER 12

PUBLIC NONEDUCATION

*[E]ducators who call themselves "critical theorists" . . . advocate
using mathematics as a tool to advance social justice. Social justice math relies on political and cultural relevance to guide math
instruction. One of its precepts is "ethnomathematics," that is,
the belief that different cultures have evolved different ways of
using mathematics. . . . From this perspective, traditional mathematics . . . is the property of Western Civilization and is inex-
orably linked with the values of oppressors and conquerors.*
—Diane Ravitch, "Ethnomathematics,"
Wall Street Journal, June 20, 2005

*There's a lot wrong with our schools, but the general decline in
order is the most unappreciated. Every day, in schools across
America, students wander around the classroom or confront
teachers with an in-your-face attitude. The disrespect is shocking. The losers are not mainly the teachers, however, but all the
other students. Disruptive behavior by one student diverts all attention. Learning is crippled.*
—Philip K. Howard, "Class War,"
Wall Street Journal, May 24, 2005

LIKE BIG BROTHER, the tyranny of tolerance must begin
thought control at an early stage. That is why it is so deeply

entrenched in the educational system: The public schools prove crucial to the advancement of the tyranny's agenda.

Here again, the liberal judiciary vigorously enforces the spread of "tolerance." By approving the tyrannical agenda and strangling reform movements on constitutional grounds, the courts have ensured that the schools are firmly in the control of the tyranny of tolerance—and also that they fail to teach basic courses, to instill basic moral principles, and to inculcate sentiments of patriotism. The movement to turn public schools into hotbeds of political correctness began with the deliberate exclusion of God, and it threatens to end with the deliberate exclusion of country. In between, the courts have seized control of curriculum in the name of desegregation and free speech (yet speech codes have even filtered into elementary and secondary schools), and have made the simple task of maintaining order and discipline virtually impossible.

JUDGES TAKE OVER THE CLASSROOM

Although public education did not become commonplace until after the Civil War and the adoption of the Fourteenth Amendment, the law was clear at least until 1969 that teachers and principals stood in loco parentis and had virtually the same rights to discipline children in their care as were enjoyed by parents themselves.[1] The courts almost never intruded into school administration, except in extraordinary cases, such as when teachers inflicted brutal beatings, and then only by way of actions for damages against the perpetrators.

But then the Supreme Court got into the act. In 1969, in the case of *Tinker v. Des Moines School Dist.*,[2] the Court decided that public school authorities could not discipline high school or junior high school students for wearing black armbands. That would be to violate the students' First Amendment rights. The justices decreed, with delicious irony in light of contemporary speech codes, that "state-operated schools may not be enclaves of totalitarianism."[3] Discipline, they said, would be authorized only if the schools could demonstrate that the students materially and substantially interfered with the requirements of "appropriate" discipline or invaded the rights of others. Of course, *Tinker* transferred the decision about what is "appropriate" from the schools to the courts.

Justice Hugo Black, one of the most zealous defenders of the First Amendment, dissented, stating with all too much truth, "One does not need to be a prophet or the son of a prophet to know that after the Court's holding today some students . . . will be ready, able, and willing to defy their teachers on practically all orders."[4] As Justice Black fore-saw, the inevitable effect of *Tinker* was to strip teachers and principals of authority to control student behavior on school premises. Liberal judges would go further, depriving school authorities of the ability to control the content of student newspapers, which are bought and paid for with taxpayer dollars. Fortunately, the post-Reagan Supreme Court shrank from that extreme.[5]

Tinker was bad enough, but later cases that relied on the Four-teenth Amendment's due process clause did even more to destroy the authority to control schools and students. The due process clause was designed to ensure notice and hearing when the government deprives a citizen of life, liberty, or property. But when liberals wielded them as a weapon, the concepts of liberty and property took on new meaning, being extended to embrace welfare benefits, driver's licenses, and public education.[6] (As we have seen, though, the traditional idea of property somehow got lost in the shuffle, so that welfare recipients generally achieved greater constitutional protection than the owners of real es-tate sought by eminent domain.)

Once the courts established that "free speech" was the order of the day in schools, they used the due process clause to do for school disci-pline what they had done for criminal law using the same clause: create new procedures out of whole cloth to protect rights discovered for the first time by liberals.[7]

In an article for the *Wall Street Journal*, attorney and author Philip K. Howard described an incident in Florida in which an out-of-control five-year-old was allowed to tear up her classroom while teachers and the principal stood by, apparently afraid to touch her. Her rampage continued until the police arrived and handcuffed her. Is this idiocy, or what? Anyone over forty can recall incidents in primary or high school in which teachers used rulers, pointers, rolled-up newspaper, or, in the case of older kids, paddles and belts to discipline unruly students. Nobody thought anything of it, and no one was the worse for it. But now little terrors can run riot, and teachers are seemingly afraid to do anything about it. Why? Are the teachers so pusillanimous that they have surrendered control of the schools to the punks and snots? No, control has been wrested from them by the same people who have taken control of prisons away from the guards, the same people to whom objective standards of conduct have no meaning: the radical liberals, once again working through their faithful allies in the courts.

First it was black armbands. Next the federal courts turned their sights on school discipline. Babbling of "liberty interests" and "fairness," the Supreme Court decided that the Fourteenth Amendment's due process clause applied to public school suspensions of high school students, and required that such students be given a "hearing" *before* any action could be taken.[8] Well, it doesn't take much to turn a hearing into a nightmare, once the lawyers get their noses under the tent. Before long, it became almost as difficult to suspend students as it did to fire public employees.[9]

If a school principal could not suspend a student without a hearing in advance, what about administering corporal punishment? Oddly enough, in a case from Florida, the Supreme Court said it was permissible to smack a kid without a hearing in advance, but only because after-the-fact remedies satisfied due process.[10] Although superficially favoring school authorities, the Florida paddling case actually sounded the death knell of corporal punishment in public schools. Why? Because it turned every such matter into not just a federal case, but into a *constitutional* case. Is this what the Reconstruction Congress and ratifying states had in mind when the Fourteenth Amendment was adopted?

Nowadays, if a public school teacher hits a kid, the kid can SUE! Since nobody really likes to be sued, corporal punishment is virtually unknown in public schools (and the specter of lawsuits has chilled the practice in private schools as well). As a result, little terrors (and big ones, too) can now take over classrooms until the cops come—and, of course, the cops will get sued, too.

The effect of liberal jurisprudence on schools is similar to its effect on prisons: The authorities lose control, and everyone suffers.

Eager to seize upon any opening to expand its control, the liberal judiciary has not only told teachers how to keep order in the classroom but also intruded on academic decisions. The Supreme Court has actually reviewed a medical school's decision to flunk out a student.[11] And a federal court of appeals has decided that teachers can't have students grade one another's papers. The appeals court cited "privacy laws" to make even this simple schoolroom task subject to judicial scrutiny. Is this what judicial review is all about? No. In fact, the Supreme Court rejected this nonsensical idea. Still, it's a testament to the power of the liberal assault that such a case could make it all the way to the highest court in the land.[12]

The problem here is that liberal judges find "liberty interests" everywhere. Yet children who are in school logically must be seen as in a special relationship of subordination to lawful authority—especially because they *are* children, attending schools run by *adults*. Since students are lawfully subject to the school authorities, routine matters of discipline simply do *not* implicate "liberty" in the constitutional sense. The student's liberty is lawfully curtailed as soon as he sets foot in the schoolroom. But don't try to convince liberals of that. The only people who have no "liberty interests" are people who want to pray in public schools.[13]

FREEDOM OF CHOICE? NOT FOR PARENTS

Liberals' determination to keep public schools firmly in the grip of the tyranny of tolerance is cast in sharp relief by the struggle over school voucher programs. For many, many Americans—especially those unfortunate enough to live in large, urban school districts—vouchers represent the best means to ensure that parents and their children obtain the best quality education for their tax dollars.[14] As Justice Clarence Thomas observed in his concurring opinion in the pivotal school vouchers case, *Zelman v. Simmons-Harris,*[15] "urban children have been forced into a system that continually fails them." Does anyone seriously contend that urban public schools are a success? Does anyone seriously contend that urban private schools are *not* superior to urban public schools? So how in the world can anyone oppose a general, evenhanded program of school vouchers?

Yet liberals fight voucher programs tooth and nail. Why such opposition? To begin, vouchers threaten favored liberal constituencies like the National Education Association. But even more important, vouchers, by allowing students to escape the public schools, would make children susceptible to religious and other influences that may (horrors!) cause them to question the social and political axioms of liberalism.[16]

Indeed, in the *Zelman* case, liberals mounted their attack on vouchers on the basis of the idea of separation of church and state. They lost the case, but the dissenting opinions of Justices John Paul Stevens, David Souter, and Stephen Breyer are remarkable for their barely concealed hostility to religion. Their opinions characterize the purpose of parochial schools as "religious indoctrination," while they describe the purpose of public schools merely as "education."[17] In addition, the dissenters—liberals all—go to great lengths to criticize vouchers on the basis that they will somehow increase "religious strife."[18] Claiming that the "wall of separation" supposedly incorporated in the First Amendment was meant to control or eliminate conflict among religious sects, the dissenting justices repeatedly describe the history of religion in America as one of social conflict and insist that the inherently divisive effects of religion have been moderated only because religious expression was "relatively private." The dissenters concluded dramatically, "With the arrival of vouchers in religious schools, that privacy will go, and along with it will go confidence that religious disagreement will stay moderate."[19]

A supremely telling facet of Justice Souter's dissent in *Zelman* is that he relied on screeds by People for the American Way to buttress his arguments.[20] Well, that's surely an objective, reliable, and scientific source! People for the American Way is a radical liberal organization par excellence, dedicated to the preservation and advancement of liberal control of the judiciary. By citing such an outrageously tendentious source as an *authority* for any proposition, Justice Souter revealed his own true colors in the clearest possible way.

Apart from hostility to religion, the liberal opposition to vouchers to save urban children from failed public schools is clearly motivated by a concern that with school choice may come *political* choice. In public schools, students will not receive differing viewpoints about the welfare state, equality under the law, or patriotism. They will receive almost no viewpoints at all, except political correctness, and they will be condemned to a standard not of excellence but of mediocrity. Again, Justice Thomas most trenchantly describes what liberals are doing: "Converting the Fourteenth Amendment from a guarantee of opportunity to an obstacle against education reform distorts our constitutional values and disserves those in the greatest need."[21]

The tyranny must compel students to remain in its system. Schools that stand for religious beliefs are, by definition, "intolerant." If vouchers succeed, it is the equivalent of the old Soviet Union allowing its citizens to opt out of the state-run economy. Such freedom of choice is incompatible with the objectives of the tyranny of tolerance. As with the courts, liberals must maintain control of the schools, and to do that, they must keep the schools in the domain of the government. Otherwise, we shall subject millions of poverty-stricken inner-city youth to the opiate of the people, religion, and, still worse, to the ideas that freedom, opportunity, and responsibility are inextricably intertwined.

The hypocrisy of the liberal attitude toward the urban poor is particularly obvious in the matter of vouchers. When urban voters have been given a chance to vote on the issue, as in Milwaukee, they overwhelmingly support vouchers. Polls indicate that black and Hispanic support for vouchers is better than 60 percent.[22] Indeed, opposition to vouchers usually is strongest in white suburbs, where voters perceive their public schools as adequate or superior, and fear (wrongly) that vouchers will be deleterious to the schools. Yet liberals insist that vouchers cannot even be considered by urban voters—the liberal plantation mentality at work.

Why do liberals insist on deploying the courts to destroy voucher programs? By investing heavily in antivoucher campaigns, they have actually defeated broad voucher plans in elections in both California and Michigan. What are liberals afraid of? The crux of the matter is not elections or votes. They use the judiciary to strangle any educational reform that does not further the ends of the tyranny of tolerance. Also, as discussed in Chapter 5, the liberal judiciary has entered into taxing and spending by decree in the name of the public schools, so that the public school monopoly is free not only of parental control but of any effective control by the representatives of the people.

It is certainly odd that liberals oppose choice in public education, while favoring abortion on demand, homosexual "marriage," and other ostensibly libertarian goals.

THE UGLY EFFECTS

Judicial control of classrooms is crucial to the tyranny of tolerance.[23] How else to enforce "tolerance" in the educational system? That is why judges have asserted their authority on everything from discipline to grading students' performance. (Besides, judges, omniscient as they are, know better than teachers how to run classrooms, right?)[24] It doesn't matter that the liberal ideas of "tolerance" and "equality" keep schools from punishing even the most intransigent students. Like terrorists, punks have rights; let's not worry about the rights of the kids who abide by the rules. Nor does it matter that those liberals who preach the fundamental nature of "choice" work tirelessly to deny parents even the opportunity to consider school choice as a way to save their children from failed public schools.

Whether in the matter of school discipline, school finance, or school choice, can it honestly be argued that judicial interference has improved the schools? No. And there is no hope that the situation will get better as long as the courts continue to superintend the schools, and liberals superintend the courts.

CHAPTER 13

WHERE THE MONEY IS

Because that's where the money is.
—Willie Sutton, upon being asked why he robbed banks.

IN EARLY 1997, just after I became chief judge of my circuit, the Missouri attorney general's lawsuit against the tobacco industry came across my desk. The Missouri government's lawsuit was a copycat suit, modeled on lawsuits that had been filed by nearly every other state, seeking "restitution" for the costs incurred by state governments as a result of Medicaid payments for care to smokers. Judged by traditional legal principles, or even by common sense, these lawsuits had no merit whatsoever. But the attorneys general knew a thing or two: They knew that the liberal judiciary would not let slip an opportunity to mulct a fat industry like tobacco in order to funnel huge sums of money into government coffers.

At the time, it appeared that the growing assault on the tobacco industry would culminate in federal legislation to resolve the whole issue. So I sent the case to a judge who could be depended on to ensure that the case was speedily dismissed after Congress acted.

Congress did not act. And the ensuing madness, in which the government essentially extorted billions of dollars from the tobacco industry, offered a frightening example of what has happened to the law of torts—that is, the law of damages for wrongs committed—thanks to an alliance of radical liberals and trial lawyers.

As we will see, the tobacco litigation was by no means an aberration. In fact, the illiberal liberals have made sure to hijack the law of torts in order to advance the tyranny of tolerance—and to line the pockets of trial lawyers and other favored groups in the process.

LEGALIZED EXTORTION

The trial bar—the plaintiffs' bar, if you will—is not all bad. The Continental Congress that adopted the Declaration of Independence, and the Constitutional Convention that produced our Constitution, were dominated by lawyers, most of them trial lawyers.[1] Throughout our history, the trial bar has often led the fight against tyranny. Abraham Lincoln is perhaps the paradigmatic lawyer statesman.

But in the latter half of the twentieth century, the creativity of the trial bar combined with the liberal concept of an omnipotent judiciary to produce a social policy juggernaut the likes of which has never been seen before in Anglo-American legal history.

Once upon a time, the law of torts was about holding individuals responsible for their misdeeds, whether negligent or intentional. If I let my cattle cross onto your property and devour your hay, I was liable to you in damages. In Blackstone's phrase, I had committed a private wrong, and for such private wrongs, the common law provided remedies. Usually those remedies came in the form of damages: The injured person was compensated in money for what he had lost.[2] Because the law for the most part measured liability by individual fault, injured persons needed to bring their suits individually or in small groups, and cases were adjudicated in that context.

As socialist and Marxist doctrines emerged, however, pressure grew to modify tort law to favor some groups in society as against others. Liability began to be seen in terms not of individual responsibility, but of "social" responsibility.[3] When the New Dealers took control of government in the 1930s, they also swept into power the kind of people who believed that law was merely an instrument to promote the social policy of whoever happened to be in power. Soon the law of torts would be characterized by two sets of rules: one for lawsuits between "equals," and one for lawsuits between favored groups (the "little guys") and disfavored groups (usually "big business").

By the late twentieth century, the law of torts had become an almost wholly owned subsidiary of liberal legal thought. Not only had the radical liberal mentality (socialist at best, Marxist at worst) taken hold in the substantive law, but the idea of an unlimited judiciary free to do "justice" according to its own unrestrained notions was solidly ensconced in academe and the judiciary itself. Revolutionary procedural changes made it easier for lawyers to bring lawsuits on behalf of thousands of people at the same time. Forget case-by-case adjudication of individual claims: If business can mass-produce automobiles, lawyers can mass-produce lawsuits claiming injuries due to defects in those automobiles. And never mind about any principled system of assessing fault, or moral culpability. "Strict liability," a concept of liability without fault of any kind, became the order of the day, especially against product makers and sellers. This strict liability would be decreed in cases involving not just one or two injured people, but thousands or hundreds of thousands of people, who might not even be injured but were merely "exposed" to the possibility of injury.[4] In these situations, we get "class actions" that amount to little more than lawful variations of gangster protection rackets—that is, extortion.

Originally the class action was a creature of equity, not law. Juries could not be expected to hear and decide actions by or against classes of persons, except perhaps in the case of associations such as labor unions or guilds, where the class was self-defined by enrollment in the organization, or of corporate shareholders, whose membership in the class was likewise a product of the individual's choice to buy or hold stock. But liberals thrust class actions into the forefront as a weapon to work social change through the courts. First came civil rights litigation. It was only a matter of time before that example was transferred to other realms.

THE MONEY ROLLS IN

Liberals were not solely responsible for the proliferation of class-action suits. Trial lawyers, not necessarily all liberals, are never slow to act on legal developments that mean more money. And class actions meant a *lot* more money.

Consider asbestos litigation, which took off in the early 1980s and became, in the words of a superb RAND Corporation study, "the longest-running mass tort litigation in U.S. history." The RAND analysis pegged the total cost of asbestos litigation at a whopping $54 billion through the year 2000.[5]

Not all of that money comes from jury verdicts. In some ways, trial courts react to new lawsuits like white corpuscles react to foreign substances in the blood: They try like mad to get rid of them as fast as possible. So when the courts were flooded with asbestos claims, they tried to "move the cases," that is, get them settled or tried as soon as possible. I presided over all asbestos cases in the city of St. Louis for ten years. During that time, I tried a dozen or so cases to verdict, but hundreds more than that were settled without a trial.

Certainly, as the RAND study indicated, asbestos litigation made a lot of money for trial lawyers. But it destroyed the entire asbestos industry, and bankrupting an industry is not a particularly good way to ensure that truly injured persons receive compensation. The question was, how to make large sums of money while at the same time keeping the host industry alive and able to pay those large sums of money? Enter the tobacco lawsuits.

The tobacco litigation that concerns us here is not the lawsuits for damages by smokers, but the litigation brought by the states and the federal government. The suit that crossed my desk in 1997, remember, had been filed by the State of Missouri.

So if Congress did not act to resolve all the various government lawsuits against the tobacco industry, what did happen? Instead of federal legislation, we got something called the Master Settlement Agreement (MSA) signed by the tobacco companies and the attorneys general of nearly every state. The agreement is a classic cartel, and its lessons have not been lost on liberals.

Unlike the asbestos litigation, the tobacco MSA did not bankrupt the industry. Indeed, it did little or nothing to prevent the manufacture or marketing of cigarettes. Instead, it acted very much like the taxation by decree liberals have favored in school desegregation cases and other contexts: It ensured that the people paid the price. The MSA imposed a hidden excise tax on tobacco, a tax paid not by the tobacco companies but by the consumer. It also obligated the states to legislate similar taxes on any new tobacco companies, so in effect there is no possibility of competition in the industry.

The tobacco MSA amounted to brazen legislation through judicial decree. In traditional tort law, the government's role is to provide a forum to enable an injured plaintiff to vindicate his rights and collect his damages. The tobacco MSA, however, not only awarded the plaintiffs money, but also spelled out in advance the manner in which the defendants would obtain the money to pay the plaintiffs. More important, tort law typically operates on past behavior only. But the tobacco judgment did more than punish a past wrong: It will control the defendants' behavior in the future. Under the agreement the tobacco companies are obligated to impose a special litigation fee on their customers and the plaintiff governments are themselves obligated to impose the same fee on any future tobacco companies that start doing business within their jurisdictions. Moreover, the tobacco companies are obliged to take certain specific steps to discourage smoking.[6]

The tobacco MSA may be a very good thing in its purpose, but the manner of its adoption is a very bad thing for liberty and democratic government. In the best liberal tradition, the MSA is another instance of government by decree. Nobody voted on it; nobody can lose an election because of it; plenty of money is lavished on plaintiffs' lawyers and the plaintiff governments—money that comes from the best possible source: an off-budget source.[7] The people who pay the price, the consumers, have nothing whatever to say about it.[8]

Now, I have no great love for smoking. I do have a great love of freedom, however, and the tobacco litigation does not bode well for freedom.

GUNS, BOOZE, AND CHEESEBURGERS

With the tobacco litigation as a guide, liberals and trial lawyers have launched similar assaults on the fast-food industry, the firearms industry, and the liquor industry.

Whatever consumers may have known or not known about tobacco products prior to 1964, when the Surgeon General formally proclaimed them dangerous, is there any doubt that people of even borderline intellectual functioning can tell that eating too much makes you fat and that cheeseburgers, french fries, and shakes are not health food?

Apparently there is some doubt.

In New York, a group of parents and their (presumably) morbidly obese offspring filed suit against McDonald's Corporation, the premier fast-food business in the world. The New York porkers claimed that McDonald's created "false impressions" in its advertising, which supposedly represented McDonald's food as nutritious and not as bad for you as science shows. Indeed, according to the plaintiffs, McDonald's portrayed its food as nutritionally beneficial and part of a healthy lifestyle if consumed daily. McDonald's misleading advertising caused plaintiffs' little pudges to eat at McDonald's three to five times per week, supposedly. If McDonald's had been truthful, the plaintiffs' children would not have partaken *as much* or *as often* as they did. The horrific result: obesity, high cholesterol, high blood pressure, heart disease, etc., etc.

The federal district judge did what any sensible person, even if a judge, would do: He dismissed the lawsuit. On appeal, however, liberal judges like Judge Guido Calabresi, who has openly denounced President Bush at meetings of liberal legal organizations,[9] saw that this would never do. They reversed on what can only be described as technical grounds, insisting that the litigation go forward to the "discovery" stage (which readily exposes frivolous claims, don't you know).[10]

Of course, this ruling meant that McDonald's would incur enormous costs in order to respond to plaintiffs' lawyers' massive demands for information.

The fast-food litigation can easily be duplicated across the country—just as was done with tobacco. Indeed, federal, state, and local governments can do the same thing with fast food that they did with tobacco: seek unconscionable sums in damages, cut a deal that calls for the industry to pay huge amounts over time, financed by increased prices to the consumer. The lawyers walk away with massive fees, and the liberals walk away with huge sums of money flowing to government for social welfare programs, and with new, court-imposed regulations fastened on the industry.

The attack on the firearms industry features the same methods, with one glaring difference: The plaintiffs want huge damages for harm that was inflicted by third persons—namely, criminals. Here, as discussed in Chapter 6, Congress and state legislatures have stepped in to prevent utter destruction of the industry, but compliant federal and state courts may circumvent those legislative efforts. What, Congress and the president, the branches of government directly responsible to the people, demand an end to contrived litigation against the firearms industry? How dare they? The courts need not pay any attention to the will of the people. The courts are "independent." The right to keep and bear arms is politically incorrect, and need not be enforced by the courts.

The liquor industry is also feeling the effects of this new wave of regulation by litigation. Even though the alcohol industry is one of the most pervasively regulated in the country, the illiberal liberals want to make it pay for the harm it does to society, not in the form of taxes voted on by accountable representatives, but in the form of hidden levies imposed by consent decree.

THE REPARATIONS SCAM

Lurking in the background is the Godzilla of all liberal tort suits: "reparations" to favored groups to "compensate" them for the sins of white males, living and dead—payable by virtually everyone in the nation.

Perhaps the leading legal light of the "reparations" litigation is Professor Charles Ogletree of Harvard. Ogletree has written, "Virtue lies in making defendants pay up; defendants may not feel their 'investment' in racial reconciliation until they are hit in their pockets."[11] Think about that quotation. It calls to mind the famous comment of Willie Sutton, who remarked that he robbed banks "because that's where the money is." The philosophy behind each statement is the same: *Stick 'em up!* It's just that Willie Sutton used a gun; Charles Ogletree uses the courts.

The strategy behind the reparations litigation is clear: use the courts to impose massive, incalculable taxes on the public, or "fees" on corporations (to be passed on to the consumer, of course). What will this treasure trove be used for? Creation of business funds to aid blacks only, broad-ranging educational, housing, and health care initiatives for favored classes. Why? To achieve the redistribution of wealth to those who need it most. The legal device to achieve these objectives (which sound very much like standard liberal objectives) is the class action. The legal theories are theories of conspiracy, human rights violations, conversion (grabbing somebody else's property), unjust enrichment, and accounting.[12]

I am not here concerned with the almost laughable mutations of legal principle that the reparations extortionists attempt to palm off as the basis for their claims. Nor am I concerned with the legitimacy of their moral and economic claims—although the basis of claims for compensation from the descendants of the hundreds of thousands of Northern white boys who died in the Civil War seems flimsy at best. What concerns me, and should concern every American, is that the reparations game is the same game the illiberal liberals have played in our courts for decades, with devastating success. It is the tobacco litigation magnified a hundredfold, for the reparations raiders have taken aim primarily at corporations, and secondarily at government. Insurance companies, banks, and other targets of the reparations claims could be tempted to enter into their own master settlement agreements designed to pay protection money to the self-appointed guardians of black Americans. Though such settlements would, by law, be subject to court approval, the judiciary has shown itself capable of declaring anything to be fair and reasonable so long as it advances the liberal agenda.[13]

The reparations game is about money and power. Its proponents claim that they seek racial "reconciliation," but lawsuits are seldom means to ensure such a goal. Surely reconciliation means letting bygones be bygones. Lawsuits are adversary proceedings, usually with winners and losers. The reparations raiders want apologies and cash.[14]

The agenda of the reparations raiders fits perfectly with the broader liberal agenda. The raiders demand special treatment for a special class. They demand such special treatment at the expense of innocent persons (indeed, at the expense of those they claim to represent, since they, too, would pay any taxes or fees imposed by reparations decrees). And they seek to impose their will through the judiciary, rather than through the democratic process (where, like other liberals, they have achieved little success).

SUBVERTING THE LAW FOR FAVORED GROUPS

In the law of torts, as in constitutional law, the key to the tyranny of tolerance is control of the judiciary. To be sure, liberals have not so far succeeded in the reparations game[15] or in taking land from its owners and giving it to Indians (whose ancestors voluntarily sold the land centuries ago).[16] But that does not mean they have given up.[17] So long as liberals control the judiciary, we can expect more, and more successful, social welfare strike suits against nearly every governmental and corporate entity in the nation—all with the design of extracting billions of dollars and imposing liberal-approved regulations. A judiciary that can countenance fat kids suing McDonald's because they ate too many cheeseburgers can easily find room for the far more pernicious claims that Americans owe large sums of money to their fellow citizens who happen to be black, just because they are black. Such lawsuits are the natural outgrowth of the past seventy-five years of liberal dominance of the judiciary, and they cannot be stopped unless and until the judiciary is restored to the role of the "least dangerous branch" of government.

CHAPTER 14

THE (UN)AMERICAN BAR ASSOCIATION

The ABA must follow a policy of noninvolvement in political and emotional and controversial issues unless they relate directly to the "administration of justice." . . . [The ABA's responsibilities] could not be carried out in course if the membership was lost, fractionated, or embittered by involvement in political controversy.

—Lewis Powell, president of the American Bar Association
and later Supreme Court justice, 1965

BEFORE THERE ARE JUDGES, there are lawyers. If you want to control the judiciary, you need a supply of lawyers who are receptive to, if not actively promoting, your agenda. Liberals have ensured such a supply by controlling both law schools—thus shaping the way lawyers think about and courts interpret the law—and bar associations. Bar associations exist at the federal, state, and local level, and some states require licensed lawyers to belong to the state bar association. Even in relatively conservative states, the state and local bar associations are strongly influenced by the biggest bar association, the American Bar Association (ABA).

The ABA was founded in 1878 by the plutocrats of the American bar. For many years, it served as the fortress of the upper crust of the American corporate bar. Its presidents were a who's who of the legal elite representing big business.[1] Even today, most people think of the ABA as a bunch of white-shoe lawyers. This patrician facade actually helps the liberals who now run the ABA, as it gives them more freedom to pursue their largely left-wing agenda without being accused of radicalism. Over the past two decades, the ABA has consistently supported the powerful iron triangle of media, academe, and judiciary that advances the tyranny of tolerance.

JUDICIAL CONFIRMATION BATTLES

The first clear sign that the radical liberals had taken control of the ABA came in 1987, during the battle over President Ronald Reagan's nomination of Robert Bork to the Supreme Court. Since the 1950s the ABA had enjoyed a special status in the federal judicial nomination process, serving the Justice Department and the Senate Judiciary Committee as a quasi-official screener of nominees.[2] But when Reagan appointed Bork—a judge with a strong commitment to judicial restraint and the original meaning of the Constitution—the liberals in the ABA abandoned all pretense of neutrality.[3]

Make no mistake, Robert Bork was the most qualified nominee for the Supreme Court since Charles Evans Hughes. He had a distinguished academic career and had performed brilliantly as solicitor general—the top lawyer in the Justice Department appearing before the Supreme Court. A friend of mine, a liberal Democrat who clerked for the conservative William Rehnquist, once told me that during his time at the Supreme Court, only one lawyer presented an oral argument that was decisive with the Court, and that lawyer was Robert Bork. Judge Bork had been confirmed for a seat on the D.C. Court of Appeals overwhelmingly. But in 1987, Senator Joe Biden, Delaware Democrat, was in charge of the Judiciary Committee, and the liberals saw Judge Bork as a mortal threat to their control of the Supreme Court.

The ABA Standing Committee on Judicial Nominees scrutinized Judge Bork and delivered a splintered report for the first time in history.

Further, the Committee leaked negative comments about Bork to the press. Also for the first time, members of the ABA Committee took the position that philosophy should disqualify nominees, even if their credentials were outstanding. One-third of the Committee voted to give Judge Bork a "not qualified" rating.[4]

As we all know, the liberals won the Bork battle, and they have preened themselves on this success ever since, the more since Judge Bork's eventual replacement, Anthony Kennedy, has defected to the side of judicial activism or been "Blackmunized."

After the defeat of Judge Bork, the ABA became more and more politicized in its ratings of Republican judicial nominees. For example, Richard Posner, a renowned scholar of law and economics from the University of Chicago, was given a split rating of qualified/not qualified, as were the similarly well-qualified John Noonan, Laurence Silberman, and James Buckley.[5] By contrast, when the Clintonites came to town, the judicial ratings went up dramatically, even though the qualifications of the nominees did not. For instance, David Tatel received the highest rating of "well qualified" when he was nominated to the D.C. circuit to replace Judge Bork. Now, I know Judge Tatel. He was my opponent in the St. Louis school desegregation case. I do not question his integrity or ability. But for David Tatel to receive a higher rating than Richard Posner or Frank Easterbrook (another brilliant University of Chicago Law School professor who was appointed to the federal Seventh Circuit Court of Appeals) is simply ridiculous. The only material difference in qualifications is that David Tatel is a dyed-in-the-wool liberal, and Richard Posner and Frank Easterbrook are not.

The ABA ratings have been studied by scholars of all persuasions, and the conclusion is inescapable that they have been decidedly biased against Republican nominees.[6] Naturally. Of late, the ABA has shown some signs of restoring a bit of integrity to its judicial rating process, as evidenced by the "well-qualified" ratings given President George W. Bush's two Supreme Court nominees in 2005, John Roberts and Samuel Alito. But with those two nominees, the ABA, like the liberals in the Senate, saw the handwriting on the wall and chose to avoid a confrontation that it could not possibly win. A better indicator of the true colors of the ABA's Committee on the Federal Judiciary is its treatment of the distinguished lawyer Michael Wallace; the ABA trashed his nomination to the Fifth Circuit Court of Appeals, probably as payback for Wallace's efforts to reform the Legal Services Corporation during the Reagan years.[7]

Wait and see what reception a highly qualified conservative nominee to succeed Justice John Paul Stevens receives.

PROMOTING THE LIBERAL AGENDA

The ABA promotes the liberal agenda in many ways beyond its screening of judicial nominees. For example, the association unnecessarily adopted a policy of supporting abortion. Does abortion have anything to do with the administration of justice or the welfare of the legal profession? The ABA has continued to support abortion and has called for public funding of abortions. By contrast, a resolution seeking to commit the ABA to the defense of innocent life from conception forward is routinely ruled "out of order" at the ABA convention and denied an up-or-down vote.[8] True, many lawyers and judges opted to leave the ABA when it became the Abortion Bar Association, but one would think that a truly representative organization would at least have members willing to speak up for innocent life.

The ABA's liberal bias is reflected still more in the positions it takes when filing friend-of-the-court briefs in legal cases. These so-called amicus curiae briefs are filed by persons or organizations that have some interest in the outcome of a case, or at least claim an interest. Since the ABA arrogates to itself the role of speaking for the American legal profession,[9] the ABA files amicus briefs in many cases before the U.S. Supreme Court.

Let's see: How about affirmative action in law school admissions? Did the ABA oppose racial quotas? Nope. For them all the way.[10] Indeed, the ABA's recent actions regarding "diversity" in law schools are especially revealing.

In almost every state, law schools must be "accredited." Students who attend "unaccredited" law schools may not sit for the state bar examination. So, naturally, most law schools, especially those affiliated with universities, will seek accreditation. Who does the "accrediting"? The ABA. What does that mean? It means that the law school must conform to "standards" laid down by the ABA. Those standards are dictated by liberal law professors who control the ABA's Section on Legal Education and Admissions to the Bar.

Early in 2006, the ABA Section offered this stunning commentary on its new standards for "diversity" in law school admissions and faculty hiring: "[T]he requirements of a constitutional provision or statute that purports to prohibit consideration of gender, race, ethnicity or national origin in admissions or employment decisions is not a justification for a school's noncompliance with [the ABA's so-called diversity decree]."[11] In other words, ABA standards are above the law; indeed, law schools must defy positive law and give race- and sex-based preferences even in the face of laws forbidding such discrimination. This is "tolerance" as practiced by the ABA; it makes a mockery of the ABA's professed veneration of the "rule of law" but reinforces liberal hegemony over the law schools and the legal profession itself.

How about the death penalty? The ABA has not filed a single brief in support of a death sentence. Instead, the organization has called for a moratorium on executions until more rules, procedures, and delays can be built into the system. The ABA supported the special exemption from execution for the "mentally retarded" and for juveniles. It demands that the process of postconviction review of death penalty cases (and, as a result, all criminal cases) be made even slower and more cumbersome than it already is. Rather than urging speedier DNA testing to help solve pending crimes, the association insists that DNA testing resources be allocated disproportionately, if not exclusively, to relitigating already completed capital cases.[12]

The ABA also is consistently pro-criminal in its demands for more funding for public defenders, for limits on the kinds of evidence (e.g., jailhouse informers) that prosecutors may use in criminal cases, and for state bar associations to impose more demanding ethical rules on defense lawyers to ensure that they employ the maximum amount of delay and obfuscation in criminal cases.

The ABA is a particularly potent ally of the tyranny of tolerance in the matter of suppressing speech deemed "intolerant" or "biased." It tosses out the First Amendment in favor of speech codes for judges and lawyers. These codes typically forbid "manifesting bias" on the basis of the usual laundry list of favored groups: race, sex, handicap (oops, disability), sexual orientation, and economic status. Notably, the ABA's published disciplinary codes, which most states use as their model for a canon of legal ethics, forbid lawyers and judges from saying anything that would "manifest bias" against someone because of sexual orientation. The ABA-derived codes were put in place even at a time when the U.S. Supreme Court had upheld state statutes that declared sodomy a crime.[13]

You see how easy it is for liberals, who control the judiciary (which adopts lawyer and judicial disciplinary rules), and the ABA (which writes those rules in the first place), to advance their agenda of "tolerance" through the simple device of forbidding lawyers and judges to be "intolerant." The ABA is now in the process of taking the next step: to forbid lawyers and judges from being members of private organizations that "discriminate" by excluding favored groups from membership.[14] Thus, soon it will be forbidden for a judge to belong to the Augusta National Golf Club or the Boy Scouts (that vicious, homophobic organization, which the ABA opposed in the case involving the homosexual scoutmaster). But for an express exception for the military written into the proposed rule, it would also be unethical for lawyers and judges to belong to the National Guard or the United States military reserves. Once again, "tolerance" run amok, courtesy of the ABA. (Of course, the ABA opposes constitutional amendments to preserve marriage and prevent desecration of the American flag, and supports "gun control" in almost all of its manifestations.)[15]

Finally, the ABA has virtually abandoned any role in support of the war on terror, and instead scolds the Bush administration at every turn for not coddling terrorists. In every terror case decided by the Supreme Court to date, the ABA supported the terrorists.[16] Thus, the association thinks that trying terrorists by military commission is wrong; detention of illegal immigrants is wrong; and eavesdropping on suspected terrorists' communications while in prison is wrong, since terrorists should have the same right of attorney-client privilege as ordinary criminals.[17]

In the 2005–2006 Supreme Court term, the ABA again supported foreign terrorists, insisting that terrorists held at Guantánamo could not be tried by special military commissions and demanding that such terrorists be treated as prisoners of war in accordance with the Geneva Conventions. The ABA also opposes legislation to give the president full power to deal with foreign terrorists and to limit federal judicial interference with the conduct of the war.[18]

The ABA plays an important role in promoting the tolerance of terror—a liberal campaign to hamstring our government in this life-and-death struggle that we will examine in more detail in the next chapter.

THE LIBERAL BAR ASSOCIATION

Having evolved from a relatively nonpartisan professional organization, the ABA now supports the tyranny of tolerance in all of its manifestations, from discrimination in favor of blacks and women to special protections for terrorists to the suppression of speech that might be deemed "biased" or "offensive" to favored groups.[19]

Contrary to its claims, the ABA does not speak for the legal profession. It speaks for the liberals in the legal profession, and it is one of the reasons why illiberal liberals continue successfully to co-opt the legal system in order to advance their agenda, without the messy requirement of winning elections.

CHAPTER 15

TOLERANCE OF TERROR

When it comes to a decision by the head of state upon a matter involving its life, the ordinary rights of individuals must yield to what he deems the necessities of the moment. Public danger warrants the substitution of executive process for judicial process.
—Justice Oliver Wendell Holmes, *Moyer v. Peabody* (1909)

After seeing the plurality overturn longstanding precedents in order to seize jurisdiction over this case . . . it is no surprise to see them go on to overrule one after another of the President's judgments pertaining to the conduct of an ongoing war. . . . The plurality's willingness to second-guess the determination of the political branches that these conspirators must be brought to justice is both unprecedented and dangerous.
—Justice Clarence Thomas, dissenting in
Hamdan v. Rumsfeld (2006)

SEPTEMBER 11, 2001. Thousands of Americans killed and wounded by the first act of war on American soil since Pearl Harbor. Congress effectively declares war on Islamic terrorists wherever they can be found, authorizing the president to use whatever force necessary to root out and crush the enemy.[1] American troops are dispatched to Afghanistan to overthrow the government supporting the terrorists. America invades Iraq to remove another government able and willing to support terrorist attacks on us, and to try to implant democratic chemotherapy in the heart of the Middle Eastern terrorist carcinoma. Not surprisingly, American troops and their allies capture a considerable number of prisoners, taken on the battlefield in the act of fighting American or allied forces. By the international law of war, these people are unlawful combatants—that is, enemies who come secretly for the purpose of waging war by destruction of life and property.[2] By the same law, they are not entitled to the status of prisoners of war[3]—at least, they weren't until Justice John Paul Stevens and his liberal gang on the Supreme Court overturned centuries of precedent to side with Osama bin Laden's driver-bodyguard, but we'll get to that.

Some of those captured by our forces overseas happen to be American citizens; most are aliens. Other terrorists are captured in this country itself, intercepted in the early stages of their terrorist career. Some of these persons are aliens (such as Zacarias Moussaoui, the "twentieth hijacker") and some are citizens (such as Yaser Hamdi, the "dirty bomber"). All are unlawful combatants: irregular, nonuniformed saboteurs and assassins, dispatched to attack civilians.

Are the captured terrorists treated as unlawful combatants, tried by military commissions, and executed? Of course not. Sure, as we will see, that happened during World War II, but this is the twenty-first century, the era of tolerance. We don't do those things anymore—the courts won't let us.

Despite the attacks on America, liberals insist we can't start *racial profiling*! We can't discriminate on the basis of *religion*! We're in a war, a war that could involve detonation of a nuclear weapon in our midst by persons more than likely to come from the Middle East and to be fanatical Muslims, but we mustn't be intolerant! Oh, no.

So what do the illiberal liberals do? What do they always do when they want to impose their views on America? No, they don't pay any attention to Congress or the president. They go to the courts. And what do the courts do? They decree tolerance for terrorists. They manipulate the law to prevent effective prosecution of somebody like Moussaoui.

Worse, they create new law to help captured terrorists force their release so they can take up arms again and renew the struggle.

SUPREME COURT OF THE WORLD

Let's take the most outrageous situation first. Alien (noncitizen) terrorists are captured in foreign countries and taken as far away as possible to the security of camps at Guantánamo Bay, Cuba. Guantánamo is not part of the territory of the United States; the United States leases it from Cuba. Sure, the United States controls it, but the United States controlled its sector of West Berlin for fifty years and nobody ever thought it was part of the United States. It's a military outpost in a foreign land, pure and simple. There are no civilian courts there. There is no federal court that has any jurisdiction whatsoever over Guantánamo Bay. But liberals, like the Great Prevaricator's attorney general, Janet Reno, can't stand the notion that these foreign enemies of our country can be held in captivity until the president thinks it's safe to let them go.[4] So what do the liberals do? Why, they run to the federal courts, of course.

Now, a basic principle of Anglo-American law is that a citizen cannot be imprisoned without good cause, and the great common law writ of habeas corpus is the remedy to make the government publicly show why a citizen is imprisoned. But the law of habeas corpus was never applied to enemy aliens being held outside the territorial jurisdiction of the court—that is, until the tyranny of tolerance was extended to them in the case of *Rasul v. Bush* in 2004.[5]

The reason for the federal courts' intervention in the war on terror is obvious. Tolerance demands it. God forbid that we should run another internment program like we did in World War II for American citizens of Japanese origins on the West Coast. That was *racism*. And we know that racism is the capital sin of all capital sins. It's even worse than child molestation, or telling a woman that she has good legs. Shafiq Rasul and the others at Guantánamo might not be citizens, but they are even better: They're Muslims of mostly Middle Eastern or

Afghan origin. And the tyranny of tolerance brooks no dissent, no deviation from its cardinal principle that racial or ethnic background can never, never be taken into account for anything (except getting into law school).

Surprisingly, the lower federal courts in the *Rasul* case acted with common sense. Rasul and his colleagues were foreigners, captured in the course of hostilities in Afghanistan. The courts held, in substance, that we're at war, and these people are prisoners of that war.[6] They said the judiciary shouldn't second-guess the president, who is commander in chief, or Congress, which authorized all necessary force, in prosecuting the war. If that means alien prisoners stay in camps indefinitely, that's too bad. Let the other branches of government sort the sheep from the goats. After all, Congress and the president are sworn to uphold the Constitution and are directly accountable to the people, as well as being subject to international pressure.

The lower courts were applying the law correctly. Shortly after World War II, a batch of German prisoners captured on the battlefield and later imprisoned for war crimes sued the United States, demanding their release. Exhibiting a sanity and common sense that liberals have since banished, the United States Supreme Court said that the federal courts had no jurisdiction in the matter. In that case, *Johnson v. Eisentrager,* Justice Robert H. Jackson, of Nuremberg fame, wrote, "Executive power over enemy aliens, undelayed and unhampered by litigation, has been deemed, throughout our history, essential to wartime security. . . . But even by the most magnanimous view, our law does not abolish inherent distinctions recognized throughout the civilized world between citizens and aliens, nor between aliens of friendly and of enemy allegiance."[7] In short, foreign prisoners of war have no right of access to American courts. The Constitution confers war powers on Congress and the president,[8] and the courts cannot interfere.

But along came *Rasul* and all that changed.

In a simple judicial fiat, the liberals on the Supreme Court, led by the worst of all at the moment, John Paul Stevens, simply ignored *Eisentrager.* Stevens insisted that *Eisentrager* didn't apply, in part because Rasul and his fellow terrorists were not nationals of *countries* at war with the United States. According to Stevens's reasoning,[9] because Kuwait and other Arab havens of terrorists are not formally at war with us, their terrorist citizens have as much right of access to the federal courts as do American citizens—indeed, greater rights, as we shall see. The *Rasul* ruling showed yet again that liberal judicial activists won't let disagreeable precedents, the plain meaning of the Constitution, the absence of statutory jurisdiction, or anything else get in the way of the tyranny of tolerance.

The absurdity of the *Rasul* decision is cast in sharp relief by another decision handed down *on the very same day*. In *Rumsfeld v. Padilla*,[10] Padilla, an American citizen, was in custody in New York after his arrest as a potential terrorist "dirty bomb" operative. He had been arrested by the FBI and charged under the ordinary criminal law. Then the government decided to treat him as an unlawful combatant and transferred him to military custody in South Carolina. Padilla's attorney filed for a writ of habeas corpus in New York. The Supreme Court held that the district court of New York had no jurisdiction, because Padilla was not in custody in New York. By the plain terms of the federal habeas corpus statute giving the district courts jurisdiction, a writ could only be issued in the district where the plaintiff was physically confined.[11]

How does one reconcile *Rasul* and *Padilla*? One doesn't (unless one is Justice Anthony Kennedy or Justice Sandra Day O'Connor). In *Rasul,* plaintiffs who weren't even in the United States were allowed to sue in the District of Columbia, but Padilla had to sue where he was locked up. Padilla was even a citizen; Rasul was not. Of course, in Padilla's case, there was no real need to rewrite the law, since Padilla was going to get to sue in federal court anyway—just not in New York.

The third of the terrorist trilogy of cases decided by the Supreme Court in 2004 was the *Hamdi* case.[12] Yaser Hamdi was an American citizen captured in combat in Afghanistan, fighting against American allies, and transferred to the United States. In *Hamdi,* the Supreme Court seemed grudgingly to admit that we are in a war, and that Hamdi, even though a citizen, could be held by the military as a prisoner.

So far, this was consistent with previous law. During World War II, a group of German saboteurs landed in the United States. One of them, Richard Quirin, was an American citizen. After they were arrested, they were tried by a military commission and sentenced to death. The Supreme Court heard the case, known as *Ex parte Quirin*,[13] on an expedited basis and upheld the death sentences. The Court held that offenses against the laws of war could be tried by a military commission; the ruling recognized a distinction between lawful and unlawful combatants—that is, between regular military forces and spies, saboteurs, or, in effect, terrorists.[14]

Hamdi, however, broke new ground in requiring federal courts to supervise the imprisonment of citizen terrorists during wartime. The majority agreed that Hamdi could be held without criminal charges, but it ruled that he was entitled to notice of why he was being held and an opportunity to show a "neutral decisionmaker" why he should not be held. Of course, the ruling makes the *courts* the final arbiter of who stays imprisoned and who goes free.

Justice Antonin Scalia's dissent in *Hamdi* illustrates the fundamental dichotomy between liberals and conservative judges (though Justice Stevens, surprisingly, joined in the dissent).[15] Justice Scalia based his dissent on the plain language of the Constitution regarding suspension of the writ of habeas corpus, on the common law, and on the rights of citizens of the United States, as opposed to aliens. His views were informed by the law, not by Hamdi's ethnicity or other favored "minority" status. Moreover, Scalia insisted that it is Congress, not the courts, that must deal with the propriety of Hamdi's detention. Justice Scalia's view was simple: Under the law, absent a criminal charge or statutory suspension of the writ of habeas corpus, an imprisoned citizen is entitled to release. No need to create "due process" rights out of thin air.

Certainly few would disagree with the view of all nine judges in *Hamdi* that a *citizen* detained on U.S. soil is entitled to habeas corpus unless Congress says otherwise. It seems obvious that Justice Clarence Thomas's view is the most sensible: *So long as hostilities persist,* the courts can and should do no more than secure from the government an explanation for the citizen's detention. The president and Congress can be trusted to deal fairly with our citizens.

With this trilogy of terrorist cases, the liberals seemed intent on exorcising the ghost of *Korematsu v. United States.*[16] In that 1944 case, the Supreme Court upheld the relocation and detention orders affecting American citizens of Japanese ancestry on the West Coast. In the late twentieth century, there was much wailing and gnashing of teeth about the injustice of this measure, and the government belatedly provided compensation for citizens who suffered losses in the process. No doubt the Japanese internment was unnecessary and tyrannical, but, as Justice Felix Frankfurter commented in his concurring opinion in *Korematsu,* the Constitution gives the president and Congress the authority to wage war successfully, and the validity of actions taken under the war power must be judged in the context of war.[17]

Even more than in World War II, the great danger in the war on terrorism emanates from people who are or may be in our midst, almost all of whom are Islamic radicals hailing from the Middle East. Every single terrorist involved in the 9/11 attacks came to this country openly, and many came legally. None of them had to be landed by submarine. Padilla arrived on a commercial airline. The point is that if the president has a basis for locking up a suspected terrorist, particularly a foreign terrorist, there seems no good reason why the courts should intervene. The *Hamdi* majority seemed to recognize this, but still insisted on dictating special procedures for such cases to give the judiciary the last word.

Here we see the same liberal mentality that drove the courts to dictate to public schools how they must have "hearings" before they suspend or expel unruly students: The courts rule the world, and anybody who does anything must answer to the courts.

After *Rasul,* the floodgates opened and the Guantánamo terrorists flocked to federal court, not only to attack their detention but also to prevent their trial for war crimes by military commissions. Salim Ahmed Hamdan, Osama bin Laden's personal driver and bodyguard, was among the first to sue. He won in the district court, but then he ran into John Roberts, who was then sitting on the federal appeals courts in Washington, D.C. Judge Roberts rejected his claims that he was a prisoner of war who could not be tried by the special military commissions created to deal with the terrorist prisoners at Guantánamo.[18]

Anticipating the sort of litigation that would be triggered by the *Rasul* decision, and knowing that the *Hamdan* case was before the Supreme Court, Congress passed the Detainee Treatment Act,[19] which provided in plain language that "no court, justice, or judge shall have jurisdiction to hear or consider . . . an application for a writ of habeas corpus filed by or on behalf of an alien detained by the Department of Defense at Guantánamo Bay, Cuba." The Act also implicitly accepted the creation of special military commissions by providing that their decisions could be reviewed only by the federal court of appeals in Washington, D.C. Did this stop the illiberal liberals? Of course not.

It took him forty pages of sophistry, but John Paul Stevens had no difficulty in holding that the Detainee Treatment Act did not mean what it said, and that the federal courts still had jurisdiction to hear Hamdan's and other habeas applications from Guantánamo terrorists.[20] Further, he held that the president had no authority to establish the special military commissions. Stevens and the other members of the liberal gang of four (namely, Ruth Bader Ginsburg, Stephen Breyer, and David Souter) even claimed that Hamdan hadn't committed any war crimes, but they couldn't get Justice Anthony Kennedy to swallow that, so maybe Hamdan can still be tried for something.

Before the 2006 *Hamdan* decision, military commissions had tried the conspirators in the assassination of Abraham Lincoln, Henry Wirtz (the head of the notorious Andersonville prison camp during the Civil War), the German saboteurs in 1942, General Tomoyuki Yamashita (Japanese commander in the Philippines), and many others.[21] The Supreme Court uniformly rejected attacks on the authority of such commissions. Before *Hamdan*, when Congress said the courts had no jurisdiction, the courts accepted what Congress said, even if the case was pending when the law was passed.[22] It took a lot of weasel words, but John Paul Stevens dumped all of this precedent to reach his result. Most breathtaking of all was his assertion that the president could not show any "military necessity" for the commissions. Not the commander in chief, but Justice Stevens decides what is a military necessity!

Now the president not only faces the burden of justifying to federal judges the detention of captured *foreign* terrorists in federal court, but he cannot decide to charge them and try them by military commission. We can expect that judges, not military commanders, will decide whether prisoners can be held. We can expect that judges, not military commanders, will decide the crimes with which they can be charged. The military will have to present evidence in court concerning the prisoner's status, and, to convict of war crimes, will have to present evidence in accordance with standard criminal procedure.

How do we prove that a prisoner should be a prisoner? Will we have to bring the soldiers who captured him into court? If he was captured by our allies (as is often the case), are we supposed to subpoena *their* soldiers to testify? And how do we prove that terrorists actually committed or planned to commit acts of terrorism? Do undercover agents come into court? Do we show all of our electronic surveillance in open court? Do we need fingerprints on murder weapons? How many terrorists are going to come into court and say, yeah, I'm a terrorist, keep me locked up? How insane is this?

Even before the *Rasul* decision came down, the military command scrambled to give prisoners "hearings" on their status, trying ineffectively to head off the omnipotent federal judges. Several prisoners were released, and, guess what? *They went back to Afghanistan and started fighting our troops again.*[23]

The fundamental premise of the liberal judges who voted to let Rasul and other alien terrorists have their day in court is that the federal courts control *everything,* including the fighting of foreign wars. It doesn't even matter if federal courts have no jurisdiction over the prisoner (which they didn't in *Rasul* and *Hamdan*); they can simply assert authority over the president and secretary of defense. Who needs the World Court? We have the Supreme Court of the World right at home.

A TALE OF TWO TERRORISTS

The tolerance of terror became particularly clear in the incredible judicial nightmare known as *United States v. Moussaoui*. This case illustrates why the president wisely decided to use military commissions instead of the civil courts to deal with terrorists. When contrasted with the prosecution and execution of a white, Christian terrorist, Timothy McVeigh, the case also illustrates the very real consequences of the tyranny of tolerance.

Zacarias Moussaoui was an alien arrested in Minnesota shortly after entering this country. The timing of his entry into the United States and his efforts to secure pilot training strongly suggested that he was to have participated in the 9/11 attacks. He was charged with conspiracy to do so and was eligible for the death sentence. His case was filed in federal court in Virginia. Unfortunately, his case was assigned to a liberal district judge appointed by the Great Prevaricator. The rest is (bad) legal history.[24]

Moussaoui was arrested in August 2001. He was charged with complicity in the 9/11 attacks in December of that year. He pleaded guilty, yes, GUILTY, in April 2005. When he was finally sentenced in May 2006, the verdict allowed Moussaoui to cheat the hangman (lethal injector?) despite admitted complicity in the worst mass murder in American history.

The Moussaoui case illustrates nearly everything that is wrong with the courts, particularly the federal courts. It is the logical outcome of nearly fifty years of corrupted precedent, creating constitutional rights out of whole cloth, warring against the death penalty, and asserting federal judicial authority over the whole world and everyone in it.[25]

The first absurdity of the Moussaoui case was the silly wrangling that the district judge allowed about whether Moussaoui could be his own lawyer. I know from experience that defendants like Moussaoui can be very difficult to deal with. (I haven't had to try any terrorists, but I have seen a choice collection of urban street gang thugs and multiple murderers.) In order to keep control of the case, the trial judge must come down hard at the outset on all eccentric behavior. Above all, you must avoid allowing the defendant to proceed as his own lawyer.

Moussaoui was an alien, patently unfamiliar with American judicial procedures, and a terrorist with ulterior motives. He was in this country to sabotage and kill Americans. His power of physical sabotage was eliminated, but he retained considerable power of propaganda sabotage. At his first appearance in court, he made it clear that he would try to obstruct the judicial proceedings as best he could, making American criminal law the laughingstock of the world. Why would any rational judge even consider letting him act as his own lawyer? One is tempted to answer that Clinton appointees tend to be irrational, but more specifically, the trial judge decided she was bound by imbecilic Supreme Court precedent to let Moussaoui act as his own lawyer.[26] This judge was undoubtedly a liberal (she had a long record of involvement in femifascist and other liberal activities before appointment), but in truth almost any trial judge likely would have felt compelled to reach the same conclusion.

One searches in vain for language in the Constitution or Bill of Rights that compels the conclusion that a defendant has a "right" to be his own lawyer. The defendant has a right to defend himself, but the Sixth Amendment was revolutionary in establishing that the defendant has a right to the assistance of counsel in defending himself.[27] And common sense dictates that you don't let an unguided missile loose in the courtroom. (By the way, the appellate courts don't put up with any "right" to self-representation before them.)

Having fouled up the proceedings by getting to act as his own lawyer, Moussaoui proceeded to drive everyone crazy by filing lunatic motions and pleadings, objecting to everything, attacking the trial judge, and demanding all sorts of special treatment. This went on for months. Finally, even Moussaoui's liberal judge had enough, and she revoked his self-representation. By then, of course, Moussaoui couldn't have cared less.

By this time, the government must have been wishing that it had treated Moussaoui as an unlawful combatant and tried him by military commission—where the usual constitutional rights of criminals do not strictly apply (at least, that's what the Supreme Court said before the *Hamdan* case). But the government lumbered on. The next issue to crop up was whether Moussaoui would be able to get testimony from al Qaeda operatives captured by American forces and held at Guantánamo. You guessed it: The Clinton judge said that of course Moussaoui gets access to these people; he has a *right* to it in defending himself. (But one wonders: Just what is the worth of testimony from a terrorist about his fellow terrorist?)

In a case called *Brady v. Maryland*,[28] the infamous Warren Court decided that due process required the government to disclose to the criminal defendant any exculpatory information known to it. Now, if this had been limited to evidence directly establishing or even tending to establish that the defendant did not in fact commit the crime, it probably would have done little harm. But the liberals on the Supreme Court could not be content with that sort of limited rule. No, their attitude was that exculpatory evidence meant anything unfavorable to the prosecution, whether the evidence would be admissible at trial or not. Moreover, this exculpatory evidence included information that was in the possession of any part of the government, not just the police and the prosecutor.[29]

The *Brady* notion reflects the underlying liberal philosophy that criminals, many of whom are members of "protected classes," deserve the utmost consideration when society is trying to punish them for their crimes. Indeed, radical liberals see the principle of due process as an end in itself. Society can go up in flames, but every defendant should get every possible opportunity to cheat justice before seeing the inside of the jail.

Moussaoui's case also reflected the decades-long war on the death penalty by the federal courts. Naturally, the government sought the death penalty against Moussaoui. But as we have seen, twenty-first-century death penalty jurisprudence makes it practically impossible to get a death sentence that will actually be carried out—especially when judges hostile to the death penalty are presiding. One would think that even illiberal liberals might be slightly less tolerant of a defendant who participated in a direct terrorist attack that murdered thousands of people. After all, even the New Deal Supreme Court decided that speedy trial by military commission and execution of a German saboteur was proper, even if he happened to be an American citizen. But because liberal Supreme Court justices had invented procedural rights to impede executions, Moussaoui's guilty plea still meant a jury trial on his punishment.

Contrast the Moussaoui debacle with the McVeigh case. The Oklahoma City bombing occurred on April 19, 1995. McVeigh was arrested the same day, but not charged until several days later. His trial commenced on March 31, 1997. He was found guilty and sentenced to death in June. His direct appeal was decided in 1998. His postconviction review was dismissed by the trial court in October 2000. He chose not to pursue appeals thereafter and was executed in June 2001. Thus, leaving aside the effect of McVeigh's decision not to pursue appeals from the denial of postconviction relief, McVeigh's case was complete in 1998, just three years after the bombing. He was executed within six years—about half the time most state death sentences involve, if they ever get executed.

Why was the government able to convict McVeigh in three years, including appeal, when it took nearly five years just to get Moussaoui before a jury? Was it because the district judge in McVeigh's case was a Republican appointee? Was it because the prosecutors were more skillful? Or was it because the liberals had no use for McVeigh, whereas Moussaoui is a member of several protected classes: racial, religious, and ethnic? Few liberal groups and law professors tried to derail the McVeigh prosecution and execution, whereas liberals turned out in force to support Moussaoui's intermediate appeals in an effort to thwart the death sentence.

In truth, there is simply no reason why a competent trial judge could not have ensured that Moussaoui was treated the same as McVeigh. Instead, the system had to exhibit "tolerance" in handling Moussaoui. *Eisentrager* represents the sanest way to deal with unlawful combatants taken on our soil while acting on plans to kill Americans.

Contrary to the liberal conception of law, due process is not an end in itself. The end of due process is the preservation of public order and prevention of private revenge in criminal cases, with some assurance of fairness to *both* the criminal and the victim, to say nothing of society. It is supposed to limit government, but not cripple it in protecting us from predators. Yet there are no limits to the mandates of tolerance. Tolerance of terror is the logical result of the past fifty years of liberal jurisprudence. In a saner time, Moussaoui would have been tried by a military commission and, if found guilty, executed long ago.

It is no answer to bleat that we should not become what we are fighting against. We aren't and we won't. Just because we exercise the primeval right to defend ourselves against people who don't and won't ever play by the rules, we are not brought down to their level. Even Franklin Roosevelt, responsible for planting the seeds of the tyranny of tolerance in the judiciary, did not shrink from shipping Japanese-ancestry citizens off to internment camps, nor did he hesitate to authorize development of the atomic bomb. The first task of government in time of war is to win, not to be tolerant.

SUPREME COURT AS SUPREME COMMANDER

The contrast between the judicial mentality of the *Rasul* and *Moussaoui* decisions and of the *Eisentrager, Korematsu,* and *Quirin* decisions could not be clearer. The latter cases all recognized the unquestionable primacy of the president and Congress in the conduct of a war. But the terror trilogy, plus *Hamdan* and *Moussaoui*, makes clear that the federal courts are omnipotent, and that they, and they alone, can decide who is properly a prisoner of war and order the release of anybody, even aliens held prisoner outside the United States and its territories, regardless of the potential threat to our national security.

The intrusion of the judiciary into the conduct of the war on terror has advanced beyond the issue of supervising the president's custody of terrorist prisoners and now threatens the gathering of intelligence—the most vital function of our government in this new kind of war. A federal district judge (a Clinton appointee, naturally) has purported to enjoin the National Security Agency from eavesdropping on telecommunications between people in the United States and people in terrorist havens.[30] The district judge's opinion drips with contempt for the president and exalts the "rights" of plaintiffs who, by their own admission, are in direct contact with enemies of the United States in wartime. The decision rests on a highly suspect analysis of the plaintiffs' right to bring the suit, and purports to create a judicial power to "enforce" separation of powers, while at the same time managing to inject the First Amendment into what is essentially a Fourth Amendment (search and seizure) case. The need for the president to stand up to these judicial usurpations cannot be clearer.

The terror trilogy and *Hamdan* blather piously about the importance of the independent judiciary, the sanctity of constitutional rights, and the rule of law. Underlying the piety is the matter of tolerance. We must tolerate letting terrorists into the country and letting terrorist prisoners go free, because otherwise we might be discriminating against these fanatics on account of their religion and race. If we deny aliens the protection of American courts, somehow we are undermining the constitutional guaranties that protect Americans.

What utter nonsense. The federal courts are not the supreme law of the land. The Constitution is the supreme law of the land. The Constitution gives the war-making power and command of the armed forces to Congress and the president. The Constitution expressly authorizes Congress to punish violations of international law. The terrorists like Moussaoui and his compatriots at Guantánamo are no better than Blackbeard the Pirate or Major John Andre. They seek to kill American citizens and destroy their property by the foulest means. There is no doubt that they are capable of using nuclear and biological weapons against us. It does no violence to the rights of Americans if our elected officers take stern measures to eradicate terrorists. The execution of the saboteur Richard Quirin did nothing to diminish the rights of all other Americans, nor did the refusal to entertain habeas corpus petitions from Nazi war criminals or General Yamashita.

The president and Congress are answerable to the people if they behave arbitrarily or oppressively in the conduct of the war on terror. They also have their own solemn oaths to support the Constitution. The president has already acted to ensure that aliens held as terrorists are humanely treated and released if they pose no threat to America. Congress has taken action to ensure humane treatment of terrorist prisoners. The president is better situated to decide who the threat is than federal judges. But driven by the tyranny of tolerance, the federal courts know no bounds.

In *The Time Machine,* H. G. Wells hypothesized a world after what amounted to nuclear war. There were two strains to the populace, the Eloi and the Morlocks. The former were peaceful children of light; the latter were violent denizens of darkness. Indeed, the Eloi were so obsessed with peace and serenity that they were unable to defend themselves against the violence of the Morlocks. Our federal courts resemble the Eloi. They are so obsessed with abstract notions of fairness and tolerance that they will permit our mortal enemies to go free to kill and maim us at will, and there is nothing we can do about it, since the tyranny of tolerance has done its work well.

CONCLUSION

SO WHAT ARE WE GOING TO DO ABOUT IT?

Sed quis custodiet ipsos custodes?*
—Juvenal

*It is not easy to stand aloof and allow want of wisdom to prevail,
to disregard one's own strongly held view of what is wise in the
conduct of affairs. But it is not the business of this Court to pronounce policy. It must observe a fastidious regard for limitations
on its own power, and this precludes the Court's giving effect to
its own notions of what is wise or politic. That self-restraint is of
the essence in the observance of the judicial oath.*
—Justice Felix Frankfurter, dissenting in *Trop v. Dulles* (1958)

THIS BOOK HAS BEEN A very depressing one to write. I have
had to review dozens of cases handed down by liberal jurists flout-
ing the most basic precepts of constitutional, natural, and moral law—
excising God from public life; denigrating the institution of marriage;
siding with murderers, abortionists, and pornographers; insisting on
treating people unequally; usurping the power of taxation. I have revis-

---

*But who guards the guards themselves?

ited one of the most unpleasant passages in my own life, resurrecting memories of my own clash with the femifascist wing of the PC police. I have been in almost daily communion with my worst fears for my country and the law.

Is there no hope? Are radical liberal judges and lawyers in total control?[1]

Dire as the situation may seem, I also remind myself of Ronald Reagan's simple prescription for the cold war: We win, they lose. Reagan prevailed against the evil empire of the Soviet Union the same way the Founders prevailed against the High Court of Parliament—by not giving up.

We can, and must, fight back against the illiberal liberals and their tyranny of tolerance. We can win the battle against the tyranny of tolerance, but only through sustained effort.

We will win if we demonstrate to the universities and the media that we won't pay them to propagate the tyranny.

We will win if we demonstrate to the politicians (as the people of South Dakota did to Tom Daschle) that their electoral survival depends on their combating the tyranny.

And we will win, of course, if we curtail the hegemony of the courts.

If, as the Declaration of Independence states, government derives its just powers from the consent of the governed, it follows that a judiciary that repeatedly strips the people of the right to decide issues of social policy, that approves religious persecution, that embraces taxation without representation, and that approves discrimination in favor of some—all without any textual basis in the Constitution, and even in opposition to what the text plainly states—is rightly subject to censure. The Declaration laid it down that governments are ordained to secure the unalienable rights of life, liberty, and the pursuit of happiness, and that when "*any form of* government becomes destructive of these ends," it is the *right* of the people "to alter or abolish it [emphasis added]." The courts have become the willing instruments of a new tyranny—the tyranny of tolerance—and their departure from the proper, limited role of the judiciary must be remedied.

But how to control an institution that itself decides what is constitutional and what is not, that says what the law is? Who guards the guards?

President Franklin Roosevelt recognized this problem when he confronted the "conservative" Supreme Court of his day. In a March 1937 radio address he said, "We cannot rely on an amendment as the immediate or only answer to our present difficulties. . . . Even if an amendment were passed, and even if in the years to come it were to be ratified, its meaning would depend upon the kind of Justices who would be sitting on the Supreme Court bench. An amendment like the rest of the Constitution is what the Justices say it is rather than what its framers or you might hope it is."

In any case, the fact is that it is extremely difficult to amend the Constitution. That is why Supreme Court decisions have been reversed so rarely by constitutional amendments: The *Dred Scott* case was reversed by the Thirteenth, Fourteenth, and Fifteenth Amendments (made possible only by the bloody Civil War itself), and the Court's decision to declare the federal income tax unconstitutional *(Pollock v. Farmers Home & Trust Co.[2])* was reversed by the Sixteenth Amendment.[3] So, although there are intriguing proposals for amendments to rein in the judiciary,[4] we cannot realistically regard amending the Constitution as a tool for fixing the problem.

No, the goal here is not to change the Constitution. That's what liberals do by their rewrite jobs. The goal is to reestablish the Constitution's true meaning and put the judiciary back in its proper place.[5]

Fortunately, we have weapons at our disposal to do so. The three most important weapons are choosing judges who reject the tyranny of tolerance, using statutes to limit the courts' jurisdiction, and, in the last ditch, defiance—just as the Founders defied Parliament, so must the elected, coequal branches of the federal government defy the dictatorship of the judiciary, in defense of the same principles fought for in 1776.

PERSONNEL

The first weapon against the judicial tyranny of tolerance is to change the personnel. This has been obvious since Thomas Jefferson's clashes with John Marshall, and became even clearer after FDR and the liberals remade the Supreme Court. Liberal judges almost invariably will vote the activist, liberal party line, as evidenced by a study published in 2003 by Professor Cass Sunstein of the University of Chicago (not what one would call a conservative).[6] Now, this does not mean that judges—even extreme liberal judges—let their philosophies control outcomes at the expense of fairness to a particular litigant. But most (if not all) cases that advance judicial autocracy do not really involve an issue of fairness to an individual litigant. These cases—abortion, homosexual "marriage," discrimination in the guise of affirmative action, church and state, and so forth—generally involve policy matters that affect government or society as a whole.

The people can and should demand judges who will decide issues with devotion to the text of the Constitution and to the traditions of our people, not to the tyranny of tolerance.[7] We need judges who embrace and defend a republican judicial philosophy. (Note the small *r* in *republican*; this is not about partisan politics, but judicial philosophy.) This philosophy rejects the power of the courts and Congress alike to change the Constitution at will, or to ignore the parts they don't like. It recognizes that the courts are not omnicompetent, that there is a separation of powers, and that the powers to tax and to make war are not given to judges. It recognizes that the Constitution is color-blind and will not tolerate discrimination against white citizens any more than against black citizens—for if the Constitution commands equal treatment, it commands it for everyone. It recognizes that courts do not sit to remedy every perceived wrong. It recognizes that the Bill of Rights is not an offensive weapon to enable favored minorities to impose their will on the majority. It recognizes that judges can't selectively "incorporate" parts of the Bill of Rights into the Fourteenth Amendment just because they think it's the right thing to do. It recognizes that the federal government is not all-powerful. It recognizes there are such things as immutable truth and natural law, not just "constructs." Above all, it recognizes God as the ultimate source of all law—as does the Declaration of Independence.[8]

Of course, the judicial nomination process has proven remarkably unreliable in ensuring appointees' solid republican credentials. Professor Sunstein's study verified what we already knew: Liberals almost always remain liberals when they get on the bench. And the good professor's numbers showed something else: Republican appointees vote in favor of the tyranny of tolerance far more often than liberals vote against it (especially since Democratic appointees are quite predictable in their defense of "tolerance"). Consider the cases of Justices Sandra Day O'Connor and Anthony Kennedy, both of whom accommodated the homosexual agenda. O'Connor was an especially faithful servant of the tyranny of tolerance on abortion and racial discrimination matters—although at the last she showed surprising signs of holding firm in death penalty cases. Then, of course, there are Justices David Souter and John Paul Stevens, both Republican appointees and now icons of liberalism.

Why do Republican appointees "Blackmunize," or embrace the liberal agenda? In part this is a testament to the power of the tyranny of tolerance. It seems that people like O'Connor and Kennedy would rather be accused of child molestation than be called racist or intolerant. Another problem is that many Republican judicial appointees have no firm judicial philosophy and thus are vulnerable to the blandishments of liberal colleagues (we judges call this being "collegial," but it often entails selling out principle for the sake of personal amity). In addition, many "conservative" judges who are not committed to a republican judicial philosophy feel a need to demonstrate that they do not let *any* philosophy control them, so they do the opposite of what they assume everybody expects. If they do this often enough, they are rewarded with the coveted title of "moderate." The liberals never, ever worry about what the media and law school elites say about them, because they are at one with the elites, and so they are "moderate" by definition.

Here the role of the media should not be underestimated. Nobody in the judiciary likes being the target of media attacks. Judges have little ability to respond to such attacks, and the relentless drumbeat of media condemnation can affect all but the hardiest. And in fact, lavish media praise can have an even greater effect on judges' behavior. On rare occasions, even I have been praised by the liberal *St. Louis Post-Dispatch* for various rulings. Glowing editorials, read by many thousands, do not make you feel bad. If you are the sort of person who prefers praise to blame (and who doesn't?), the siren song of the media's praise is bewitching indeed. I can only imagine the headiness of the existence of Supreme Court justices who choose to cater to the elites. Much of Justice Kennedy's behavior can undoubtedly be explained by his affinity for the international legal elites. You cannot be lionized by the elites and then rend their imbecile ideas. You might not be invited to next year's international law conferences.

To avoid seeing the Blackmunization of more judges, the president must nominate and the Senate must confirm only persons with a demonstrated republican judicial philosophy. FDR won the war with the Supreme Court by appointing none but certifiable liberals to the appellate bench. Republican nominees should not be afraid of the cry of "conservative activism": It is not activism to reject liberals' illegitimate changes to the Constitution and restore the authority of the other branches of government to decide controversial issues (or not to decide them, for that matter).

In spite of the liberal indoctrination attempted at nearly every law school,[9] people can be found who demonstrate a republican judicial philosophy: Clarence Thomas and Antonin Scalia come to mind, along with appeals court judges Alex Kozinski and Edith Jones. Early indications are that John Roberts and Samuel Alito may be of this mold. Such judges must be nominated, and they must be confirmed.

The president and Senate can ensure that truly republican judicial candidates ascend to the federal district and appellate courts by insisting on thorough scouting reports from local lawyers and on the very sort of "paper trail" that outrages liberals. All too often, judicial nominees have been selected on the basis of senatorial patronage or their lack of demonstrated commitment to republican principles. The president should not accept the home-state senator's recommendation unless the candidate—and the candidate's judicial philosophy—have been thoroughly vetted.

Appointing committed republican jurists can be the swiftest and most effective means of stopping the tyranny of tolerance in its tracks, for liberal notions of tolerance cannot win an honest election. If you voted for George W. Bush to support the war on terror, to support the institution of marriage and defeat the legitimization of sexual perversion, to restore some measure of responsibility as a complement to freedom, and to promote true equality under the law by eliminating favored treatment for special classes of citizens, then it is your responsibility to see to it that Bush and the Senate deliver a federal judiciary that behaves as though it were in fact the least dangerous branch of government. If you don't, your vote for George W. Bush simply did not count—and that's the way Ted Kennedy, Joe Biden, Chuck Schumer, and other liberals want it.

Indeed, one of the obstacles to appointing judges committed to a republican judicial philosophy is the Senate confirmation process, which enables a determined minority to obstruct judicial nominees indefinitely. The Senate confirmation process has become vicious in the extreme. It was bad enough back in 1987, when the Republicans caved in to the Democrats' attacks on Robert Bork and instead we got Anthony Kennedy, Ronald Reagan's third choice, a "moderate," slithering in and out of liberalism. But at least the Democrats were in the majority then; now the minority party turns judicial confirmation hearings into high-tech lynchings, as Justice Thomas put it. Who wants to put up with that? Citizens who are willing to serve their country as judges are entitled to the courtesy of honest opposition. Nominees shouldn't have to sit helplessly as liberals launch tirades against them under the pretense of testing their qualifications. Let liberals frankly state that they won't support any conservative nominee, for reasons of political philosophy, and be done with it.

Apart from turning the confirmation process into a gauntlet that few have the stamina to run, liberals have also discovered the filibuster.

They are every bit as determined to use that weapon to preserve the tyranny of tolerance as the old Southern senators were determined to use it to preserve segregation. Here, it is high time that the Republican leadership in the Senate dust off the liberals' own weapon against the filibuster—the one they tried to use in the 1940s and 1950s to defeat Southern filibusters of civil rights bills.[10] Senator John Cornyn of Texas and others have outlined measures along these lines to reform the Senate confirmation process,[11] but so far the Republicans have not used the tools available to them. Why not? Lack of guts, pure and simple. They don't want to violate the mores of the club. Well, is the control of the judiciary important or not? Do you really want to have an effective death penalty, an end to affirmative action, a stop to homosexual "marriage," and a renunciation of judicial taxation, or don't you?

The Constitution authorizes each house of Congress to establish its rules of procedure. Nothing in the Constitution, however, contemplates that nominations will be killed by "holds" or endless debate. In particular, there is nothing in the text of the Constitution that authorizes the Senate to emasculate the executive or judicial branches simply by refusing to vote on nominees. Yes, "going nuclear" on the issue of filibustering judicial nominees could come back to haunt conservatives in the future, but shouldn't the Senate be forced to assume the responsibility of an up-or-down vote? And if a majority of the Senate is willing to confirm a nominee, shouldn't that majority prevail? This is the essence of democracy, and it should hold whether the Democrats or the Republicans control the Senate.

One thing is certain: When the Democrats regain control of the Senate and the presidency, they will not hesitate to adopt the arguments for "going nuclear," and they *will* have the nerve to ram their nominees through.

The battle for personnel change in the judiciary must be fought without quarter—just as FDR fought. This battle must be waged in order to make the courts once again subject to the Constitution—the Constitution that was adopted by the people, not the Constitution that liberals make up as they go along.

During the seventeenth century, under another oppressive regime, the great jurist Sir Edward Coke had the courage to tell his king, *"Quod rex non debet esse sub homine, sed sub Deo et lege"* ("The king is under no man, but he is under God and the law").[12] Coke was later forced to kneel before that king and recant his views, but his words have echoed down to us across the centuries. Like King James, even the Supreme Court of the United States must be under God and the law.

JURISDICTION

Personnel change in the judiciary, while crucial, is not the only weapon that could be deployed against the tyranny of tolerance. And here again, Republicans could employ a technique first devised by liberals.

Soon after the Democrats captured control of Congress in 1930, they adopted the Norris-LaGuardia Act,[13] severely limiting the power of federal courts to issue injunctions in labor disputes.

A federal judge had first granted such an injunction in 1894 in the infamous Pullman Strike. The next year the U.S. Supreme Court upheld the lower court's authority to grant the injunction and affirmed the imprisonment of the union leader Eugene V. Debs for violating it.[14] Thereafter, federal injunctions became a prominent part of the employers' arsenal of weapons against strikes—until, that is, the Democrats passed the Norris-LaGuardia Act. The constitutionality of this limitation on federal judicial power has never been questioned by liberals or conservatives. It provides the template for legislative limits on the activities of the federal courts in other areas, since the lower federal courts have always been recognized as creatures of Congress, with only so much jurisdiction as Congress chooses to grant.[15]

Today, Congress could take several steps to corral liberal judges. Congress has already imposed some limitations on federal judicial review of death sentences. These limitations, riddled with exceptions and loopholes, have done little but produce more litigation to determine the meaning of the statutes.[16] Indeed, in recent cases, the Supreme Court has created a whole new procedure for attacking death sentences via the Reconstruction-era Civil Rights Acts, leading to challenges to lethal injection and federal injunctions mandating impossible conditions on the execution of death sentences. Congress can and should block such efforts, simply by amending the existing federal Anti-Injunction Act to prohibit injunctions against the execution of death sentences.[17]

Congress would strike another heavy blow at the tyranny of tolerance by explicitly abolishing "affirmative action." The Civil Rights Act of 1964 could be amended to reject any program that discriminates on the basis of race for any purpose whatsoever. Ironically, the original act contained several provisions that seemingly were intended to accomplish that very result, but they have been ignored by liberal judges. Perhaps one more, very explicit statute would have better effect. (Years ago, when I was engaged in the struggle to prevent judicial taxation in St. Louis, I drafted a statute designed to prohibit judicial taxation altogether and to limit federal judges' ability to administer local government in place of elected officials.[18] I still think it's a good idea.)

So why hasn't Congress taken such steps to sweep away the tyranny of tolerance? One possible explanation is that the tyranny of tolerance has so intimidated Republican legislators that they refuse to lift a finger against it. It's impossible to know exactly how politicians respond, but I do know that shortly after the Republicans took control of Congress in 1994, some of them proposed legislation to eliminate the purported authority of federal courts to impose taxation by decree. By the time this legislation emerged from the House Judiciary Committee, it had been so amended as to *authorize* judicial taxation.[19] The tyranny of tolerance is a powerful force, especially now that liberals in the Senate have shown their willingness to use the filibuster. They will fight viciously against any legislative changes designed to check their judicial empire.[20]

Another problem with legislative solutions is the obvious: If the judges say what the law is, how can they be prevented from merely changing established law to nullify limitations on their power? Established law means nothing to liberal judges, so they can be expected to strike down any legislative limits on the tyranny of tolerance.

As we saw in the discussion of tolerance and terror in Chapter 15,

Congress reacted to the 2004 terror trilogy of cases by adopting a statute that expressly stripped the federal courts of jurisdiction to entertain any writ of habeas corpus filed by a Guantánamo prisoner.[21] In light of the Norris-LaGuardia Act and Civil War legislation concerning habeas corpus, there can be no doubt that Congress had that power to limit the courts' jurisdiction. (Congress also has the power to suspend the writ during time of invasion—and such a suspension would limit even the Supreme Court's authority to issue the writ.)[22] Of course, in *Hamdan v. Rumsfeld*,[23] the liberals, joined by the great internationalist Anthony Kennedy, simply ruled that the statute limiting federal jurisdiction didn't mean what it said. In the course of the opinion, Justice John Paul Stevens clearly hinted that the liberals will simply strike down any statute on jurisdiction that they don't like.

Still, legislation is worth a try. At a minimum, it will impede liberals' ability to advance their agenda via the judiciary. They will have to attack the constitutionality of the congressional acts, and these issues can be resolved only by the Supreme Court. By the time the challenges reach the Supreme Court, there may be one or two more justices who recognize limits on their power and who would be willing to yield to the legislature on the jurisdictional issue.

DEFIANCE

When the South engaged in "massive resistance" to the federal desegregation decrees of the 1950s, it put President Dwight Eisenhower in a difficult position. If he enforced those decrees, he was advancing the judicial power; if he declined, he was advancing the agenda of the segregationists. He chose to enforce the federal decrees. During the 1894 Pullman Strike, President Grover Cleveland was faced with a similar choice: If he enforced the federal judge's injunctions, he was acceding to the power claimed by the judiciary to enjoin strike activity; if he declined to enforce them, he was acceding to riots and lawlessness. He, too, chose to enforce the decrees.

In each case, the president was not so much vindicating the authority of the Supreme Court as preserving order.

In other cases, presidents have refused to obey the Supreme Court. The first instance occurred in 1832, when Andrew Jackson refused to enforce the Court's ruling in *Worcester v. Georgia.*[24] In that case, Chief Justice John Marshall held (rightly) that the repatriation of the Cherokee Indians out of Georgia was unconstitutional and contrary to federal treaties with the tribe. President Jackson is said to have declared, "John Marshall has made his decision, now let him enforce it." Jackson did nothing, and the Indians went down the Trail of Tears to Oklahoma. Given the circumstances then obtaining, even the eminent liberal historian Samuel Eliot Morison later wrote that this was the best decision at the time. Whether it was or not, it demonstrates that a president may decline to enforce a Supreme Court order in his discretion as head of the executive branch.

During the Civil War, Abraham Lincoln offered even more pertinent examples of defiance. On his own authority, he authorized suspension of the writ of habeas corpus in certain areas of Maryland. Chief Justice Roger Taney, sitting as a circuit justice, granted a writ of habeas corpus in the arrest of a Maryland farmer, John Merryman, suspected of bridge-burning. Lincoln simply ignored the decision.[25] The justification for Lincoln's action was obvious: The president is charged with fighting wars and preserving public order. At times, the federal courts can do more harm than good by asserting jurisdiction to second-guess the president.

Lincoln also argued persuasively that the *Dred Scott* decision should be given no effect beyond the parties to the case themselves. He recognized the decision for what it was: judicial amendment of the Constitution. Other presidents have struggled with the conundrum of keeping the Supreme Court within constitutional bounds, but in modern times, few have found the courage of Jackson or Lincoln.

Obviously there are two types of judicial decisions that can affect government policy. The classic case involves true judicial review, in which the courts declare that a law or act of the government is unenforceable because it conflicts with the Constitution. As noted, this power is necessarily implied in the constitutional structure. Otherwise, the Constitution would be at the mercy of the legislative or executive branches.

But there is another sort of judicial decision: the sort that imposes a new policy on the government and actively seeks to manage that policy. It is this sort of "reform" decision that the illiberal liberals employ to further the tyranny of tolerance. They also have a way of creating "fundamental" rights out of whole cloth and then using the power of judicial review to frustrate any legislative attempts to regulate or limit those rights.

This is how the judiciary has declared sodomy laws unconstitutional. While the decision has no root in the Constitution, it has the virtue of being consistent with the power of judicial review. Not content with immunizing perverted sex against criminal prosecution, the tyranny of tolerance next proceeds to the "reform" stage, by mandating homosexual "marriage" and special treatment for homosexuals in a host of public and private contexts, and by actively persecuting any who have the temerity to be "intolerant."

Here, though, the other two coequal branches of the federal government can properly refuse to implement blindly Supreme Court decisions. The president can properly refuse to enforce liberal judicial mandates and Congress can refuse to fund them. Particularly in the area of war-making, the president can and must refuse to comply with unconstitutional intrusions by the Supreme Court. Here, the text of the Constitution itself refutes the pretensions of the liberals. The president can effectively repel the tyranny of tolerance by telling the courts, "No! I will not submit to your authority to decide what foreign enemies of the United States should be set free to kill Americans." The power of the tyranny of tolerance is in large part a chimera, created by decades of slavish deference to the Supreme Court's usurpations. The other branches must at last demand that the judiciary stay within constitutional bounds, no matter what the supposed noble goal of the usurpation of power is.

The *Rasul* and *Hamdan* terrorist decisions provide the perfect opportunity to restore the constitutional balance of power and remind liberals that the judiciary is not omnipotent. President Bush should paraphrase Andrew Jackson and tell Justice Stevens that he has made his decision, and he can try to enforce it if he wants to take a motorboat to Guantánamo. If liberals scream about the rule of law, the president can simply invite the House of Representatives to impeach him if they feel he has transgressed his oath.

There was a time when even local officials would resign their office rather than obey a judicial decree. In many cases in the nineteenth century, when federal courts tried to order collection of taxes (taxes authorized by statute, by the way), the tax collectors resigned, and the taxes were not collected. Today, of course, the courts would try to appoint their own receivers, but if no one accepted the appointments (as Americans once upon a time refused to be stamp masters), the judiciary would be put in its place.[26]

I emphasize that defiance of the Supreme Court is permissible only by the two elected branches of the federal government, and then only when the Court purports to control powers expressly confided to the other branches, such as war-making and taxation. This is not a call for mob rule or governors to stand in schoolhouse doors. By refusing to permit the courts to dictate their actions in their constitutional spheres of war-making and taxation, the president and Congress do no violence to constitutional government. Rather, they uphold it—but only they have the constitutional authority to do so. The president can stand against the tyranny of tolerance, and begin its dismantling, by simply telling the Supreme Court, "No."

NOT TOO LATE

The tyranny of tolerance has been seven decades in the making. Yet its foundation is fragile. If the president exposes the hypocrisy of liberals by direct challenge to the Supreme Court, he will win, and freedom for all will be the winner. Terrorists will not be freed to kill again. Taxes will not be imposed by decree, or if imposed, will not be collected without the people's consent. Perversion will not be exalted in the public square while Christmas and the Boy Scouts are excluded.

The Founding Fathers created a judiciary that could not be controlled in its decision making by either the executive or the legislative branches. But judicial independence is not the same thing as judicial hegemony. In creating this third, independent branch of government, the Founding Fathers did not have in mind government by judicial decree.

Once, the judiciary was a force for liberty, confining government within boundaries fixed by the Constitution. Now, however, in the service of the tyranny of tolerance, judges have betrayed their oaths and tried to convert themselves from neutral arbiters of disputes into philosopher kings. Only the most drastic action is likely to bring home to the people the ever-increasing danger of the tyranny of tolerance.

When asked what the constitutional convention had given the people, Benjamin Franklin replied, "A republic, if you can keep it." The tyranny of tolerance has gone far toward dismantling that republic. Whether we rescue it and keep it or not for future generations depends on whether we defeat the principal tool of the tyranny, the imperial judiciary.

It is not too late to reverse course, but time may be running out. And if the problem is not solved, if the Brennans, Souters, Kennedys, Bidens, and Schumers win, then the Constitution is indeed gone, and succeeding generations will suffer the consequences of the tyranny of tolerance, imposed by a judiciary that has long since forgotten that the Constitution has any meaning.

APPENDIX

MY RUN-IN WITH THE TYRANTS OF TOLERANCE

More than any other experience, one very direct run-in with the tyrants of tolerance offered me a frightening view of what is happening to American law. The run-in occurred when, in one of my legal opinions, I dared to criticize one of liberals' favorite weapons, sexual harassment litigation.

When writing opinions, judges have long enjoyed the freedom to criticize the parties' theories and to explain or instruct the public concerning the state of the law. With my opinion in this case, which is shown in the pages that follow, I felt especially comfortable because my criticism of radical feminist sexual harassment theories did not affect my legal judgment.

Nevertheless, my opinion prompted an attack on my integrity and accusations of official misconduct. My correspondence with the Missouri Commission on Retirement, Removal, and Discipline is also shown in this appendix, after my opinion.

As the correspondence reveals, I beat a retreat of sorts at the time. But as this book reveals, I feel I should no longer keep quiet about what the tyranny of tolerance is doing to our country.

STATE OF MISSOURI   )
)   SS
CITY OF ST. LOUIS   )

MISSOURI CIRCUIT COURT
TWENTY-SECOND JUDICIAL CIRCUIT
(St. Louis City)

JOAN DOE,	)
	)
Plaintiff,	)
	)
	) Cause No. 982-00xxx
vs.	)
	) Division No. 1
JAY ROE, M.D.,	)
	)
Defendant.	)

ORDER

"[I]t is an accusation easy to be made, hard to be proved, but harder to be defended by the party accused, though innocent."[1]

Thus far it has been held that no action will lie for the insult involved in inviting a woman to illicit intercourse, "the view being, apparently, that there is no harm in asking."[2]

Recognizing that women suffer sexual harassment in the workplace, based on outmoded sexual sterotypes [sic] and male

---

[1] 4 Bl.Comm. *215, quoting Hale.

---

[2] W. Prosser, *Handbook of the Law of Torts* 64–65 (1941), quoting Magruder, "Mental and Emotional Disturbance in the Law of Torts," 49 Harv.L.Rev. 1033, 1055 (1936) (footnotes omitted).

domination of subordinate female employees, we reject the view . . . that, as a matter of law, the degrading and humiliating behavior herein detailed was at worse [sic] a "social impropriety" which did not amount to intentional infliction of emotional distress.[3]

From Anita Hill to Monica Lewinsky, the cry of "sexual harassment" has been selectively raised to advance certain groups' political agendas under the guise of promoting equal opportunity in the workplace, or under the banner of "equality" in academe. See R. Bork, *Slouching Towards Gomorrah* 215, 222 (1996); see also Note, 80 Cornell L.Rev. 1268 (1995), presenting a fairly comprehensive summary of the law concerning sexual harassment while advocating special rules to advance the cause of plaintiffs. Spawned in the protean atmosphere of federal employment discrimination litigation, and there producing a body of law with no anchor in statute or common law and virtually no coherent standards of proof, see *Faragher v. City of Boca Raton,* 118 S.Ct. 2275 (1998); *Burlington Industries, Inc. v. Ellerth,* 118 S.Ct. 2257, 2273 (1998) (Thomas, J., dissenting); *Harris v. Forklift Systems, Inc.,* 510 U.S. 17 (1993); *Meritor Sav. Bank v. Vinson,* 477 U.S. 57 (1986); *Jones v. Clinton,* 990 F.Supp. 657 (E.D.Ark. 1998); the theories of the "sexual harassment" police have stretched their tentacles from college faculties to Supreme Court confirmation hearings to legal and judicial ethics, see Supreme Court Rule 2, Canon 3C, and now seek to ensnare the common law of torts. The question before this Court is whether a wholesale extension of notions of "sexual harassment" into tort law is warranted, without direction from the people through the General Assembly. The Court concludes that the common law does not enact Cardinal Newman's definition of a gentleman, nor Catharine MacKinnon's vapid maunderings, and that Plaintiff's petition at present fails to state a claim.

---

[3] *Howard University v. Best,* 484 A.2d 958 (D.C.App. 1984).

Plaintiff alleges[4] that the Defendant inflicted emotional distress on her while she worked as an employee of IW Hospital under Defendant's supervision, and while she had a "physician-patient" relationship with him. Count I alleges intentional infliction of emotional distress. Count II alleges the same facts, but attempts to state a claim for negligent infliction of emotional distress. The distressing conduct alleged by Plaintiff consists of the following, all of which allegedly occurred between August 1994 and March 30, 1995: (1) Defendant "repeatedly" touched Plaintiff's person; (2) Defendant asked Plaintiff to perform sexual acts in his office; (3) Defendant "repeatedly" telephoned Plaintiff at her home, at other places of employment and at friends' homes. Defendant's conduct occurred despite Plaintiff's informing Defendant not to do such things. Plaintiff alleges in conclusional fashion that the Defendant's conduct was extreme and outrageous and that it caused her to suffer medically diagnosable and medically significant injury.

Defendant has moved to dismiss, arguing that the claims of offensive touching are barred by the statute of limitations and that the petition otherwise fails to allege facts sufficient to state a claim for intentional or negligent infliction of emotional distress. Defendant Roe contends that Doe's claims of offensive touching are barred by the two-year statute of limitations applicable to battery claims. He further claims that the one-year "savings statute," § 516.230 RSMo (1994) does not apply to the present action, because Doe's battery claim was previously filed and dismissed for lack of jurisdiction. Dr. Roe also maintains that the conduct alleged in Doe's petition is not outrageous or extreme for purposes of her claim for intentional infliction of emotional distress.

---

[4] The facts, of course, must be derived solely from the petition in deciding a motion to dismiss. However, the Court notes that Plaintiff's memorandum opposing the motion incorporated a memorandum and order of the United States District Court for the Eastern District of Missouri (Jackson, J.). *Doe v. IW Hospital,* No. 4:96-CV-735 (CEJ). Judge Jackson's opinion alludes to the fact that Plaintiff and Defendant engaged in a sexual relationship from approximately January to August 1994.

Doe counters that she has made a claim for intentional infliction of emotional distress, independent of the tort of battery. Further, she contends, any claim which might be construed as battery is within the savings statute and is not barred by the two-year statute of limitations. Finally, she claims, the conduct alleged is sufficiently egregious to support a claim for emotional distress.

STATUTE OF LIMITATIONS

A claim may be dismissed when it is obvious on the face of the pleadings that it is barred by the statute of limitations. *Lehnig v. Bornhop*, 859 S.W.2d 271, 272 (Mo.App. 1993). At issue is whether the five-year statute of limitations for tort actions, including actions for emotional distress, § 516.120(4) RSMo (1994), applies, or the two-year limitation period governing actions for battery, § 516.140 RSMo (1994).

Doe's emotional distress claims are based on the following alleged conduct on the part of Dr. Roe: (1) offensive touching without consent; (2) requests to perform sexual acts; and (3) nuisance telephone calls.

With respect to Doe's claim for intentional infliction of emotional distress, no independent action lies where the existence of the claim depends on a battery. *K.G. v. R.T.R.*, 918 S.W.2d 795, 800 (Mo.banc 1996). In *K.G.*, the court found that, *but for* the allegations of the commission of a battery, no cause of action for intentional infliction of emotional distress would lie, and the two-year statute of limitations for battery claims applied. The court reasoned that recovery for emotional distress may be allowed as an element of damages in a distinct battery action. *Id.* The plaintiff in *K.G.* also purported to allege a claim for negligent infliction of emotional distress arising from the same intentional touching. The court found that the specific allegations of intentional touching contradicted the possibility that the defendant's conduct was mere negligence, and found no independent claim for negligent infliction of emotional distress as a result of intentional sexual contact between a father and his minor child. *Id.*

Doe's petition alleges that Dr. Roe, intentionally and without Doe's consent, touched her in an offensive manner. This conduct constitutes a battery, defined as the willful touching of another and the consummation of an assault. *Adler v. Ewing*, 347 S.W.2d 396, 402 (Mo.App. 1961). The other alleged conduct, however, does not fall within the definition of another tort with a limitations period of less than five years.

The last alleged act of battery or intentional touching occurred in March 1994, more than two years before the present action was filed in February 1998. However, Doe had previously filed a suit against IW Hospital and Dr. Roe in the U.S. District Court for the Eastern District of Missouri, for sexual harassment and retaliation under Title VII and the Missouri Human Rights Act, together with common-law claims for negligent supervision, battery, and intentional and negligent infliction of emotional distress.[5] On December 4, 1997, U.S. District Judge Carol E. Jackson granted Dr. Roe's motion to dismiss Doe's claims for sexual harassment and retaliation under Title VII, and for violations of the Missouri Human Rights Act, for lack of subject matter jurisdiction. Judge Jackson concluded that Dr. Roe was not an "employer" for purposes of Title VII. Consequently, the court ruled that the pendent state-law claims were dismissed for lack of subject matter jurisdiction.

Doe contends that, even if her claim is construed as one for battery, it is not time barred by virtue of the savings statute, § 516.230 RSMo, which allows a party who suffers a nonsuit to refile the action within one year, thereby tolling the statute of limitations.[6] The savings statute applies where the cause of action and the parties defendant in the second suit are the same as those in the first suit. *Foster v. Pettijohn*, 213 S.W.2d 487, 490-1 (Mo. 1948). The parties apparently do not dispute that the present suit and the prior federal court action share similar causes of action; in this case, a claim for battery arising from Dr. Roe's intentional offensive contact with Doe. See, e.g., *State ex rel. Blackburn Motor Co. v. Litzinger*, 417 S.W.2d 126, 129 (Mo.App. 1967).

---

[5] No. 4:96-CV-735 (CEJ).

---

[6] The parties apparently do not dispute that the claims in the federal court action were filed within the applicable limitations period.

For purposes of the savings statute, a "nonsuit" occurs when a court order terminates a cause of action without prejudice. *Litton v. Rhudy,* 886 S.W.2d 191, 193 (Mo.App. W.D. 1994); *Webb v. Mayuga,* 838 S.W.2d 96, 98 (Mo.App. 1992). A dismissal for lack of subject matter jurisdiction is a dismissal without prejudice. *Stonebarger v. Emerson Elec. Co.,* 668 S.W.2d 187 (Mo.App. 1984). However, the effect of a dismissal for want of subject matter jurisdiction is to render any other actions taken by the dismissing court as null and void. *Zahn v. Associated Dry Goods Corp.,* 655 S.W.2d 769, 772 (Mo.App. E.D. 1983).

The savings statute has been liberally construed to include voluntary nonsuits or dismissals of pending cases. *Conrad v. McCall,* 226 S.W. 265, 266 (Mo.App. 1921). Whether the case was pending depends on whether the court was ever in a position to try the case. *Mertens v. McMahon,* 115 S.W.2d 180, 183 (Mo.App. 1938). The effect of a dismissal for lack of subject matter jurisdiction is as if suit had never been filed. *Id.* As stated in *Conrad,*

> . . . where the court has acquired no jurisdiction of the named defendant and is powerless to do anything, except perhaps to clear its docket of a pretended case not properly before the court, it can hardly be said that there is a pending case. . . . There was no case pending and consequently no nonsuit suffered.

226 S.W. at 266.

The District Court dismissed, for want of subject matter jurisdiction, all federal and pending state-law claims against Dr. Roe. Having concluded that subject matter jurisdiction was lacking, the court was never in a position to try the case against Dr. Roe on its merits, and any attempt to do so would have been null and void. Thus, there was nothing to be saved under the savings statute.

This Court concludes that Doe's claims, to the extent they are based on offensive touching, are now and always have been actionable as a battery (or, in case of threatened touching, as an assault). There is no need to cloak that which has always been actionable in voguish, late-twentieth-century terminology, nor does such a cloak suffice to evade the common sense bar of the statute of limitations. Because emotional distress arising from intentional touching is actionable as a battery, it is a claim governed by the two-year statute of limitations. In the context of this case, the Court further finds that the savings statute, § 516.230, does not apply to these battery claims. Doe's claims arising from allegations of intentional offensive touching, as contained in both counts of her Petition, are barred by the two-year statute of limitations for battery actions.

EMOTIONAL DISTRESS

Defendant Roe also contends that Doe fails to state claims for emotional distress, because the alleged conduct is not sufficiently extreme and outrageous as a matter of law. Doe counters that Roe's alleged acts are within the extreme conduct which may support a claim for emotional distress.

A motion to dismiss for failure to state a claim is solely a test of the adequacy of the plaintiff's petition. The Court assumes that all of plaintiff's averments are true, and liberally grants to plaintiff all reasonable inferences therefrom. *Murphy v. A. A. Mathews, a Division of CRS Group Engineers, Inc.,* 841 S.W.2d 671, 672 (Mo.banc 1992). No attempt is made to weigh any facts as to whether they are credible or persuasive. Instead, the petition is reviewed to see whether the facts alleged meet the elements of a recognized cause of action, or of a cause that might be adopted in that case. *Nazeri v. Missouri Valley College,* 860 S.W.2d 303, 306 (Mo.banc 1993).

The elements of intentional infliction of emotional distress are as follows: (1) defendant acted intentionally or recklessly; (2) defendant's conduct was extreme and outrageous; (3) the conduct caused severe emotional distress; and (4) the conduct was intended only to cause extreme emotional distress to the victim. *Gibson v. Brewer,* 952 S.W.2d 239, 249 (Mo.banc 1997); see also *Hyatt v. Trans World Airlines, Inc.,*

943 S.W.2d 292, 297 (Mo.App. E.D. 1997). The court initially determines, in the first instance, whether the alleged conduct is so extreme
and outrageous "as to go beyond all possible bounds of decency, and to
be regarded as atrocious, and utterly intolerable in a civilized community." *Id.,* citing Restatement (Second) of Torts § 46 (1965). A cause of
action for intentional infliction of emotional distress may be supported
by facts that allow an inference that the defendant's behavior "was not
just mean-spirited or boorish" but rather "reflected a calculated plan to
cause plaintiff emotional harm." *Polk v. INROADS/St. Louis, Inc.,*
951 S.W.2d 64, 68 (Mo.App. E.D. 1997); but see *Gibson v. Brewer,*
supra.[7]

Doe has alleged that Roe requested sexual acts of her and made
nuisance telephone calls, despite her protests.[8] She has also alleged that
she and Roe had had a physician-patient relationship since 1989 and
that he was her supervisor. These facts indicate that Doe was both a
subordinate and a patient of Dr. Roe and was to some degree under his
control personally and professionally.

The well-pleaded factual allegations do not allow the inference that
Dr. Roe's acts reflected a conscious, calculated plan to harm Doe emo-
tionally, or show an exclusive intent to inflict emotional harm. Indeed,
as pleaded, the facts alleged at most show that Defendant was seeking
to gratify his own sexual urges despite rejection by Plaintiff. Merely because his sexual advances were unwelcome to Plaintiff, it does not follow that they were exclusively intended to inflict emotional harm.
Although Professor Magruder, quoted at the outset, would undoubtedly

---

[7] The Court is doubtful that the reasoning of *Polk* and its assessment of what
constitute's outrageous behavior comport with the Supreme Court's views as
set forth in *Gibson;* nor does *Polk* address the requirement that the petition
reflect that the defendant's "sole purpose" was to invade the plaintiff's interest in freedom from emotional distress. *Gibson,* 249.

---

[8] As adumbrated above, the injurious conduct arising from battery is barred by
the statute of limitations and is not addressed as to the remainder of Doe's
claims for emotional distress.

be pilloried by modern academicians were he writing today that "there is no harm in asking," it seems clear that, except for the denizens of the cloud-cuckooland of radical feminism, no court has held that sexual advances are *ipso facto* actionable. More is required to establish a tort than a rejected advance. See, e.g., *Andrews v. City of Philadelphia*, 895 F.2d 1469 (3d Cir. 1990); *Paroline v. Unisys Corp.*, 879 F.2d 100 (4th Cir. 1989); *Jones v. Clinton*, supra.

As an employee of IW, Plaintiff had potential employment discrimination claims as a result of the alleged misconduct by her supervisor. She attempted to assert such claims, but they were largely rejected by the federal court. Plaintiff is now attempting to recast her claims so as to avoid both statutes of limitations and also the Missouri employment-at-will doctrine. See, e.g., *Johnson v. McDonnell Douglas Corp.*, 745 S.W.2d 661 (Mo.banc 1988); *Hanrahan v. Nashua Corp.*, 752 S.W.2d 878 (Mo.App.E.D. 1988). (Plaintiff may also be seeking to evade the jurisdictional bar of the Workers Compensation Act, as well. Cf. *Miller v. Lindenwood Female College*, 616 F.Supp. 860 [E.D.Mo. 1985].) If the clear policy of the law in these areas is not to be defenestrated, it follows that Plaintiff's petition must be subjected to more rigorous analysis than might otherwise be the case. Moreover, as once remarked by Prosser (a leading proponent of the tort of infliction of emotional distress as it evolved in an earlier era):

> The danger of imposition, of fictitious claims and vexatious suits in such cases, is evident, and serious. There must be some convincing evidence that the mental suffering is genuine and extreme. Liability of course cannot be extended to every trivial indignity. . . . The plaintiff must necessarily be expected and required to be hardened to a certain amount of rough language, and to acts that are definitely inconsiderate and unkind. . . . [Prosser, *Handbook* at 63].

A plaintiff seeking recovery from a fellow employee or supervisor for emotional distress in the employment context surely must plead sufficient facts to permit the inference that the defendant was doing more than creating a "hostile and oppressive work environment," which is actionable under employment discrimination statutes. The pleaded facts must show outrageous conduct, i.e., conduct which is regarded as atrocious and utterly intolerable in a civilized society. Mere solicitation to begin, or renew, a sexual relationship is not such conduct. There must be more. Consistent with the reported cases concerning the tort of infliction of emotional distress, the Plaintiff must plead (and eventually prove) conduct which was especially calculated to cause and did in fact cause mental damage of a very serious kind. Telephone calls at home may be sufficient if they are so numerous and intrusive as to evidence a calculated plan to inflict harm. Similarly, the invitations to intercourse could be presented with such frequency, and in circumstances in which the Defendant obviously knows that his request or solicitation will cause affront or alarm, cf. § 566.095, V.A.M.S., so that the conduct could be considered outrageous.[9] Plaintiff's pleading does not present sufficient facts to bring her claims within this realm. *Pretsky v. Southwestern Bell Tel. Co.*, 396 S.W.2d 566 (Mo. 1965).

Turning to Plaintiff's other theory, a claim for negligent infliction of emotional distress must allege that the defendant should have realized that his conduct involved an unreasonable risk of causing emotional distress, and that the resulting distress or mental injury is medically diagnosable and significant. *K.G.*, 918 S.W.2d at 800; *Bass v. Nooney Co.*, 646 S.W.2d 765 (Mo.banc 1983). Doe has pleaded the conclusion that she sustained medically diagnosable and significant distress or mental injury but has not pleaded any facts, which, if proved, would lead to this conclusion. Count II, purportedly alleging negligent infliction

---

[9] The Court assumes, without deciding, that a violation of the criminal law by indecent exposure, § 566.093, V.A.M.S., would be actionable, if sufficiently serious emotional injury was thereby inflicted, without a requirement of repetitive misbehavior. This Court suggests that Missouri law on this point would be more expansive than that of Arkansas. Compare *Jones v. Clinton*, supra, with *Beeman v. Safeway Stores, Inc.*, 724 F.Supp. 674 (W.D.Mo. 1989). Here, however, we are dealing with objective criminal conduct, not mere words.

of emotional distress, is therefore insufficient with respect to the element of injury.

More importantly, however, Plaintiff's theory in Count II is at war with the factual allegations (such as they are) underlying both Counts I and II. In other words, it beggars credulity to accept that Defendant's conduct could be "negligent." The Court recognizes that claims may be pleaded in the alternative and need not be consistent. Rule 55.10, Mo.R.Civ.P. To date, however, the reported Missouri cases concerning negligent infliction of emotional distress have arisen in the context of conduct involving another, independent error of commission or omission, which inflicts emotional injury. Thus, the seminal case of *Bass v. Nooney Co.*, supra, involved failure to maintain an elevator, which resulted in plaintiff being trapped. In the case at bar, the only conduct alleged involves no breach of any cognizable duty of care and can hardly be characterized as "negligent." Compare *Young v. Hockensmith*, 929 S.W.2d 840 (Mo.App.W.D. 1996) with *Young v. Stensrude*, 664 S.W.2d 263 (Mo.App.E.D. 1984). Plaintiff would seek to have the Court impose a duty of care on persons inviting others to engage in sexual relationships. Plaintiff's attempt to inveigle the Court into a realm which is best left to church and family is supported by neither reason nor authority. Absent outrageous intentional conduct, resulting in substantial, objective injury—or legislation imposing a standard representing the will of the people—the courts cannot and should not attempt to regulate behavior in this peculiarly private area.

* * *

For centuries, words alone, with few exceptions, have not been regarded by the courts as actionable. Although it is by now well established that conduct which inflicts demonstrable emotional harm may be actionable, the law must rest on objective principles, objectively applied. It is a curious phenomenon of modern law that the proponents of expansion of liability for "sexual harassment" seem to be resurrecting bygone notions of inequality of the sexes to impose different standards on men and women in the matter of intimate relationships. Even in the Title VII context, the courts have recognized that such standards as there are must be applied on the basis of what a reasonable person, not just a reasonable man or a reasonable woman, would deem offensive. *Harris v. Forklift Systems, Inc.,* supra. Moreover, the sexual harassment police seem oblivious to the First Amendment as they eagerly enlist the courts as censors of words and literature in the workplace.

It would be idle to maintain that Professor Magruder's dictum, quoted above, is a definitive or correct statement of the law. In some circumstances, it *can* hurt to ask. But those circumstances must be clearly defined and so egregious as to be abhorrent to reasonable people. Plaintiff's petition does not allege such circumstances. However, the opinion of the District Court concerning her Title VII claims suggests that Plaintiff may be able to allege sufficient facts to come within the standard recognized by *Gibson v. Brewer.* Accordingly, the Court will dismiss Count I with leave to amend.

ORDER

For the foregoing reasons, it is

ORDERED that Defendant's Motion to Dismiss is hereby granted, and Plaintiff's action is dismissed without prejudice as to claims of intentional infliction of emotional distress; all claims of intentional infliction of emotional distress on the basis of offensive touching and all claims of negligent infliction of emotional distress are dismissed with prejudice; Plaintiff is granted 15 days to file an amended petition restating Count I consistent with this opinion.

SO ORDERED:

Robert H. Dierker, Jr.
Presiding Judge

Dated:_____, 1998

COMMISSION ON RETIREMENT, REMOVAL AND DISCIPLINE

STATE OF MISSOURI

RICHARD F. ADAMS
CHAIRMAN
4600 MADISON, SUITE 600
KANSAS CITY, MO 64112

JOHN R. O'MALLEY
SECRETARY

VIVIAN L. EVELOFF

JAN M. MARCASON

WALTER D. McQUIE, JR.

JAMES K. PREWITT

JAMES M. SMITH
ADMINISTRATOR AND COUNSEL

2190 S. MASON ROAD, SUITE 201
ST. LOUIS, MO 63131

Telephone: (314) 966-1007
Facsimile: (314) 966-0076

E-mail: jsmith@osca.state.mo.us

November 30, 1998

Honorable Robert Dierker
████████████
St. Louis, Missouri 63105

Dear Judge Dierker:

Please be advised that the Commission on Retirement, Removal and Discipline has received a complaint against you concerning your order in the case Joan ████ v Jay ███████, Cause #982-00███. A copy of that order is enclosed.

The complaint alleges that the language used in the order indicates a preconceived bias against women, female lawyers or sexual harassment suits. The following specific passages are alleged to be indicative of a lack of impartiality:

"From Anita Hill to Monica Lewinsky , the cry of 'sexual harassment' has been selectively raised to advance certain groups' political agendas under the guise of promoting equal opportunity in the workplace, or under the banner of 'equality'." Page 1.

"… the theories of the 'sexual harassment' police have stretched their tentacles from college faculties to Supreme Court confirmation hearings to legal and judicial ethics, see Supreme Court Rule 2, Canon 3C, and now seek to ensnare the common law of torts." Page 2.

"The court concludes that the common law does not enact Cardinal Newman's definition of a gentleman, nor Catherine MacKinnon's vapid maunderings, …" Page 2.

"… it seems clear that, except for the denizens of the cloud-cuckoo-land of radical feminism, no court has held that sexual advances are *ipso facto* actionable." Page 11.

"Moreover, the sexual harassment police seem oblivious to the First Amendment as they eagerly enlist the courts as censors of words and literature in the workplace." Page 15.

The complaint suggests that these statements were extraneous to the ruling of the case and that: "The language of this order raises concerns as to the impartiality of Judge Dierker. We question whether this order is reflective of his courtroom deportment as well."

Pursuant to Supreme Court Rule 12, this is your opportunity to present whatever matters you may wish in way of explanation. The Commission would appreciate your response concerning these various allegations within 15 days.

Sincerely,

James M. Smith
Administrator and Counsel

TWENTY-SECOND JUDICIAL CIRCUIT OF MISSOURI

CIVIL COURTS BUILDING

ST. LOUIS, MISSOURI 63101-2044

ROBERT H. DIERKER, JR.
PRESIDING JUDGE

December 14, 1998

AREA CODE 314
622-4311
FAX
589-6599

Commission on Retirement, Removal & Discipline
c/o Hon. James M. Smith
2190 S. Mason Rd., Suite 201
St. Louis, MO 63131

      Re: Complaint

Dear Mr. Smith:

      This is a difficult letter to write, as this is the first time in my 12 years on the bench that I have received a letter of this sort from the Commission or any other source. I appreciate the opportunity to respond to the complaint.

      Your letter states that the complaint alleges that certain specific passages in my Order of October 5, 1998, in the case of Joan ▮▮▮ v. Jay ▮▮▮▮▮ are indicative of a preconceived bias and lack of impartiality. In effect, an attack on my judicial integrity is being made, and that is deeply disturbing to me. At the same time, there is no indication in your letter that the complaint contends that I have either willfully distorted established law to reach an unjust result, or in any way acted without regard to the record in the case.

      At the outset, I fully acknowledge that certain language in the opinion is too polemical and detracts from the analysis of the legal issues presented for my determination. During my term as Presiding Judge of the Twenty-Second Judicial Circuit, I have written more than 500 opinions. I acknowledge that the pressures of my responsibilities (including problems attendant to supervising the rehabilitation of the Courthouse without minimizing the full operation of the Court) may well have led me to dispense with appropriate editorial revisions.

      Likewise, in retrospect, I realize how some of the language undermined the central purpose of the opinion, which was to define meaningful standards in a difficult and evolving area of the law. Ironically, in context, I attempted to articulate a plea for objective principles objectively applied.

      In the final analysis, my opinion challenged ideas, not people, and reflected no unwillingness to follow the law. Rather, it indicated concern at the direction in which I fear the law may go. I do not believe that this can be deemed unethical conduct on my part.

Notwithstanding the lapses which I recognize, I respectfully submit that the complaint does not invoke any grounds that would justify your further consideration.

First, from the description in your letter, the complaint is founded on objections to commentary in the opinion, not on any contention that my ruling on the record in the ▇▇▇ case was due to bias or lack of impartiality. Your letter indicates also that the complaint raises the question as to whether such language is reflective of my courtroom deportment. Without hesitation, I can assure you that I have never conducted my Court in a manner that ever inferred a hint of bias of any nature. Perhaps the absence of any factual basis for the complaint's speculation is a sufficient recognition that the allegation is wholly groundless. However, my concern that it has even been made has led me to share your letter with the senior female member of the Court, Hon. ▇▇▇▇▇▇▇▇▇▇. Judge R▇▇▇ indicated to me that she intends to write to the Commission directly. Without knowing the exact content of her letter, I am confident that it will provide any necessary additional assurance to the Commission that the excessive commentary in the opinion was only an example of rhetorical hyperventilation and not indicative in any way of either unethical conduct or any preconceived bias against women.

Second, this is a pending case. As authorized by the operative language of my Order, an amended petition has been filed and the case remains on the active docket. When I became aware of the controversy in regard to the opinion, I wrote to the parties to advise them of my concern that they might be questioning my fairness, and offering them the opportunity to seek reconsideration before Judge C▇▇▇▇ (a departure from usual practice). Judge C▇▇▇▇▇ will be Presiding Judge as of January, 1999.

I have deep concern that further consideration of the complaint by the Commission would amount to a direct interference in a pending case. I feel certain that the Commission is acutely aware of the danger that the Commission process can have the effect of intimidating a sitting judge in a pending case. In such circumstances, further action by the Commission would inevitably affect any other Judge before whom the case might come.

Finally, I must allude to the serious constitutional implications of disciplining a judge for expressing views in a written opinion, on a matter of public interest and importance, especially in a developing area of the law. Nothing in the Code of Judicial Conduct was, in my judgment, intended to inhibit the right and duty of Judges to write freely on legal issues. This principle is at the core of judicial independence.

C.R.R.D.
December 14, 1998
Page 3

    I want to assure the Commission that the criticism leveled at the language in my opinion has not fallen on deaf ears. I can and will take measures to avoid overblown dicta in the future.

    Ms. ▓▓▓▓▓▓▓▓▓▓▓▓▓▓▓▓▓▓▓▓▓▓▓ St. Louis, Missouri 63105, has graciously agreed to represent me if there is any further need of response. Please include her on any future correspondence. Six (6) copies of this letter have been included for distribution to the Commission.

                        Sincerely,

                        Robert H. Dierker, Jr.

COMMISSION ON RETIREMENT, REMOVAL AND DISCIPLINE

RICHARD F. ADAMS
CHAIRMAN

4600 MADISON, SUITE 600
KANSAS CITY, MO 64112

JOHN R. O'MALLEY
SECRETARY

VIVIAN L. EVELOFF

JAN M. MARCASON

WALTER D. McQUIE, JR.

JAMES K. PREWITT

STATE OF MISSOURI

JAMES M. SMITH
ADMINISTRATOR AND COUNSEL

2190 S. MASON ROAD, SUITE 201
ST. LOUIS, MO 63131

Telephone: (314) 966-1007
Facsimile: (314) 966-0076

E-mail: jsmith@osca.state.mo.us

February 10, 1999

Honorable Robert Dierker
~~███████████~~
St. Louis, Missouri 63105

Dear Judge Dierker:

Please be advised that the Commission on Retirement, Removal and Discipline has completed its review of your response to my letter of November 30, 1998 regarding the case <u>Joan ███ v Jay</u> <u>██████</u>, Cause #982-0███. At the conclusion of its review, the Commission voted to dispose of this file informally by reminding you to avoid the use of language in your official duties that might give rise to an appearance of bias. The file on this matter is now closed.

Thank you for your cooperation in this investigation.

Sincerely,

James M. Smith
Administrator and Counsel

NOTES

CHAPTER 1

1. See George Neumayr, "Socializing Summers," *The American Spectator,* Jan. 18, 2005 (online posting); see also Harvey Mansfield, "The Debacle at Harvard," *Harvard Magazine,* May–June, 2006, p. 60.
2. See Kay Hymowitz, "The Meaning of Their Motherhood," *Wall Street Journal,* May 17, 2005, p. D10, reviewing *Promises I Can Keep.*
3. See Robert Bork, *Slouching Towards Gomorrah,* Ch. 11 (Regan Books, 1996).
4. *Meritor Sav. Bank v. Vinson,* 477 U.S. 57 (1986).
5. See *Harris v. Forklift Systems, Inc.,* 114 S.Ct. 367, 371–72 (1993) (Scalia, J., concurring).
6. See *Meritor Sav. Bank,* 477 U.S. 73. The EEOC of course jumped in and added regulations defining sexual harassment and outlining how employers can avoid liability. See 29 C.F.R. §§ 1604ff.
7. See *Burlington Industries, Inc. v. Ellerth,* 524 U.S. 742 (1998); *Faragher v. City of Boca Raton,* 524 U.S. 775 (1998); see also Barbara Schlei and Paul Grossman, *Employment Discrimination Law,* 150 (1989 Cum.Supp.) (discussing EEOC interpretation of the statute); *Martin v. Norbar, Inc.,* 537 F.Supp. 1260 (S.D.Ohio 1982).
8. Professor MacKinnon led the charge. See Catharine MacKinnon, *Sexual Harassment of Working Women* (Yale Univ. Press, 1979).
9. See, e.g., *Clark County School Dist. v. Breeden,* discussed below.
10. See Bork, *Slouching Towards Gomorrah* 222 (1996); BNA Labor Relations Reporter, weekly reports, such as Jan. 24, 2005; Merrick Rossein, *Employment Discrimination: Law & Litigation* § 5:32 (Clark Boardman, 2003).
11. *Harris v. Forklift Systems, Inc.,* 114 S.Ct. 367 (1993).
12. *Howley v. Town of Straford,* 217 F.3d 141 (2d Cir. 2000).
13. See William Prosser, *Handbook of the Law of Torts* 51, 57 (West, 1941).
14. See Chapter 10; Eugene Volokh, "Freedom of Speech and Workplace Harassment," 39 *UCLA L. Rev.* 1791 (1992).
15. 121 S.Ct. 1508 (2001).
16. A simple search on the Internet for "Gender and Justice" will produce many of these reports. Another convenient tool is the website of the National Center for State Courts, whose site for "gender fairness," www.ncsconline.org/WC/Education/GenFaiGuide.htm, visited June 27, 2006, presents a cornucopia of reports, papers, and other politically correct "gender and justice" nostrums, including access to many of the reports of "gender fairness"

commissions. My discussion relies primarily on the Missouri *Report of the Missouri Task Force on Gender and Justice* (June 1993). Remarkably, this monstrosity was produced when the Missouri Supreme Court was composed exclusively of judges appointed by John Ashcroft.

17. *Report of the Missouri Task Force on Gender and Justice* (1993), describing the Iowa proposal.

18. *Hazelwood Sch. Dist. v. United States*, 433 U.S. 299 (1977).

19. See also MacKinnon, "Reflections on Sex Equality Under Law," 100 *Yale L. J.* 1281, 1303–05 (1991). MacKinnon's work can best be described as sexual McCarthyism meets *Animal Farm.*

20. See Missouri Supreme Court Rule 2.

21. MacKinnon, "Reflections," 100 *Yale L. J.* 1290ff.

22. See Associated Press, "ACLU Report: U.S. Drug Laws Harm Women," *USA Today,* Mar. 17, 2005. An ACLU operative was quoted as "acknowledg[ing] that legislation addressing the situation would *probably* need to be gender-neutral." [Emphasis added.]

23. MacKinnon, "Reflections," 100 *Yale L. J.* 1290ff.; see also Ruth Bader Ginsburg and Barbara Flagg, "Some Reflections on Feminist Thought of the 1970s," 1989 *U. Chi. L. F.* 9.

24. *Bradwell v. Illinois*, 16 Wall. (83 U.S.) 130 (1873).

25. The plaintiff in the case, Myra Bradwell, simply left Illinois and got admitted to the Missouri bar.

26. 208 U.S. 412 (1908).

27. *Rostker v. Goldberg*, 453 U.S. 57 (1981).

28. *Kahn v. Shevin*, 416 U.S. 351 (1974).

29. *Califano v. Webster*, 430 U.S. 313 (1977).

30. See, e.g., Jessica Gavora, *Tilting the Playing Field: School, Sports, Sex and Title IX* (Encounter Books, 2002).

31. *Geduldig v. Aiello*, 417 U.S. 484 (1974).

32. *United States v. Virginia*, 518 U.S. 515 (1996).

33. *Mississippi University for Women v. Hogan*, 458 U.S. 718 (1982).

34. *Craig v. Boren*, 429 U.S. 190 (1976).

35. *J.E.B. v. Alabama ex rel. T.B.*, 511 U.S. 127 (1994).

36. See, e.g., *United States v. Virginia* (Scalia, J., dissenting).

37. *J.E.B.*, above note 35 (Scalia, J., dissenting).

38. *Goesaert v. Cleary*, 335 U.S. 464 (1948).

39. *United States v. Virginia* (Scalia, J., dissenting).

CHAPTER 2

1. *The Federalist No. 78* (Cooke ed. 1961). *The Federalist* was a series of newspaper articles published by James Madison, Alexander Hamilton, and John Jay in support of the ratification of the Constitution in 1787–88. There

are several editions. The one I rely on is the 1961 edition, edited by Jacob Cooke.

2. See Gordon Wood, *The Creation of the American Republic,* Part III, esp. Ch. 11 (Univ. of North Carolina Press, 1969). I had occasion to research the origins of judicial review while studying for my LL.M. Insofar as a humble LL.M. student could do, my research confirmed that judicial review was accepted during the Revolutionary era as necessarily implied by the establishment of a Constitution itself. The Anti-Federalists attacked the idea, but only because they realized that the power had to exist.

3. *The Federalist,* no. 78 (Cooke ed. 1961).

4. *Marbury v. Madison,* 1 Cranch (5 U.S.) 137 (1803).

5. For a sample of the debates surrounding the adoption of the Fourteenth Amendment, see 7 *Great Debates in American History,* Ch. XII, "The Fourteenth Amendment" (Miller ed. 1913); see also Charles Fairman, "Does the Fourteenth Amendment Incorporate the Bill of Rights? The Original Understanding," 2 *Stan. L. Rev.* 5 (1949).

6. 109 U.S. 3 (1883).

7. The transformation of the equal protection clause during the post–New Deal reign of liberals has been recognized by the major constitutional law casebooks. Indeed, equal protection has been described as "old" and "new" to account for the change. See Gerald Gunther and Noel Dowling, *Cases and Materials on Constitutional Law,* Ch. 14 (8th ed. Foundation Press, 1970); in the later edition, Kathleen Sullivan and Gerald Gunther, *Constitutional Law* (Foundation Press, 2004), the "new" equal protection is presented rather less emphatically, for reasons that are not readily apparent.

8. *Johnson v. California,* 125 S.Ct. 1141, 1152–53 (2005) (Ginsburg, J., concurring).

9. *Lawrence v. Texas,* 539 U.S. 558 (2003), in which Justice O'Connor insisted that moral disapproval of homosexual sodomy was the same as disapproval of homosexuals as a group and so was irrational, because it made homosexuals "unequal" to heterosexuals in the matter of deviate sexual intercourse. If that makes no sense, don't blame me.

10. Willard Hurst, *The Growth of American Law: The Law Makers* 31–33 (Little, Brown, 1950).

11. It is all but forgotten that Cardozo concurred in the first decision, striking down a New Deal legislative measure, *Schechter Poultry Corp. v. United States,* 295 U.S. 495 (1935), calling the statute "delegation run riot." 295 U.S. at 553 (Cardozo, J., concurring).

12. *Palko v. Connecticut,* 302 U.S. 319 (1937).

13. Justice Felix Frankfurter forcefully restated Cardozo's "fundamental rights" and "absorption" concepts against the determined attack of Justice Hugo Black, who advocated incorporation of the Bill of Rights in the due process clause of the Fourteenth Amendment. See *Adamson v. California,* 332 U.S. 46 (1947) (Frankfurter, J., concurring; Black, J., dissenting).

14. See the competing opinions on the issue of "substantive" due process in *Michael H. v. Gerald D.*, 491 U.S. 110 (1989), featuring a debate between Justices Scalia and Brennan.

15. *Washington v. Glucksberg*, 521 U.S. 792 (1997); *Vacco v. Quill*, 521 U.S. 793 (1997). Superficially, the Court was unanimous in rejecting the constitutional "right" to assisted suicide, but Justice O'Connor and the four liberals filed opinions clearly intended to hold out the possibility that such a "right" could be found under other circumstances.

16. See Chapter 4.

17. *Cantwell v. Connecticut*, 310 U.S. 296 (1940).

18. E.g., *Shapiro v. Thompson*, 394 U.S. 618 (1969).

19. *United States v. Virginia*, 518 U.S. 515 (1996).

20. *Lawrence v. Texas*, 539 U.S. 558, 123 S.Ct. 2472, 2484 (2003) (O'Connor, J., concurring); see also *Goodridge v. Dept. of Pub. Health*, 798 N.E.2d 941 (Mass. 2003).

21. *Plyler v. Doe*, 457 U.S. 202 (1982); *Graham v. Richardson*, 503 U.S. 365 (1971).

22. *Cleburne v. Cleburne Living Center*, 473 U.S. 432 (1985).

23. See Chapter 3.

24. *Tennessee v. Lane*, 124 S.Ct. 1978 (2004).

25. Some of the more outré demands of the liberals have been turned aside, to be sure, such as a "right" to assisted suicide, a "right" to public funding of abortions, and a "right" to some federal standard of public education. But often these idiotic ideas were rejected by but a single vote on the Supreme Court. Almost always, the liberal idea commanded at least three votes on the Court. See *San Antonio Ind. Sch. Dist. v. Rodriguez*, 411 U.S. 1 (1973). Note the dissent of Justice Marshall, demanding a sliding-scale equal protection depending on the Court's assessment of the importance of the interests at stake.

26. See Theodore Plucknett, *A Concise History of the Common Law*, Book 2, Part 5 (Little, Brown, 1956).

27. One can search the books fruitlessly for instances of injunctive relief against the government in the eighteenth or early nineteenth centuries.

28. *In re Debs*, 158 U.S. 564 (1895).

29. *Mississippi v. Johnson*, 4 Wall. (71 U.S.) 2 (1867). This is one of many forgotten cases recognizing limits on judicial power.

30. *Ex parte Young*, 209 U.S. 123 (1908).

31. These established principles are expressed in *Marbury v. Madison* itself, as witness Chief Justice John Marshall's extensive discussion of the role of the writ of mandamus. 1 Cranch (5 U.S.) 137 (1803).

32. See *Cooper v. Aaron*, 358 U.S. 1 (1958).

33. 473 U.S. 432 (1985).

34. Here Marshall cites good ol' Oliver Wendell Holmes, who also wrote, "three generations of imbeciles is enough."

35. See Chapters 5 and 7.

36. This is a matter of individual rights, not "states' rights" as some would have us believe. States don't have rights. Under our constitutional scheme, as the Ninth and Tenth Amendments make clear, only individuals have rights. Government has powers, and those powers are supposedly limited. The federal government in particular was intended to be a limited government, with specified powers. All other powers were reserved to the states or the people, and the enumeration of certain rights was not intended to abrogate other rights retained by the people, as against the federal government. Liberals have, for the most part, turned the federal government, and especially the federal judiciary, into an unlimited government. This was and is necessary to enable liberals to impose their tyranny of tolerance on the people. That what the radical liberals are doing is wrong has nothing to do with the rights of states.

CHAPTER 3

1. Writing in the *Wall Street Journal,* University of Pennsylvania law professor Amy Wax and Berkeley business professor Philip E. Tetlock rightly noted that to liberals, "anything short of straight group representation—equal outcomes rather than equal opportunity—is 'proof' that the process is unfair." This is what happens when you assume everyone is biased, consciously or unconsciously. See Wax and Tetlock, "We Are All Racists at Heart," *Wall Street Journal,* Dec. 1, 2005, p. A16.
2. *Griggs v. Duke Power Co.,* 401 U.S. 424 (1971).
3. For detailed discussion of the concept of guilt by the numbers, see Paul Grossman, *Statistical Proof of Discrimination,* various editions; see also Thomas Sowell, *The Vision of the Anointed,* Ch. 3 (Basic Books, 1995).
4. See Sowell, *The Vision of the Anointed.* In several examples, he demonstrates that, when all variables are controlled, there is seldom adverse impact in objective employment selection procedures. Also, it should be noted that until race discrimination litigation came along, the law generally disdained the use of statistics to prove someone's state of mind or to prove that someone committed an illegal act. Indeed, the Supreme Court continues to hold that statistics alone seldom prove intentional discrimination. *Washington v. Davis,* 426 U.S. 229 (1976).
5. See, e.g., Schlei and Grossman, *Employment Discrimination Law,* Ch. 4 (1989 Supp.), discussing the EEOC's Uniform Guidelines in force during the late 1970s and early 1980s.
6. Title VII, CRA of 1964, § 703(h).
7. Among the St. Louis officials who decided to fight the case was the director of public safety, Alfonso Jackson, who would later become secretary of housing and urban development under George W. Bush.
8. *Firefighters Institute v. City of St. Louis,* 616 F.2d 350 (8th Cir. 1980), cert. denied sub nom. *City of St. Louis v. United States,* 452 U.S. 938 (1981)

(another case in which I represented the losing side!). The Supreme Court took nearly a year to act on the petition for certiorari, causing a certain amount of angst in the Justice Department.

9. *Cooper v. Aaron*, 358 U.S. 1 (1958).

10. *Plessy v. Ferguson*, 163 U.S. 537 (1896).

11. 416 U.S. 312 (1974).

12. It wasn't long before the Supreme Court approved racial gerrymandering in order to increase the election of black politicians. *United Jewish Organizations v. Carey*, 430 U.S. 144 (1977), featuring Justice William Brennan's paean to the "remedial use of race." This racial gerrymander is with us to this day. See *Shaw v. Hunt*, 517 U.S. 899 (1996), appeal after remand, *Hunt v. Cromartie*, 526 U.S. 541 (1999), *Easley v. Cromartie*, 532 U.S. 234 (2001). Note particularly the dissenting opinions of Justices Stevens and Souter in the first case, insisting that it is perfectly okay to draw legislative districts to discriminate against white voters. The *Shaw* case illustrates the uphill battle imposed on white plaintiffs who claim illegal discrimination in voting districts. In the end, the liberals, aided by the swinging Justice O'Connor, simply rewrote the facts and found that politics, not race, produced the districts at issue. In an example of the law of unintended consequences, however, the political ghettoization of black voters has demonstrably damaged the ability of the Democratic Party to retain control of the U.S. House of Representatives and many statehouses. Once elected, like all politicians regardless of race, black politicians want to stay in office forever. Since this is made difficult by the annoying decennial census, an alliance between black politicians (nearly all Democrats) and the Republican Party has ensured that black voters remain concentrated, so heavily concentrated that their influence is in fact diminished, rather than enhanced.

13. 438 U.S. 265 (1978).

14. See, e.g., *Franks v. Bowman Trans. Co.*, 424 U.S. 747 (1976).

15. *Fullilove v. Klutznick*, 448 U.S. 448 (1980).

16. 448 U.S. at 522–23 (Stewart, J., dissenting).

17. *Coalition for Sensible and Humane Solutions v. Wamser*, 771 F.2d 395 (8th Cir. 1985) (this time I won!).

18. Lani Guinier, "[E]racing Democracy: The Voting Rights Cases," 108 *Harv. L. Rev.* 109 (1994).

19. Our friends the ACLU are particularly good at fomenting distrust and antagonism toward the police. A particularly outrageous example is noted in a story in St. Louis about efforts to beef up neighborhood police patrols. Instead of encouraging community cooperation with and respect for the police, the ACLU sent out operatives to teach the community how to report police abuse, refuse to assist the police, and to sue them. See Mitch Schneider, "ACLU Program to Monitor Police-Community Relations," *The West End Word*, Aug. 3–9, 2005, p. 1.

20. See *Atonio v. Wards Cove Packing Co.*, 490 U.S. 642 (1989).

21. *Firefighters Local 1784 v. Stotts*, 467 U.S. 561 (1984) (hiring quotas);

Wygant v. Jackson Board of Education, 476 U.S. 267 (1986) (racial preferences in teacher layoffs); *Richmond v. J.A. Croson Co.,* 488 U.S. 469 (1989) (set-asides); *Adarand Constructors, Inc. v. Pena,* 515 U.S. 200 (1995) (set-asides).

22. *Hopwood v. Texas,* 236 F.3d 25 (5th Cir. 2000), striking down racial preferences at the University of Texas.

23. 123 S.Ct. 2411 (2003).

24. 123 S.Ct. 2325 (2003).

25. *Gratz,* 123 S.Ct. at 2434 (Breyer, J., concurring).

26. *Grutter,* 123 S.Ct. at 2338–41.

27. See the chart set out by Chief Justice Rehnquist in *Grutter,* 123 S.Ct. at 2368–69.

28. *Grutter,* 123 S.Ct. at 2346–47.

29. *Grutter,* 123 S.Ct. at 2347–48 (Ginsburg, J., concurring).

30. Another round in this struggle will be fought during the next Supreme Court term in October 2006. The Court has granted review of two cases in which public school students are assigned to schools on the basis of race, in one case in defiance of a voter initiative forbidding such racial preferences. *Parents Involved in Community Schools v. Seattle School Dist. No. 1,* 126 S.Ct. 2351 (2006) (granting certiorari); *Meredith v. Jefferson County Bd. of Education,* 126 S.Ct. 2351 (2006) (granting certiorari). With Justice Sandra Day O'Connor gone, Justice Anthony Kennedy will be the decisive vote. He sided with the white kids in the Michigan cases, but his "moderate" credentials are now at stake.

31. *Loving v. Virginia,* 388 U.S. 1 (1967).

CHAPTER 4

1. The author learned of the episode from conversations with persons present at a small neighborhood gathering.

2. Theodore Plucknett, *A Concise History of the Common Law* 712 (Little, Brown, 1956).

3. See 2 Frederick Pollock and Frederic Maitland, *The History of English Law* Ch. VII (Milsom ed. 1968). In recent years, the Supreme Court has held that parental control of children could not be superseded by the state in the name of rights of grandparents. Of course, the leading liberals were *in dissent* in that case. For example, Justice John Paul Stevens, liberal extraordinaire, said that the rights of parents could be subordinated to what a court determines to be the best interests of the child. See *Troxel v. Granville,* 530 U.S. 57 (2000).

4. See Kathleen Sullivan and Gerald Gunther, *Constitutional Law* 815 (2004).

5. 391 U.S. 68 (1968).

6. *Levy,* 391 U.S. 72.

7. See, e.g., *Lalli v. Lalli,* 439 U.S. 259 (1978) (Brennan, J., dissenting);

Mathews v. Lucas, 427 U.S. 495 (1976); *Labine v. Vincent,* 401 U.S. 532 (1971) (Brennan, J., dissenting).

8. 4 *Bl. Comm.* *198. A "misprision," mentioned by Blackstone, is a misdemeanor—a less serious crime, but still a crime. Sometimes a distinction was made as to whether the child had "quickened," but Blackstone mentions no such requirement, and the fact remains that the common law regarded abortion as a crime at some point in the pregnancy and recognized no right to abort.

9. See *Roe v. Wade,* 410 U.S. 170, 175 (1973) (Rehnquist, J., dissenting).

10. 410 U.S. 113 (1973).

11. *Akron v. Akron Center for Reproductive Health,* 462 U.S. 416 (1983).

12. *Stenberg v. Carhart,* 530 U.S. 914 (2000).

13. Ibid.

14. *Stenberg,* 120 S.Ct. at 2621 (Scalia, J., dissenting).

15. See the trial transcript in *State of Missouri v. Reproductive Health Services,* 22nd Cir. No. 004-0008, aff'd in part and rev'd in part, 97 S.W.3d 54 (Mo.App.E.D. 2002).

16. *Gonzalez v. Carhart,* 126 S.Ct. 1314 (2006), granting certiorari. The statute is the Partial-Birth Abortion Ban Act of 2003, and the congressional findings are set out in § 2 of the Act. See 18 U.S.C. § 1531; 117 Stat. 1201.

17. 19 How. (60 U.S.) 393 (1856). The *Dred Scott* case is itself a study in judicial activism. A careful reading of the dissenting opinions and the opinions of the Missouri state courts reveals that Taney's holding was an innovation in the law, which had long held that a slave taken into free territory ceased to be a slave. In deciding the case as he did, Chief Justice Taney did the same thing that the Supreme Court has done in the abortion cases: He presumed to the ultimate authority to settle a question of social policy that the Constitution had left in the hands of the democratic process.

18. 163 U.S. 537 (1896).

19. See generally 4 *C. J. S.,* "Infants," § 3, discussing current law.

20. See, e.g., 38 *C. J.,* "Marriage," § 1 (1925). Yes, I know that among lawyers a citation to "C.J." or *Corpus Juris,* a sort of *Reader's Digest* of the law, is not the ultimate authority; but when it's in *Corpus Juris* it often means that almost every court in the country is in agreement on the point.

21. The radical feminist MacKinnon has described the unborn child as a parasite. See MacKinnon, "Reflections on Sex Equality Under Law," 100 *Yale L. J.* 1281, 1314 (1991).

22. Grudgingly, the Supreme Court has accepted some parental notification, but parental *consent* cannot be required. *Hodgson v. Minnesota,* 497 U.S. 417 (1990); *Bellotti v. Baird (II),* 443 U.S. 622 (1979). The issue was again before the Supreme Court in *Ayotte v. Planned Parenthood of No. New England,* 126 S.Ct. 961 (2006), without any conclusive result.

23. Ironically, the same Supreme Court that said fatherhood is not entitled to legal protection in the married state has insisted that the rights of fathers must be recognized *after* a child is born. Of course, when the Court took up the lat-

ter issue, the justices were talking about *unmarried* fathers. See *Stanley v. Illinois*, 405 U.S. 645 (1972).

24. *Meyer v. Nebraska*, 262 U.S. 390 (1923); *Pierce v. Society of Sisters*, 268 U.S. 510 (1925).

25. *Loving v. Virginia*, 388 U.S. 1 (1967). The idea of marriage as a "fundamental" right is fully in keeping with Justice Benjamin Cardozo's analysis of substantive due process, which emphasized history and tradition. See Chapter 2.

26. *Griswold v. Connecticut*, 381 U.S. 479 (1965); *Carey v. Population Services International*, 431 U.S. 678 (1977).

27. *Casey*, 505 U.S. at 840.

28. See, e.g., Richard Helmholtz, *Marriage Litigation in Medieval England* (Cambridge Univ. Press, 1974), illustrating the vast body of law of marriage that coexisted with the developing common law, and demonstrating the existence of the legal relationship without intervention of legislation.

29. 4 *Bl. Comm.* *208–*215; see also William Clark, *Handbook of Criminal Law* 125–127 (West, 1915); *Rose v. Locke*, 423 U.S. 48 (1975). Note that Blackstone also mentioned intercourse with man "or beast." Bestiality was therefore classified together with homosexual sodomy.

30. *Bowers v. Hardwick*, 478 U.S. 186 (1986).

31. *Romer*, 116 S.Ct. at 1629.

32. 539 U.S. 558, 123 S.Ct. 2472 (2003).

33. *Baehr v. Levin*, 852 P.2d 44 (Hawaii 1993).

34. *Goodridge v. Dept. of Public Health*, 798 N.E.2d 941 (Mass. 2002); *Baker v. State*, 744 A.2d 864 (Vt. 1999).

35. *Li v. State of Oregon*, 110 P.3d 91 (Ore. 2005).

36. See *Wilson v. Ake*, 1 A.L.R.Fed.2d 611 (M.D.Fla. 2005). For the "enlightened" legal elite's view of the Defense of Marriage Act, see Note, "Litigating the Defense of Marriage Act," 117 *Harv. L. Rev.* 2684 (2004).

37. Compare *Citizens for Equal Protection v. Bruning*, 290 F.Supp.2d 1004 (D.Neb. 2003); Annot., 1 A.L.R.Fed.2d 1 (2005) with *Hernandez v. Robles*, No. 86, New York Court of Appeals, July 6, 2006, and *Perdue v. O'Kelley*, No. SO6A1574, Georgia Supreme Court, July 6, 2006. There can be no doubt that only a federal constitutional amendment can prevent further judicial erosion of traditional marriage.

38. See, e.g., Boot, "A Different Kind of Whistleblower," *Wall Street Journal*, Apr. 27, 2004; "Protests About Gay Tolerance Prompt Firings," *Wall Street Journal*, Oct. 30, 2002, p. B1.

39. *Robinson v. California*, 370 U.S. 660 (1962); but see *State v. Kantner*, 493 P.2d 306 (Hawaii 1972), another Hawaii case, discussing "privacy" and drugs, which I noted in 41 *UMKC L.Rev.* 133 (1973).

40. *Stanley v. Georgia*, 394 U.S. 557 (1969).

41. See Justice Thurgood Marshall's dissent in *United States v. Reidel*, 402 U.S. 351 (1971).

42. *Osborne v. Ohio*, 495 U.S. 103 (1990).

43. *Lawrence*, 123 S.Ct. at 2484. By the way, has anyone noticed that the conduct in *Lawrence* was not really private? The defendants engaged in their deviate intercourse in the presence of police officers and were arrested only after refusing to stop.

CHAPTER 5

1. Sadly, even otherwise solid, conservative judges felt obliged to employ the usurped power to tax. This illustrates how much respect conservative judges display to precedent, even illegitimate precedent. See *Kroll v. St. Charles County*, No. 88-1875-C-5, order of June 4, 1991 (Limbaugh, J.), ordering a tax increase for a new courthouse if the voters rejected a sales tax, even though the voters had previously rejected a tax increase by a two-to-one majority. The voters caved in.

2. 731 F.2d 1294 (8th Cir.) *(en banc)*, cert. denied, 469 U.S. 816 (1984).

3. Two of the leading lawyers for the St. Louis school board were David Tatel and Allen Snyder, of the powerful Washington, D.C., law firm of Hogan & Hartson. Both Tatel and Snyder were nominated for seats on the U.S. Court of Appeals for the District of Columbia Circuit, by Bill Clinton of course. Tatel (unquestionably a very able lawyer) was confirmed, but Snyder fortunately failed confirmation. I would anticipate that Tatel would be a favorite for the Supreme Court if we get another Clinton administration, as his blindness would appeal to politicians with quota mentalities—although I daresay that he would be the last to seek favored treatment on that basis.

4. *Liddell v. Bd. of Education*, 620 F.2d 1277 (8th Cir.) *(en banc)*, cert. denied, 449 U.S. 826 (1980).

5. The record in the district court in the *Liddell* case is replete with motions and requests by the St. Louis Board of Education for further court intervention in the operation of the school district, as long as all costs were borne by the state or the taxpayers. See various pleadings in *Liddell v. Bd. of Education*, No. 72-100C(4), Eastern District of Missouri; see also the summary of the school board's position in *Liddell v. Bd. of Education*, 677 F.2d 626 (8th Cir. 1982).

6. *Milliken v. Bradley*, 418 U.S. 717 (1974).

7. See outline of the history of this stage of the case in *Liddell v. Bd. of Education*, 677 F.2d 626 (8th Cir. 1982).

8. *Liddell v. Bd. of Education*, 567 F.Supp. 1037 (E.D.Mo. 1983) (describing settlement terms; the full settlement agreement was entered into evidence and included in the appendices to the various petitions for certiorari following the Court of Appeals decision).

9. In perhaps the most disheartening episode at the oral argument of the case, Charles Cooper, deputy attorney general of the United States, who purported to be a conservative, told the federal court of appeals that the federal courts *did* have the power to tax. Afterward, I told him that I could not believe that

President Reagan had any idea that he would say such a thing. His only response was to stammer uncomfortably about a Virginia case. This is but another example of the ways in which indoctrination by liberal law schools has unexpectedly pernicious effects on lawyers in the public sector.

10. I was personally acquainted with Judge Heaney's practice, as some of the requests for information were directed to me. This occurred in at least two cases in which I was involved as attorney for the City of St. Louis.

11. See *National Taxpayers Union's Dollars & Sense*, May/June, 1990; Kennedy, J., dissenting, in *Missouri v. Jenkins*, 495 U.S. 33 (1990).

12. The measures of King Clark are outlined in the opinion of the federal Court of Appeals, *Jenkins v. State of Missouri*, 855 F.2d 1295, 1301 (8th Cir. 1988).

13. 495 U.S. 33 (1990).

14. I cannot recall Justice White without also recalling the chant directed against John Jay, when he was thought to have sold out America at the time of the Jay Treaty: Damn Whizzer White, damn all those who won't damn Whizzer White, damn all those who won't stay up all night damning Whizzer White. In *Jenkins*, White was joined enthusiastically by the liberal brigade of William Brennan, Thurgood Marshall, John Paul Stevens, and Harry Blackmun.

15. Contrast this attitude with the steadfastly antireligion attitude in the case of *Locke v. Davey*, 124 S.Ct. 1307 (2004), when the Court forbade the state to fund scholarships for students seeking religious study, even though all other students were eligible.

16. As prophesied in the *Wall Street Journal* editorial "Judge George III," Apr. 23, 1990. The *Journal* also astutely observed that "accepting an invitation to order tax increases risks the nobility of the law and ultimately the independence of the judiciary." Less astutely and less presciently, the *Journal* thought that "any [George H. W.] Bush Justice is likely to be the swing vote back on the next test case." David Souter?

17. The NAACP lawyer crowed about the Supreme Court's usurpation in *Missouri v. Jenkins*, "it reinforces the broad discretion that federal courts have to right wrongs." Cocounsel Allen Snyder, failed Clinton judicial nominee, joined the celebratory remarks. See Stephen Wermiel, "High Court Backs U.S. Judge's Authority to Order Funds for School Desegregation," *Wall Street Journal*, Apr. 19, 1990, p. A16. Apparently to Brother Snyder and his liberal allies, stripping away our right to vote on taxes and spending is never wrong, as long as it's done to achieve liberal ends.

18. The evidence in the *Liddell* case, with which I am familiar, showed that, during the desegregation litigation at least, per pupil expenditure in the St. Louis school district was one of the highest in the state of Missouri. See *Leggett v. Liddell*, No. 83-1386, U.S. Supreme Court, Appendix to Petition for Writ of Certiorari.

19. See *Angle v. Legislature of Nevada*, 274 F.Supp.2d 1152 (D.Nev. 2003), denying federal relief to taxpayers and legislators who were attacking the

decision of the Nevada Supreme Court, "declaring the Nevada Legislature to be in violation of the Nevada Constitution and compelling the Legislature to fulfill its constitutional duty to increase revenues to balance Nevada's budget for the biennium beginning July 1, 2003, and to fund public education during that fiscal period."

20. *Montoy v. State*, 102 P.2d 1160 (Kan. 2005), appeal after remand, 112 P.2d 923 (Kan. 2005).

21. *DeRolph v. State*, 728 N.E.2d 993 (Ohio 2000).

CHAPTER 6

1. See Henry Campbell Black, *Handbook of American Constitutional Law* 530 (West, 1927).

2. See *United States v. Miller*, 307 U.S. 174, 179 (1939).

3. Columbia University Board of Trustees, press release of December 13, 2002.

4. 394 U.S. 557 (1969).

5. The term "Blackmunization" describes the transformation of a moderately conservative judge into a flaming liberal. Justice Harry Blackmun morphed from an honest disciple of judicial restraint (as witness his opinion in the death penalty case *Furman v. Georgia*) to a liberal extraordinaire (as witness his later renunciation of "tinkering with the mechanics of death" and his glorification of abortion). The causes of Blackmunization are difficult to discern. It never operates in reverse—that is, liberal jurists never see error in their ways. One cause is doubtless the adulation the liberal media and academe heap upon judges who "grow." Another is likely the concentrated exposure to the Beltway, with very limited contact with the real world outside of Washington politics. Another is the very human impulse to "do right," heedless of any thoughts that perhaps we should be operating under a *limited* government. The impulse to "do right" can be especially strong in a small group of people who have no practical limits on their power, or who think they don't. Only judges of exceptional intellectual tenacity and self-control, like Justice Clarence Thomas, seem capable of resisting Blackmunization.

6. The "incorporation doctrine" is discussed in all standard constitutional law texts and casebooks. It is briefly summarized in Brannon Denning, "Gun Shy: The Second Amendment as an 'Underenforced Constitutional Norm,'" 21 *Harv. J. L. & Pub. Pol.* 719, 752ff. (1998), insofar as the Second Amendment has been ignored by this facet of liberal jurisprudence.

7. This is a shorthand description of two of the principal strands of liberal jurisprudence over the past eighty years. The "fundamental right" concept, enunciated by Justice Benjamin Cardozo in *Palko v. Connecticut*, 302 U.S. 319 (1937), makes some sense, as it ties construction of the Due Process Clause to history and tradition. The fair trial idea surely is implicit in the guaranty of due process, but the "incorporation doctrine" (sometimes also characterized as the "absorption doctrine") holds that selected provisions of the Bill of

Rights are per se elements of a fair trial, even though Cardozo rejected that idea. In Cardozo's scheme, specific procedural portions of the Bill of Rights (e.g., double jeopardy) were not fundamental to ordered liberty, because a free society could operate without them; a trial could be "fair" even if it was the second trial for the same offense following an appeal by the government claiming error in the first trial. Cardozo flatly denied that "due process" was simply a shorthand way of saying "the Bill of Rights."

8. *Quilici v. Morton Grove,* 695 F.2d 261 (7th Cir. 1981).

9. 695 F.2d at 271–72.

10. See Denning, "Gun Shy," 21 *Harv. J. L. & Pub. Pol.* 783, discussing legislative protection of the right of freed blacks to bear arms after the Civil War.

11. 518 U.S. 515 (1996).

12. See David Kopel, "The U.N. Wants Your Gun," *Wall Street Journal,* July 8–9, 2006, p. A11.

13. Protection of Lawful Commerce in Arms Act, § 2(a), S.397, H.R.800, 109th Congress, 15 U.S.C. § 7901 et seq.

14. 384 U.S. 641 (1966).

15. *City of Boerne v. Flores,* 117 S.Ct. 2157 (1997).

16. Protection of Lawful Commerce in Arms Act, § 2(b).

17. *In re Joint Eastern & Southern Dist. Asbestos Litigation,* 14 F.3d 726 (2d Cir. 1993).

18. See *City of New York v. Beretta U.S.A. Corp.,* 401 F.Supp.2d 244 (E.D.N.Y. 2005).

19. *City of New York v. Beretta U.S.A. Corp.,* 413 F.Supp.2d 180 (E.D.N.Y. 2006).

20. P.L. 109–108, quoted at 413 F. Supp.2d 181.

21. See Denning, "Gun Shy," 21 *Harv. J. L. & Pub. Pol.* 726–32, noting that most legal scholars recognize that the Second Amendment protects an individual right, but that many refuse to accept the logical consequences of the meaning of the amendment.

22. See "Minutemen Are People, Too," *Wall Street Journal,* May 19, 2005, p. A15.

CHAPTER 7

1. *State v. Taylor,* 929 S.W.2d 209 (Mo.banc 1996), federal habeas denied, 329 F.3d 963 (8th Cir. 2003); *State v. Nunley,* 923 S.W.2d 911 (Mo.banc 1996). The description of the facts of the case is drawn from my own opinion in the case, filed in 1992, cited in the federal opinion.

2. 481 U.S. 279 (1987). By the way, this case marked McCleskey's second trip to the Supreme Court over a litigation life of some twenty years.

3. The cynical manner in which statistics can be manipulated to "prove" discrimination is brilliantly exposed by Thomas Sowell in his telling criticism of modern liberals, *The Vision of the Anointed,* Ch. 3 (Basic Books, 1995).

4. See, e.g., James Eaton, *Handbook of Equity Jurisprudence* 24–25 (West, 1923).

5. *Nelson v. Campbell,* 541 U.S. 637 (2004).

6. 126 S.Ct. 2096 (2006).

7. *Taylor v. Crawford,* 2006 WL 1779035 (W.D. Mo. 2006), remanded, 2006 WL 2291150 (8th Cir. 2006).

8. *Trop v. Dulles,* 356 U.S. 86 (1958), quoted at the beginning of the chapter.

9. 408 U.S. 238 (1972).

10. 408 U.S. 364 (Marshall, J., concurring).

11. See Lawrence Friedman, *A History of American Law* (Simon & Schuster, 1973).

12. *Coker v. Georgia,* 433 U.S. 584 (1977).

13. *Gregg v. Georgia,* 428 U.S. 153 (1976).

14. See Alex Kozinski and Sean Gallagher, "Death: The Ultimate Run-on Sentence," 46 *Case W. Res. L. Rev.* 1 (1995); see also Bureau of Justice Statistics, Department of Justice, www.ojp.usdoj.gov/bjs/; James Liebman, Jeffrey Fagan, Andrew Gelman, Valerie West, Garth Davies, and Alexander Kiss, *A Broken System Part II: Why There Is So Much Error in Captial Cases* (Columbia Law School, 2000).

15. *Atkins v. Virginia,* 536 U.S. 304 (2002). Interestingly, this was the position advanced by the American Bar Association. See Ch. 14.

16. The facts are summarized in the opinions in both the Supreme Court of Missouri and the Supreme Court of the United States. *State ex rel. Simmons v. Roper,* 112 S.W.3d 397 (Mo.banc 2004), aff'd sub nom. *Roper v. Simmons,* 125 S.Ct. 1183 (2005).

17. *Roper v. Simmons,* 125 S.Ct. 1195.

18. 113 S.Ct. 892 (1993) (Thomas, J., concurring).

19. See "Racial Justice Act," 103d Congress, H.R. 4017. (Senator Kennedy supported this in the Senate debates on habeas limits.)

20. Missouri Sentencing Advisory Commission, *Report on Recommended Sentencing* 59ff. (2005).

21. *Nelson v. Campbell,* 541 U.S. 637 (2004).

22. If liberals do succeed in eliminating the death penalty, don't be surprised when they start complaining about the harshness of imprisonment for life without probation or parole. These criminals are capable of repentance and rehabilitation, after all. We cannot shut the prison door on them forever, can we? By the way, a disproportionately large number of prisoners doing "big life" (as we call it in Missouri) are black. Yep, discrimination!

23. See the excellent study by professors Ross Sandler and David Schoenbrod, *Government by Decree* (Yale University Press, 2002).

24. See Sowell, *Vision of the Anointed,* Ch. 2, "The Pattern."

25. E.g., *Hutto v. Finney,* 437 U.S. 678 (1978); *Bounds v. Smith,* 430 U.S. 817 (1977).

26. The case I am describing was filed in the U.S. District Court in St. Louis; its

history is outlined in *Tyler v. Murphy*, 135 F.3d 594 (8th Cir. 1998); see also the Prison Litigation Reform Act, 18 U.S.C. 3626. Names of the parties changed as sheriffs and other officials came and went. I was cocounsel in the case in 1982 and 1983.

27. This anecdote was related to me by one of the city attorneys who took over the case after I went on the bench.

28. See *Wilkinson v. Austin*, 125 S.Ct. 2384 (2005). Admittedly, the decision in *Wilkinson* was unanimous. Another instance of conservative judges respecting precedent, although the outcome favored prison authorities and perhaps was relatively harmless. Still, one questions why judges should have superintending power over assignment of prisoners to different prisons, whether higher security or not.

29. 123 S.Ct. 2162 (2003).

CHAPTER 8

1. See *Head v. Amoskeag Mfg. Co.*, 113 U.S. 9 (1885). See the summary of eminent domain jurisprudence in Justice Thomas's dissenting opinion in *Kelo v. City of New London*, 125 S.Ct. 2655, 2681–84 (2005).

2. See *United States ex rel. TVA v. Welch*, 327 U.S. 546 (1946).

3. 348 U.S. 26 (1954).

4. *Berman*, 348 U.S. 33.

5. *Calder v. Bull*, 3 Dall. 386 (1798).

6. 467 U.S. 229 (1984).

7. 702 F.2d 788 (9th Cir. 1983).

8. *Kelo*, 125 S.Ct. at 2687.

9. *Legal Services Corp. v. Velasquez*, 531 U.S. 533 (2001).

10. 524 U.S. 156 (1998).

11. 123 S.Ct. 1406 (2003).

12. See, e.g., *Elk Grove Unified Sch. Dist. v. Newdow*, 542 U.S. 1, 36 (O'Connor, J., sounding liberal); *Flast v. Cohen*, 392 U.S. 83 (1968) (Douglas, J., concurring).

13. 515 U.S. 687 (1995).

14. See Stephen Moore, "Of Mice and Men," *Wall Street Journal*, March 23, 2006, p. A17.

15. Ibid.

16. As of this writing, the Supreme Court has taken a case for review that challenges Congress's ability to regulate "wetlands" that don't come anywhere near navigable waters. It remains to be seen if the Roberts Court will decide to depart from the Court's routine abdication of the duty of judicial review in commerce clause cases.

17. See *Nat. Ass'n of Home Builders v. Babbitt*, 130 F.3d 1041, 1060 (D.C. Cir. 1997) (Sentelle, J., dissenting). This was a commerce clause/congressional

power case, but it illustrates that ruthless sweep of certain environmental laws at the expense of individual rights, and at the expense of public (human) needs, in this case a county hospital.

18. *Solid Waste Agency v. Army Corps of Engineers,* 121 S.Ct. 675 (2001).

19. 547 U.S., 126 S.Ct. 2208 (2006).

20. *Palazzolo v. Rhode Island,* 533 U.S. 606 (2001); *Lucas v. South Carolina Coastal Council,* 505 U.S. 1003 (1992).

21. In various cases, the Supreme Court has insisted that welfare benefits are property rights, and efforts to limit or terminate such benefits are subject to the due process and equal protection clauses. Thus, welfare benefits cannot be terminated without advance notice and hearing, *Goldberg v. Kelly,* 397 U.S. 254 (1970), and people who travel to other states to soak up benefits cannot be subjected to a residency requirement before collecting, as that "burdens" the right to travel, a "fundamental" constitutional right that does not appear expressly in the Constitution. *Shapiro v. Thompson,* 394 U.S. 618 (1969).

22. *Westermann v. Missouri Conservation Comm.,* 22nd Cir. No. 22964-02539 (1996).

23. *Kelo,* 125 S.Ct. 2677 (Thomas, J., dissenting).

CHAPTER 9

1. *Reynolds v. United States,* 98 U.S. 145 (1878).

2. *Elk Grove Unified Sch. Dist. v. Newdow,* 124 S.Ct. 2301, 2323 (2004) (O'Connor, J., concurring).

3. The exclusion of God and Christmas from the public square has depended entirely on the alliance of liberal judges and litigation groups such as the ACLU. The first step in the process was to sweep away limitations on the ability of people to sue the government for theoretical grievances. This has to do with a legal doctrine known as "standing."

Our constitution limits the authority of federal courts to "cases and controversies." The idea of a "case" derives from the common law adversary process: A "case" is a lawsuit by A against B to remedy some claimed wrong to A. The common law judges did not sit to hear academic disputes or public policy debates but to decide whether A could get money, land, or some other tangible relief against his opponent, because of a direct violation of A's legal rights by B. Obviously, there were times when the judges had to decide issues involving the rights of the subject and the Crown, but these cases actually involved some tangible gain or loss to one side or the other. The idea that judges should not decide imaginary or hypothetical disputes was carried forward into our Constitution. This is the idea of "standing," i.e., the parties' real stake in a lawsuit. If parties don't have standing, the courts don't have jurisdiction. See, e.g., *Valley Forge Christian Coll. v. Americans United for Separation of Church & State,* 454 U.S. 464 (1982).

The idea of standing is a major limitation on the power of the judiciary. It means that the judiciary can and should get involved in an issue only if the judiciary's decision actually means something to the parties before the court, in a real sense. For most of our history, the courts respected this limitation on their power. In the 1930s, however, the federal judiciary became peopled with liberals, who saw the judiciary and the law merely as instruments to achieve political objectives. With such an attitude toward judicial power, it is no wonder that the first doctrines to fall by the wayside at the hands of liberal judges were limitations on standing.

In the 1920s, the Supreme Court rejected efforts by taxpayers to assert standing as taxpayers to attack federal expenditures. *Frothingham v. Mellon,* 262 U.S. 447 (1923). The Court reasoned, rightly, that individual taxpayers have no real interest in the outcome of such a case. Their individual taxes won't be affected, win or lose. But after liberals took control of the judiciary and began using it as an instrument to achieve political objectives, standing doctrine was rewritten. In 1968, the Supreme Court said that taxpayers *could* attack federal expenditures to enforce the First Amendment's prohibition of "an establishment of religion," because that was a specific limitation on Congress's spending power. *Flast v. Cohen,* 392 U.S. 83 (1968).

Once the rules about standing were gone, the liberals could build on rulings applying the First Amendment to the states, through the doctrine of "incorporation." The "incorporation" gimmick freed liberal judges to write into the Fourteenth Amendment those parts of the Bill of Rights that the liberal judges saw as proper or fair. The Establishment Clause was thus "incorporated," and once incorporated, it would be applied to the states in accordance with liberal ideas of what it meant.

Once it was decided that the First Amendment establishment clause applied to the states via the Fourteenth Amendment, and once rules of standing evaporated, the stage was set for a nationwide assault on religion in the public square.

4. Florida ACLU website, www.aclucentralflorida.org, visited 6/15/05.

5. The ACLU, supposedly the premier defender of free speech, does not rush to defend the right of religious groups to speak on public property or through public means. Compare ACLU briefs in *Rosenberger v. Rector & Visitors of U. of Va.,* 515 U.S. 819 (1995) and *Lamb's Chapel v. Center Moriches Union Free Sch. Dist.,* 508 U.S. 384 (1993) (briefs accessible online through legal research services).

6. Christianity is the primary target but not the only target. See, e.g., *Bd. of Education of Kiryas Joel v. Grumet,* 512 U.S. 687 (1994).

7. When the liberals have lost on religion issues, it is usually because "moderates" like Justices Anthony Kennedy and Sandra Day O'Connor simply cannot swallow the blatant hostility to religion. In general, the courts have taken a stand against religion primarily on questions of prayer and religious texts or monuments on public property, in public schools, and at government functions.

One issue has been more of a mixed bag: public funding, since liberals have some difficulty throwing out social welfare spending of any kind, even if it indirectly supports religious institutions.

8. Jill Stewart, "Politics by Design," *Wall Street Journal*, Apr. 29, 2005, p. W13.

9. *Webb v. City of Republic*, No. 98-3306-CV-S-RGC (W.D.Mo.).

10. *Ellis v. La Mesa*, 990 F.2d 1518 (9th Cir. 1993); see also *Paulson v. San Diego*, 294 F.3d 1124 (9th Cir. 2002) *(en banc)*.

11. See *San Diegans for the Mt. Soledad National War Memorial v. Paulson*, Nos. 05A1233 & 05A1234, July 7, 2006 (Kennedy, J., in chambers).

12. *Marsh v. Chambers*, 463 U.S. 783 (1983).

13. 449 U.S. 39 (1980).

14. See Lanny Keller, "Bloody Tangipahoa," *Wall Street Journal*, Mar. 17, 2005, p. A17.

15. See, e.g., *Boy Scouts of America v. Wyman*, 335 F.3d 80 (2nd Cir. 2003) (another triumph for Judge Calabresi, a liberal Clinton appointee, who has publicly likened President Bush to Hitler and Mussolini); *Barnes-Wallace v. Boy Scouts of America*, 275 F.Supp.2d 1259 (S.D.Cal. 2003) (district judge a Clinton appointee).

16. *Capitol Square Review Bd. v. Pinette*, 515 U.S. 753 (1995).

17. Christopher Levenick, "High Noon at Sunrise Rock," *Wall Street Journal*, May 27, 2005, W15; *Buono v. Norton*, 212 F.Supp.2d 1202 (C.D.Cal. 2002).

18. *Van Orden v. Perry*, 125 S.Ct. 2854, 2866 (2005) (Thomas, J., concurring).

19. Ibid., at 2882 n. 10 (Stevens, J., dissenting).

20. *Elk Grove Unified Sch. Dist. v. Newdow*, 124 S.Ct. 2301 (2004). It is ironic that the liberals resorted to rules of standing to avoid the Newdow claim. Liberals like to grant standing to anybody or anything: Justice William O. Douglas wanted to give standing to trees and animals.

21. See *Newdow v. Congress*, 383 F.Supp.2d 1229 (E.D.Cal. 2005). A suit filed by ACLU in Florida is described at www.gopusa.com/new/2006. The House bill, which could be a historic limitation on federal court jurisdiction, if it can get through the Senate, is H.R. 2389, sponsored by Rep. Todd Akin of Missouri.

22. 330 U.S. 1 (1947).

23. See, e.g., Daniel I. Dreisbach, "The Mythical 'Wall of Separation': How a Misused Metaphor Changed Church-State Law, Policy, and Discourse," Heritage Foundation, June 23, 2006.

24. See Act of Supremacy, 1 Elizabeth, c. 1 (1559); Act of Uniformity, 1 Elizabeth, c. 2 (1563); Act against Sectaries, 35 Elizabeth, c. 2 (1593); Massachusetts Const., Decl. of Rights, art. III (1780); Mass. Colony Laws, Ch. LI (Acts against Heresy), *The Charters & General Laws of the Colony and Province of Massachusetts Bay* (1814).

25. *Elk Grove*, 124 S.Ct. at 2327–28, n. 1.

26. *Van Orden v. Perry*, 125 S.Ct. at 2865 (Thomas, J., concurring); *Elk Grove Unified Sch. Dist. v. Newdow*, 124 S.Ct. at 2330 (Thomas, J., concurring).

27. See *McCreary County,* 125 S.Ct. 2722, 2759–60 (2005) (Scalia, J., dissenting).

28. See *Van Orden,* 125 S.Ct. at 2868 (Breyer, J., concurring).

29. Ibid., at 2871 (Breyer, J., concurring in the judgment).

30. See *Rosenberger v. Rector & Visitors of U. of Va.,* 515 U.S. 819 (1995) and *Lamb's Chapel v. Center Moriches Union Free Sch. Dist.,* 508 U.S. 384 (1993).

31. Carroll, "On Wings and Prayers," *Wall Street Journal,* June 17, 2005, p. W13.

32. *McCreary County,* 125 S.Ct. at 2745.

33. *Elk Grove,* 124 S.Ct. at 2327–28, n. 1.

34. E.g., *McCreary County,* 125 S.Ct. at 2746 (O'Connor, J., concurring).

35. *McCreary County v. ACLU,* 125 S.Ct. at 2752 (Scalia, J., dissenting).

36. See *Wallace v. Jaffree,* 472 U.S. 38 (1985).

CHAPTER 10

1. E.g., *R.A.V. v. City of St. Paul,* 505 U.S. 377 (1992); *Roth v. United States,* 354 U.S. 476 (1957).

2. *Cohen v. California,* 403 U.S. 15 (1971).

3. *Plummer v. City of Columbus,* 414 U.S. 2 (1973).

4. *Tinker v. Des Moines Ind. Community Sch. Dist.,* 393 U.S. 503 (1969).

5. *Virginia v. Black,* 538 U.S. 343 (2003). Admittedly, the Court upheld the cross-burning statute insofar as it constituted a direct threat to specific people, as by burning a cross on a black person's lawn, but any general prohibition on public or private cross-burning was nullified.

6. *Texas v. Johnson,* 491 U.S. 397 (1989). It's worth noting that the flag-burning cases evince the hypocrisy of liberals like Senator Joe Biden. Biden and others insisted that no constitutional amendment was needed to overturn the first flag-burning case, arguing instead for a federal statute, all the while knowing perfectly well that no statute would suffice. Sure enough, the Supreme Court struck down the Flag Protection Act. *United States v. Eichman,* 496 U.S. 310 (1990). So did Biden & Co. then join the push to amend the Constitution on the issue? Of course not!

7. *Rankin v. McPherson,* 483 U.S. 378 (1987). Of course, this was a case in which the employee approved of attempts on President Reagan's life; would Justice Marshall & Co. have disapproved of such a statement directed at President Clinton? To give the liberals their due, I would say, probably yes, as they usually curtail only speech related to abortion or sexual advances by men.

8. *Ashcroft v. Free Speech Coalition,* 535 U.S. 234, 122 S.Ct. 1389 (2002).

9. The late Mike Royko, among others, skewered the notion of policing "insensitivity," in an article entitled "With Apologies to Berthas Everywhere," *St. Louis Post-Dispatch,* August, 1991. See also Diane Ravitch's trenchant analysis, *The Language Police* (Knopf, 2003).

10. *Davis v. Monsanto*, 858 F.2d 345 (6th Cir. 1988).

11. Another advantage of the liberal speech codes is that many disciplinary actions against lawyers and judges are taken in secret. We know that they occur, however, from occasional published reports and from data provided by bar disciplinary organizations.

12. See, e.g., Dinesh D'Souza, *Illiberal Education*, Ch. 5 (Free Press, 1991).

13. E.g., Brendan Miniter, "Crimson and Camouflage: Will Harvard bring back ROTC?," WSJ.com, *OpinionJournal*, May 27, 2002; David Montgomery, "Harvard v. ROTC," *FrontPageMagazine.com*, Jan. 7, 2003.

14. 10 U.S.C. § 558.

15. *Forum for Academic & Inst. Rts. v. Rumsfeld*, 390 F.3d 219, 225–28 (3d Cir. 2004), rev'd, 126 S.Ct. 1297 (2006) (outlining history of Solomon Amendment and the Clinton administration's reaction).

16. 10 U.S.C. §§ 503, 983.

17. See Dept. of Defense regulations, 48 CFR Part 209, 243, 252.

18. 354 F.Supp.2d 156 (D.N.J. 2003).

19. *Board of Directors of Rotary Int. v. Rotary Club*, 481 U.S. 537 (1987); *Roberts v. United States Jaycees*, 468 U.S. 609 (1984); see also *New York State Club Ass'n v. City of New York*, 487 U.S. 1 (1988).

20. E.g., *Debs v. United States*, 249 U.S. 211 (1919); *Schenck v. United States*, 249 U.S. 47 (1919).

21. 530 U.S. 640 (2000).

22. E.g., "Bashing the Boy Scouts," *Wall Street Journal*, Nov. 26, 2004; Julia Duin, "Boy Scouts Fight Back," *The Washington Times*, Mar. 7, 2004; see also Chapter 9.

23. 390 F.3d 232.

24. 120 S.Ct. 2459 (Stevens, J., dissenting, joined by the usual group of Souter, Ginsburg, and Breyer).

25. In *Burton v. Wilmington Parking Auth.*, 365 U.S. 715 (1961), the Supreme Court held that a lessee of a government-owned parking garage was a "state actor," subject to the requirements of the Fourteenth Amendment. Of course, in *Burton*, the liberal justices were engaged in stamping out racial discrimination.

26. *Rumsfeld v. Forum for Acad. & Inst. Rights*, 126 S.Ct. 1297 (2006).

27. 126 S.Ct. 1313; the "trivializing" comment is at 126 S.Ct. at 1308.

28. See "Law Dean at WU Reverses Loan Vote," *St. Louis Post-Dispatch*, Mar. 26, 2002; Bill McClellan, "Bias Seems Fine at WU Law School If Military Is Target," *St. Louis Post-Dispatch*, Mar. 25, 2002.

29. *Hague v. CIO*, 307 U.S. 496 (1939); *Schneider v. New Jersey*, 308 U.S. 147 (1939).

30. See, e.g., *Madsen v. Women's Health Center, Inc.*, 512 U.S. 753 (1994).

31. *Hill v. Colorado*, 530 U.S. 703 (2000); see also *Schenck v. Pro-Choice Network of Western New York*, 519 U.S. 357 (1997).

32. *Planned Parenthood v. American Coalition of Life Activists*, 290 F.3d 1058 (9th Cir. 2002) *(en banc)*.

33. 2 Joseph Story, *Commentaries on the Constitution of the United States* § 1880; 4 William Blackstone, *Commentaries on the Laws of England* *151–52.

34. *New York Times Co. v. United States,* 403 U.S. 713 (1971).

35. Interestingly, perhaps the most extreme liberal in the federal judiciary, Stephen Reinhardt, dissented in this case, joining Reagan-appointed judges like Alex Kozinski and Diarmuid F. O'Scannlain, in condemning the injunction as a prior restraint. 290 F.3d at 1088 (Reinhardt, J., dissenting).

36. *NAACP v. Claiborne Hardware Co.,* 458 U.S. 886 (1982).

37. See, e.g., Harold Reuschlein & William Gregory, *Handbook on the Law of Agency and Partnership* § 52 (West, 1979).

38. *Meritor Savings Bank v. Vinson,* 477 U.S. 57 (1986).

39. See Note, 80 *Minn. L. Rev.* 979 (1996), justifying suppression of "harassment" notwithstanding the First Amendment.

40. See Note, 80 *Minn. L. Rev.* 979 (1996).

41. See generally Schlei and Grossman, *Employment Discrimination Law,* Ch. 12 (1978 & Supp.), describing the course of reported cases on this topic. For an early recognition of the seriousness of the constitutional issue, see Volokh, "Freedom of Speech and Workplace Harassment," 39 *UCLA L. Rev.* 1791 (1992).

42. *Clark County School District v. Breeden,* 121 S.Ct. 1508 (2001).

43. The Supreme Court of Missouri, in construing a criminal sexual misconduct statute, has indicated that there is such a right. *State v. Moore,* 90 S.W.3d 64, 68–69 (Mo.banc 2002).

44. See, e.g., Heather MacDonald, "A Court Restrains HUD's Thought Police," *Wall Street Journal,* Jan. 8, 1999, outlining the persecution of ordinary citizens for daring to oppose a "group home" in their neighborhood, as well as other cases of deployment of "bias hounds" by government.

45. *Aguilar v. Avis Rent A Car System, Inc.,* 980 P.2d 846 (Cal. 1999), cert. denied sub nom. *Avis Rent A Car System, Inc. v. Aguilar,* 120 S.Ct. 2029 (2000) (Thomas, J., dissenting).

46. See, e.g., James Simon, *The Antagonists: Hugo Black, Felix Frankfurter and Civil Liberties in Modern America,* Ch. III (Simon & Schuster, 1989).

47. *City of Chicago v. Morales,* 527 U.S. 41 (1999).

CHAPTER 11

1. *PGA Tour, Inc. v. Martin,* 121 S.Ct. 1879 (2001).

2. *City of Cleburne v. Cleburne Living Center,* 473 U.S. 432, 105 S.Ct. 3249 (1985).

3. *Cleburne,* 105 S.Ct. at 3252 n. 2, 3256 n. 9.

4. 124 S.Ct. 1978 (2004).

5. *Tennessee v. Lane,* 124 S.Ct. at 1996. In reciting the list of horrible acts of discrimination perpetrated on "people with disabilities," the liberal justices cited

many cases in which the Supreme Court had held that the conduct was constitutional! Most notable was the case of *Buck v. Bell,* in which Justice Holmes upheld involuntary sterilization of the retarded, declaiming, "Three generations of imbeciles are enough." 274 U.S. 200, at 207 (1927).

6. *School Board of Nassau County v. Arline,* 107 S.Ct. 1123 (1987). The decision quotes legislative history about recovered cancer patients (is cancer a communicable disease?) as a justification for treating a contagious disease as a "handicap" under federal law.

7. E.g., *Doe v. Dist. of Columbia,* 796 F.Supp. 559 (D.D.C. 1992).

8. A whole other book can be written about how liberal judges create special rights for special groups, and then liberal legislators pass laws to protect the rights that the liberal judges created, and then the liberal judges carry those laws to further extremes—all without a thought as to whether the "right" in question ever really existed in the Constitution, or whether the liberal laws actually square with the constitutional power of the legislatures. The "Access to [Abortion] Clinics Act," the Fair Housing Act, the "Violence against Women Act," and many others come to mind. Interestingly, the liberals recently discovered federalism and limitations on Congress's commerce power when confronted with cases on "medical marijuana" and assisted suicide. There, they insisted that Congress could *not* regulate such things, even though they held for decades that Congress could regulate what people grow on their own land, for their own use. *Gonzales v. Raich,* 125 S.Ct. 2195 (2005); compare *Wickard v. Filburn,* 317 U.S. 111 (1942), holding that the government could punish a farmer for growing wheat for consumption on his farm.

9. See *City of Edmonds v. Oxford House,* 514 U.S. 725 (1995); West's *Federal Practice Digest 4th,* Table of Cases, vol. 103, listing federal cases in which Oxford Houses were parties.

10. *Oxford House-C v. City of St. Louis,* 843 F.Supp. 1556 (E.D.Mo. 1994), rev'd, 77 F.3d 249 (8th Cir. 1996).

11. See *White v. Lee,* 227 F.3d 1214 (9th Cir. 2000); MacDonald, "A Court Restrains HUD's Thought Police," *Wall Street Journal,* Jan. 8, 1999.

CHAPTER 12

1. See, e.g., William Prosser, *Handbook of the Law of Torts* 167 (West, 1941).

2. 393 U.S. 503 (1969).

3. 393 U.S. at 511.

4. 393 U.S. at 525.

5. *Hazelwood Sch. Dist. v. Kuhlmeier,* 484 U.S. 260 (1988).

6. For a discussion of the liberal use of the due process clause to impose policy choices, see, e.g., Lino Graglia, "Our Constitution Faces Death by 'Due Process'," *Wall Street Journal,* May 24, 2005, p. A12. Professor Graglia's arti-

cle is merely a convenient summary of an issue that is widely debated among lawyers, constitutional scholars, and judges.

7. See, e.g., Kay Hymowitz, "How the Courts Undermined School Discipline," *Wall Street Journal,* May 4, 1999.

8. *Goss v. Lopez,* 419 U.S. 565 (1975).

9. As a state judge, I have been required to review several cases involving student discipline issues. The records in such cases have been comparable in bulk to public employee dismissals.

10. *Ingraham v. Wright,* 430 U.S. 651 (1977).

11. *Board of Curators v. Horowitz,* 435 U.S. 78 (1978).

12. *Owasso Independent School District v. Falvo,* 534 U.S. 426, 122 S.Ct. 934 (2002). The plaintiffs in the case were parents of a handicapped child who was "mainstreamed" pursuant to federal mandates; the parents apparently objected to their child having his paper examined by a classmate, so they brought—surprise!—a *class action* to stop that process. Isn't the idea of "mainstreaming" intended to ensure that disabled children get treated the same as others? Or are they more equal?

13. See *Good News Club v. Milford Central School,* 121 S.Ct. 2093, 2112 (Stevens, J., dissenting), 2115 (Souter and Ginsburg, JJ., dissenting).

14. See, e.g., Jill Carroll and Leila Abboud, "School Voucher Debate Frays Traditional Alliances," *Wall Street Journal,* July 1, 2002, p. B1; "School Unions Demoted" (editorial), *Wall Street Journal,* Apr. 4, 1999. For a discussion of the merits of privatizing education, see Philip Porter and Michael Davis, "The Value of Private Property in Education," 14 *Harv. J. L. & Pub. Pol.* 397 (1991).

15. 122 S.Ct. 2460, 2480 (2002).

16. On this issue, see Joseph Viteritti, "Blaine's Wake: School Choice, the First Amendment, and State Constitutional Law," 21 *Harv. J. L. & Pub. Pol.* 657 (1998).

17. *Zelman,* 122 S.Ct. 2484–85 (Stevens, J., dissenting).

18. *Zelman,* 122 S.Ct. 2501–02 (Souter, J., dissenting), 2502–05 (Breyer, dissenting).

19. *Zelman,* 122 S.Ct. at 2501 (Souter, J.).

20. *Zelman,* 122 S.Ct. 2500.

21. *Zelman,* 122 S.Ct. at 2484.

22. See George Clowes, "Polls Show Vouchers Are Popular and Would Be Widely Used," The Heartland Institute (Oct. 1, 2004); *Wall Street Journal,* July 1, 2002, p. B1.

23. For the tyranny's approach at the college level, see "A Chill in the Classroom," *Wall Street Journal,* Dec. 3, 2004, p. W15.

24. "The Supreme Court undoubtedly thought that *Tinker* and *Goss* would free students from oppressive adult power. Yet today, thirty years later, resentful students must march through metal detectors, get sniffed for guns by trained dogs, watch police and security guards patrolling the hallways—and

fear for their lives." Kay S. Hymowitz, "How the Courts Undermined School Discipline," *Wall Street Journal*, May 4, 1999.

CHAPTER 13

1. See, e.g., Richard Morris, *Witnesses at the Creation* (Holt, Rinehart, 1985), dealing with the authors of *The Federalist Papers* (all lawyers); C. Fred Kleinknecht, *Anchor of Liberty* (Ancient Scottish Rite of Freemasonry, 1987), containing brief biographical sketches of the Framers of the Constitution.

2. See, e.g., Theodore Plucknett, *A Concise History of the Common Law,* Ch. 4 (Little, Brown, 1956); see also Roscoe Pound, *The Formative Era of American Law,* Ch. III (Little, Brown, 1938).

3. See Morton Horwitz, *The Transformation of American Law, 1870–1960* (Oxford Univ. Press, 1992). When I was at Harvard, Professor Horwitz was known as "Mort the Tort" and excelled in propagating the ideas of law as a mere instrument of the dominant political elite and of "loss spreading" notions of tort law. Horwitz and his fellows in academe are, if not Marxists, certainly economic determinists.

4. See *Restatement (Second) of Torts* § 402A and related commentary. The "restatement" idea was the product of various law school professors and some judges to provide a coherent statement of American tort law, not as it was, but as it should be. The "restatements" have been treated almost as holy writ (if law professors would ever acknowledge such a thing) in academe and many state courts, where most tort law has been made, resulting in the well-publicized "crises" in medical malpractice and asbestos litigation. For an example of "mass tort" lawsuits arising from claimed exposure to toxic substances without tangible injury, see *Metro-North Commuter R. Co. v. Buckley,* 521 U.S. 424 (1997) (rejecting claims based on mere exposure under railroad employer liability law).

5. See Stephen Carroll et al., *Asbestos Litigation Costs and Compensation: An Interim Report* (RAND Institute for Civil Justice, 2002).

6. Like many liberal nostrums for social ills, the advertising campaign against smoking that the tobacco companies are required to implement merely keeps tobacco products on the public mind. It is all very well to intone piously that smoking is bad for you, and that youth should stay away from it. But the effect of this advertising can be to convey the subtle message that smoking is forbidden fruit, and that if you do it, you somehow are thumbing your nose at the adult world.

7. See W. Kip Viscusi, *Smoke-Filled Rooms: A Postmortem on the Tobacco Deal* (Univ. of Chicago Press, 2002), reviewed by Richard Posner, 70 *U. Chi. L. Rev.* 1141 (2003).

8. It is a tribute to the liberal control in government, and the federal Justice Department in particular, that the president of the United States was appar-

ently powerless to call a halt to the federal government's own lawsuit against the tobacco industry, relying on the same theories of "restitution" for government benefit costs as did the state lawsuits. Why has this Clintonian lawsuit ground on, in spite of its obvious conflict with the principles of the Bush administration?

9. See Associated Press, June 25, 2004, accessed at MSNBC.com. Judge Calabresi's irruption was originally reported in the *New York Sun*.

10. *Pelman v. McDonald's Corp.*, 396 F.3d 508 (2d Cir. 2005).

11. Charles Ogletree, "Repairing the Past: New Efforts in the Reparations Debate in America," 38 *Harv. Civ. R.-Civ. L. L. Rev.* 279, 307 (2003).

12. Taunya Lovell Banks, "Exploring White Resistance to Racial Reconciliation in the United States," 55 *Rutgers L. Rev.* 903 (2003) (the author is a professor of something called "equality jurisprudence"); Charles Ogletree, "Repairing the Past," 279. Both authors blatantly ignore the fact that citizens of Japanese ancestry displaced during World War II were compensated by legislation enacted by Congress and signed by the President.

13. Rule 23, F.R.Civ.P. The "fair and reasonable" standard was applied in *Liddell v. Bd. of Education* discussed in Chapter 5, with resultant approval of federal judicial control of tax rates in the city of St. Louis.

14. Ward Connerly, the courageous foe of "affirmative action," has described the "reparations" claims as the "new shakedowns." Connerly, "The New Shakedown," *Washington Times*, April 1, 2002.

15. See *Colo v. United States*, 70 F.3d 1103 (9th Cir. 1995).

16. *City of Sherrill v. Oneida Indian Nation*, 125 S.Ct. 1478 (2005), remarkable for common sense displayed by Justice Ginsburg, but not Justice Stevens. Although they do not proceed on tort theories so much as statutory claims, Indian land grab suits reflect how liberals use the law to oppress the majority and win special treatment for a favored class. In 1985, the United States Supreme Court gave the green light to lawsuits by Indian tribes in the eastern United States, who sought to "reclaim" millions of acres of land that they had sold voluntarily and that for centuries had been owned and occupied by innocent purchasers. *Oneida Indian Nation v. County of Oneida*, 414 U.S. 661 (1974), after remand, 470 U.S. 226 (1985). The Indian lawsuits were the spawn of Legal Services Corporation attorneys, who looked for ways to advance the liberal agenda of favored treatment for minorities that had been "victimized" by the majority. See Walter Olsen, "Indian Claims Debacle Offers a Sobering Preview on Reparations," *The New York Sun*, Oct. 29, 2002. Even though the Indian land grab suits have seldom succeeded on the merits, the pendency of the suits has kept homeowners in agonized limbo for years.

17. See Associated Press, "Advocates Quietly Push for Slavery Reparations," July 9, 2006.

CHAPTER 14

1. See *The ABA in Law and Social Policy: What Role?* (Federalist Society, 1994).

2. *The ABA in Law and Social Policy,* Ch. 3.

3. Judge Bork has brilliantly recounted his courageous struggle in *The Tempting of America: The Political Seduction of the Law* (Free Press, 1989).

4. *The ABA in Law and Social Policy,* Ch. 3.

5. See *ABA Watch,* August 1996.

6. *ABA Watch,* August 2002.

7. "An ABA Hit Job," *Wall Street Journal,* July 26, 2006, p. A14. By a strange coincidence, the chairman of the ABA Committee attacking Wallace was one of the ardent opponents of Wallace's Legal Services Corporation reforms.

8. See Jeffrey Jacobs, "Report to the House of Delegates of the American Bar Association," posted at abanet.org/leadership/2006/annual/elevanone.doc.

9. See ABA Pres. Hirshon interview, *ABA Watch,* August 2001.

10. All amicus briefs filed with the Supreme Court are a matter of public record. WestLaw and Lexis, the primary legal research services, provide access to all briefs filed in their Supreme Court databases. My summary of ABA positions is derived from a paper presented by The Federalist Society, "Report on ABA Amicus Briefs," available on the Society's website.

11. See David Bernstein, "Affirmative Blackmail," *Wall Street Journal,* Feb. 11, 2006, p. A9.

12. In addition to amicus briefs, see *ABA Watch,* February 2001, August 1996.

13. "Sexual orientation" is seldom defined. Given the vagueness of the term, it is difficult to see how pedarests, necrophiliacs, and zoophiliacs are excluded. Yet lawyers and judges are forbidden by the ABA codes from saying anything that would "manifest bias" concerning the behavior of such groups. See Missouri Supreme Court Rules 2.03, 4-8.4.

14. See ABA News Release, July 22, 2004, available at ABA website.

15. See *ABA Watch,* February 2006, interview with ABA President Karen Mathis; *ABA Watch,* August 1996, summarizing ABA positions, none of which have changed to date.

16. See ABA amicus briefs filed in the 2004 Terror Trilogy *(Rasul v. Bush, Rumsfeld v. Padilla, Hamdi v. Rumsfeld)* and in 2006 in *Hamdan v. Rumsfeld,* 126 S.Ct. (2006). The briefs are available online at Findlaw.com, as well as standard legal research services WestLaw and Lexis. Citations to the cases mentioned can be found in Chapter 15.

17. *ABA Watch,* August 2002.

18. See "The ABA, The War on Terrorism and Civil Liberties," *ABA Watch,* The Federalist Society for Law & Public Policy Studies, Feb. 2006.

19. Some have suggested that the ABA has jumped to the side of the tyranny of tolerance to atone for its failure to take a strong stand for civil rights in the

1950s and 1960s. The Federalist Society, *The ABA in Law and Social Policy,* Ch. 2 (1994).

CHAPTER 15

1. Authorization for Use of Military Force, 115 Stat. 224 (2001). The statute authorizes the president to use all necessary force against groups or persons *he determines* to have aided the terrorist attacks of September 11 or to have harbored such persons.

2. *Ex parte Quirin,* 317 U.S. 1 (1942), quoting Geneva Conventions.

3. *Quirin,* note 2.

4. See brief of Janet Reno et al., filed in *Rasul v. Bush.*

5. 124 S.Ct. 2686 (2004).

6. See *Rasul v. Bush,* 215 F.Supp.2d 55, aff'd, 321 F.3d 1134 (D.C. Cir. 2003).

7. 339 U.S. 763 (1950).

8. See U.S. Const. art. I, § 8, art. II, § 2.

9. 124 S.Ct. at 2693.

10. 124 S.Ct. 2711 (2004).

11. See 28 U.S.C. § 2242; *Rumsfeld v. Padilla,* 124 S.Ct. at 2717. After winning in the Fourth Circuit Court of Appeals on the issue of Padilla's status, the Bush administration wimped out and shifted him back to criminal court, to avoid Supreme Court review. Judge Michael Luttig, a brilliant conservative jurist, was outraged by this cut-and-run, but in light of the *Hamdan* decision, it's not likely that the administration would have won. See *Padilla v. Hanft,* 547 U.S. ___, 126 S.Ct. 1649 (2006) (Kennedy, J., concurring in denial of certiorari).

12. *Hamdi v. Rumsfeld,* 124 S.Ct. 2633 (2004).

13. 317 U.S. 1 (1942).

14. *Quirin,* 317 at 5.

15. 124 S.Ct. 2660 (Scalia, J., dissenting).

16. 323 U.S. 214 (1944). For the liberal take on the case, see, e.g., *Hamdi,* 124 S.Ct. 2654 (Souter & Ginsburg, JJ., concurring in part, dissenting in part).

17. 323 U.S. at 224–25 (Frankfurter, J., concurring).

18. *Hamdan v. Rumsfeld,* 415 F.3d 33 (2005).

19. Detainee Treatment Act of 2005, Pub.L. 109–148, 119 Stat. 2739.

20. *Hamdan v. Rumsfeld,* 126 S.Ct. 2749 (2006).

21. See 126 S.Ct. 2834–36 (Thomas, J., dissenting).

22. 126 S.Ct. 2810–12 (Scalia, dissenting), explaining prior cases, including *Ex parte McCardle,* 7 Wall. (74 U.S.) 506 (1869), which dismissed a habeas appeal because Congress passed a law stripping the Supreme Court of jurisdiction to hear it. This case is the bane of liberals who insist that Congress cannot limit the jurisdiction of the courts.

23. See, e.g., "London and Guantánamo," *Wall Street Journal*, July 13, 2005, p. A14.

24. A great deal of the history of the *Moussaoui* case is obtainable online from the district court's own database. *United States v. Moussaoui*, No. 04-455-A. The gist of the 9/11 attack and of Moussaoui's role is set forth with tragic terseness in the agreed statement of facts, signed by Moussaoui and filed as part of the record. My summary is drawn from that plea statement. My summary of the court proceedings is drawn from the reported appellate opinions and the court minutes posted on the website of the district court. See *United States v. Moussaoui*, 282 F.Supp.2d 480 (E.D.Va. 2003), aff'd in part, vacated in part, 382 F.3d 453 (4th Cir. 2004) *(en banc)*; see also *United States v. Moussaoui*, 205 F.R.D. 183 (E.D.Va. 2002), 213 F.R.D. 277 (E.D.Va. 2002), 333 F.3d 509 (4th Cir. 2003).

25. See Andrew McCarthy, "This Is No Way to Fight a War," *Wall Street Journal*, May 6–7, 2006, p. A9. See also "Moussaoui's Mess," and David Rivkin and Lee Casey, "A Recipe for Disaster," *Wall Street Journal*, March 17, 2006, p. A12, for penetrating analyses of the "mess." Of course, the *Hamdan* case makes the mess that much worse.

26. *Faretta v. California*, 422 U.S. 806 (1975).

27. See Theodore Plucknett, *A Concise History of the Common Law* 434–35 (Little, Brown, 1956).

28. 373 U.S. 83 (1963).

29. *Kyles v. Whitley*, 514 U.S. 19 (1995).

30. *ACLU v. National Security Agency*, No. 06-CV-10204 (E.D.Mich. 2006), appeal pending.

CONCLUSION

1. One thinks of the Roman lawyers described by Gibbon: "Others . . . maintained the gravity of legal professors, by furnishing a rich client with subtleties to confound the plainest truth, and with arguments to color the most unjustifiable pretensions. The splendid and popular class was composed of the advocates, who filled the Forum with their turgid and loquacious rhetoric. Careless of fame and of justice, they are described for the most part as ignorant and rapacious guides, who conducted their clients through a maze of expense, of delay, and of disappointment; from whence, after a tedious series of years, they were at length dismissed, when their patience and fortune were almost exhausted." 1 Edward Gibbon, *Decline and Fall of the Roman Empire* 536 (Modern Library ed.). Of course, in our day, the subtleties to confound plain truth are practiced most often in federal courts by liberals.

2. 157 U.S. 429 (1895).

3. Also, the Twenty-fourth and Twenty-fifth Amendments were adopted in reaction to Supreme Court decisions, but were not so much intended to reverse the Court as to extend its holdings in the poll tax case, *Harper v. Virginia State*

Bd. of Elections, 383 U.S. 663 (1966), and the case regarding eighteen-year-olds' right to vote, *Oregon v. Mitchell,* 400 U.S. 112 (1970)—a study in itself of judicial amendment of the Constitution. Otherwise, Congress proposed an amendment to reverse the Supreme Court's decision on child labor in *Hammer v. Dagenhart,* 247 U.S. 251 (1918), but the amendment was never ratified.

4. One proposal to limit the judiciary does warrant comment. Professors Calabresi and Lindgren have proposed term limits on Supreme Court justices, to combat the judicial "gerontocracy," and to ensure turnover of personnel. The proposal is for a term of fifteen years. See Steven Calabresi and James Lindgren, "Supreme Gerontocracy," *Wall Street Journal,* Apr. 8, 2005, p. A12 (this is Steven Calabresi, not to be confused with liberal judge Guido Calabresi). The idea of term limits is a good one, but I see no prospect of its adoption in my lifetime. One might as well suggest adoption of the Missouri Non-Partisan Court Plan at the federal level. That plan sets up a shared system for judicial selection, melding a nominating commission, the executive, and the voters in a system of selection and retention of judges. (It must be a reasonable system: I got appointed!). The Missouri system provides a significant check on judicial autocracy because the voters are always able to remove judges who get out of control, even though the people have exercised the power sparingly. Also, Missouri judges are subject to mandatory retirement at age seventy.

5. The liberal notion of judicial revision of the constitution is expressed by Justice Breyer himself in his book, *Active Liberty* (Knopf, 2005). The title is a dead giveaway, and yet he claims that he is arguing for the primacy of democracy, not judicial philosopher kings.

6. See Cass Sunstein, David Schkade, and Lisa Ellman, "Ideological Voting on Federal Courts of Appeals: A Preliminary Investigation," 90 *U. Va. L. Rev.* 301 (2004), summarized in *Wall Street Journal,* "Gloves Come Off in Fight to Control Courts," Oct. 30, 2003, p. A4. Sunstein's politics are revealed in his book, *Radicals in Robes: Why Extreme Right-Courts Are Wrong for America* (Basic Books, 2005), in which he excoriates "conservative activists." Of course, Sunstein's concept of "extreme right wing" probably embraces nearly all Bush voters and pro-life Democrats, and people who "aggressively read the Constitution to protect vulnerable members of society [omit the unborn, of course]" are merely mainstream. See Cass Sunstein, "John Roberts, Minimalist," *Wall Street Journal,* Sept. 1, 2005, p. A10.

7. Much is made of the debate about "originalism" and how the Founders disagreed among themselves about the meaning of certain parts of the Constitution or Bill of Rights. There is a basic rule of law that has been overlooked in this debate. For centuries, the courts have understood that the best guide to interpretation of an ambiguous or uncertain text, whether a contract or a charter or a statute, is *the practice of the parties who drafted it.* That is why custom and tradition are critical. If a law has coexisted with the Constitution for decades, or centuries, it is a very good indication that it is constitutional.

8. Is this a "religious test"? I don't think so. I would exclude no one from the

judiciary based on religion, but I think it is legitimate to inquire into any judge's core philosophy. If he is an atheist, he must nonetheless recognize the importance of moral authority.

9. See, e.g., Dan Subotnik, *Toxic Diversity* (NYU Press, 2005).

10. Robert Caro, *The Years of Lyndon Johnson: Master of the Senate*, pp. 855ff. (Knopf, 2002).

11. Martin Gold and Dimple Gupta, "The Constitutional Option to Change Senate Rules and Procedures: A Majoritarian Means to Overcome the Filibuster," 28 *Harv. J. L. & Pub. Pol.* 205 (2004); John Cornyn, "Our Broken Judicial Confirmation Process and the Need for Filibuster Reform," 27 *Harv. J. L. & Pub. Pol.* 181 (2003).

12. *The Question of Prohibitions,* 12 Co.Rep. 64 (1607). Here Coke was quoting another great jurist, Bracton.

13. 29 U.S.C. §§ 101–15.

14. *In re Debs,* 158 U.S. 564 (1895).

15. As long ago as 1850 the Supreme Court recognized the principle of the limited jurisdiction of federal courts and the subjection of that jurisdiction to control by Congress. *Sheldon v. Sill,* 49 U.S. 441 (1850). Of course, when legislative efforts were made to limit forced busing to implement school desegregation decrees, the liberals suddenly discovered "exceptions" to Congress's authority over the jurisdiction of the federal courts. Oh, no, they cried, we cannot limit federal jurisdiction in matters of civil rights! Not hampered by any demands of intellectual honesty, they swept the Norris-LaGuardia Act under the rug.

16. *Felker v. Turpin,* 518 U.S. 651 (1996). Ted Kennedy and company tried to legislate an executioner's quota in 1994, before the GOP swept control of Congress. The Kennedy legislation would have imported "disparate impact" notions into capital sentencing, with the necessary consequence that executions would be based on the murderers' skin color rather than on their deeds.

17. See 28 U.S.C. § 2283, construed in *Mitchum v. Foster,* 407 U.S. 225 (1972). No one questions the validity of § 2283, absolutely banning federal injunctions against state court proceedings, "except as authorized" by Congress. In *Hill v. McDonough,* 126 S.Ct. 2096 (2006), the Supreme Court decided that federal courts can enjoin executions by lethal injection because they are too painful, leading to a new freeze on executions in almost all states.

18. See Robert Dierker, "*Sub Deo et Lege:* Toward Limitation of Federal Judicial Power," 4 *St. L. U. Pub. L. Forum* 205 (1984).

19. Letter of Rep. James Talent to the author, 1996.

20. There have also been proposals to reform the confirmation process by legislation. Charles Pickering, " 'Nuclear' Isn't the Only Option," *Wall Street Journal,* May 9, 2005, p. A22. Judge Pickering is hallucinating if he thinks a statute limiting filibuster tactics can pass in the face of the intransigence of the Kennedy-Biden-Schumer axis of liberalism.

21. Detainee Treatment Act, Pub.L. 109–148, 119 Stat. 2739, § 1005 (2005).

22. See U.S. Const. art. I, § 9; 2 Joseph Story, *Commentaries on the Constitution of the United States* §§ 1338 et seq. (Bigelow ed. 1891). Surely the attacks on New York and Washington and the continuing threat of attack by Islamic terrorists qualifies as an "invasion."

23. 126 S.Ct. 2749 (2006).

24. 31 U.S. (6 Pet.) 515 (1832); see also 4 Albert Beveridge, *The Life of John Marshall* 551 (Houghton Mifflin, 1919).

25. *Ex parte Merryman*, 17 Fed.Cas. 144 (No. 9487) (C.C.D.Md. 1861); see also Joseph Story, *Commentaries*, § 1342, ed. note a; Kathleen Sullivan and Gerald Gunther, *Constitutional Law* 365 (Foundation Press, 2004).

26. Recently, members of the Missouri legislature formed a compact to suffer imprisonment rather than submit to any judicial decree imposing taxes or taking control of spending for education. This is an example at the state level of the permissible role of defiance by one coequal branch of government.

ACKNOWLEDGMENTS
AND DISCLAIMERS

I promised to acknowledge my daughters, Libby, Kate, and Madeline, and so I do. They are the greatest.

I gratefully acknowledge the assistance and guidance of my editor, Jed Donahue, and of my agent, Mel Berger. I was exceptionally lucky to connect with Mel. I also wish to acknowledge the support and encouragement of my dear friend Thomas P. O'Rourke.

The views expressed herein are personal, and should not be construed as any indication of how I would rule on any case coming before me. No public resources were used in the preparation of this work. The use of my title is strictly for identification.

INDEX

269

ABOUT THE AUTHOR

Robert H. Dierker Jr. is a circuit judge of the Twenty-Second Judicial Circuit of Missouri. Before becoming a judge in 1986, he clerked for the Missouri Court of Appeals, worked in private practice, and served as assistant and associate counselor for the City of St. Louis. Judge Dierker holds his A.B. degree from St. Louis University, his J.D. degree from the University of Missouri at Kansas City, and his LL.M. degree from Harvard University.

ABOUT THE AUTHOR

Robert H. Dierker Jr. is a circuit judge of the Twenty-Second Judicial Circuit of Missouri. Before becoming a judge in 1986, he clerked for the Missouri Court of Appeals, worked in private practice, and served as assistant and associate counselor for the City of St. Louis. Judge Dierker holds his A.B. degree from St. Louis University, his J.D. degree from the University of Missouri at Kansas City, and his LL.M. degree from Harvard University.